D1551417

History of the American Newspaper
Publishers Association

History of the AMERICAN NEWSPAPER PUBLISHERS ASSOCIATION

BY

Edwin Emery

GREENWOOD PRESS, PUBLISHERS
WESTPORT, CONNECTICUT

Acknowledgments

APPRECIATION is due several persons for their aid in the writing of this history of the American Newspaper Publishers Association. Three advisers offered patient guidance during graduate student days at the University of California in Berkeley. They were Professor Robert W. Desmond, chairman of the department of journalism; the late Professor Frederic Logan Paxson, chairman of the department of history; and the late Professor Charles Harvey Raymond, first chairman of the department of journalism. Several colleagues in the University of Minnesota School of Journalism have been helpful; in particular, Director Ralph D. Casey has read the manuscript and made many valuable suggestions.

Cranston Williams, general manager of the American Newspaper Publishers Association, cooperated fully in making available the basic materials for this study. To him and to his secretary, Mrs. R. V. Lang, is due much appreciation. Thanks are also extended to the board of directors of the association and to the several members who were of assistance. It should be emphasized, however, that the responsibility for the gathering of facts and the interpretation of them is wholly my own.

EDWIN EMERY

Minneapolis, October 1949

Contents

History of the American Newspaper
Publishers Association

CHAPTER I

The Setting

THE American Newspaper Publishers Association was formed in 1887 by forty-six men as a daily newspaper trade association. Sixty years later it had a membership of 809 newspapers, representing more than 90 percent of the total circulation of dailies in the United States and Canada.

Between these two dates lies the history of a typical trade association. It is undeniably a most significant and influential organization, for its members control the major components of a fundamental agency of mass communication. The story of their group activities is primarily one of the advancement of the business interests of daily newspapers and of resulting adjustments and conflicts with advertisers, with labor, with communications competitors, with newsprint makers, and with the government.

But before that story is begun, the broad outlines of the socioeconomic setting in which the association was founded may be suggested. The United States was coming of age in 1887; so was the daily newspaper. In the years before the close of the century — the formative years of the American Newspaper Publishers Association — the new economic pattern of the nation and of its newspapers reached a first maturity.

The dynamic capitalism of an expanding America, seizing upon unparalleled natural resources and utilizing the new machines of the industrial revolution, had transformed the national economy in the years following the Civil War. Forces of economic individualism, consolidating industrial and financial power in a materialistic-minded age, then found unrestrained opportunity in the last two decades of the nineteenth century. The full intensity of this vast sweep of economic development came to be felt in every phase of American life.

3

Familiar symbols of this new economic order are John D. Rockefeller and the oil monopoly, Andrew Carnegie and the steel combine. But similar concentrations of wealth and business control developed throughout American industry and trade.

The captains of industry and the financial kings who dominated the American scene in the late nineteenth century rose to power through a variety of means. Some gained control of large segments of natural resources. A few held patents on basic inventions. Others, of whom Rockefeller was the most noted, won supremacy in part through unfair manipulation of transportation rates. Some were lucky in the world of financial speculation. Most important, the Rockefellers and the Carnegies usually were successful because they had, or could hire, the brains which were necessary to create a new manufacturing or financial empire.

America was a rich continent for the aggressive and the ingenious. Between 1880 and 1900 its national wealth more than doubled. Its population increased 50 percent. Its iron ore, its oil, its lumber, and its western agricultural lands were sources of yet untapped wealth. Its people, who by and large admired the successful enterprisers, eagerly provided investment and speculative capital.

But as the machine revolutionized the American economy, it brought with it the threat of overproduction and disastrous competition among the new producers. The dislocation of labor which resulted, and the bankrupting of weaker businesses, also promoted economic instability. The captains of industry cast about for ways of avoiding the industrial and financial panics which threatened the strong as well as the weak.

One effort to overcome these dangers took the form of the pool agreement among competitors in a given field. Individual enterprises sought by voluntary secret agreement to limit industry-wide production, to allocate satisfactory quotas, and to stabilize selling prices. Such pools, however, not only were illegal but also proved ineffective in times of stress because of their voluntary nature.

A more successful form of industry control was the trust, developed by the Standard Oil Company group about 1880. By this method the shareholders in the original companies assigned their capital stock to a board of trustees and received trust certificates in return. The trustees thus won legal control of the individual units. They could stabilize marketing and prices for the industry and eliminate competition.

The year 1887 saw the formation of the great sugar and whiskey trusts, as well as the rope and lead producers' trusts. But the next year saw the introduction in Congress of the legislation which became the Sherman Anti-trust Law of 1890, which was designed to restore open competition. The end result was hardly satisfactory to opponents of industrial monopoly, for the sugar trust simply became an incorporated company under the laws of New Jersey and the Standard Oil Company of New Jersey became a holding company for the Rockefeller empire. The amalgamation of many businesses now took the form of a single great corporation.

Dominant companies had already appeared as a natural consequence of unrestrained competition in steelmaking and other manufacturing industries of the East, in railroading, and in the mining and cattle businesses of the West. Now in the 1890s the trend toward amalgamations and holding companies brought even larger industrial corporate concentrations. Many products, ranging from tin plate to newsprint, fell under near monopolistic control.

It remained for Andrew Carnegie to complete the process, when in 1901 he unveiled the breath-taking billion-dollar United States Steel Corporation. Here were brought together nearly 250 companies, which used half the total iron ore smelted in the country. The new corporation also controlled its own iron deposits and coal mines, and its ships and railroads, as well as its smelters, furnaces, rolling mills, and factories. This was a new method of industrial organization — integration.

The basic trend in this economic revolution was one which came to be intensified in twentieth-century America. It involved an increasing change from production of a small number of units at a comparatively large profit per unit to production of a large number of units at a smaller profit per unit. The familiar story of mass production by a decreasing number of producers was chronicled in many fields of business.

The American newspaper could not fail to be affected along with the rest of the national economy. Already in the 1880s newspapers had begun to benefit from the change to mass production methods. More and more businesses needed regional or national distribution of their mass-produced soaps, foods, and other articles. The result was the rise of new techniques in advertising and merchandising to popularize brand names. Acting as the go-between for businesses and newspaper publishers were the advertising agents, whose influence had been growing steadily since Civil War days. Newspapers received added advertising revenue, not only from this new source, but also from the retail stores of the expanding cities.

But the blessings of the new order were mixed. Metropolitan papers, particularly, had begun to feel strong pressures for efficient operation which the increased mechanization of printing processes and pyramiding capitalizations entailed. It was costing more and more money to produce a competitive daily newspaper, and the publisher who wished his paper to grow, or even to survive, had to match the skills of his rivals. His increasing production costs had to be met by increased revenues from advertising and newspaper sales. This race for larger circulations and advertising volumes could only bring the eventual elimination of those competing newspapers which failed to match the pace, either in the quality of their product or in their business ability.

Because of the community character of each newspaper, however, the publishing industry scarcely could be amalgamated into one giant national corporation or consolidated into a few major production units. Here, fortunately, the new economic pattern did not apply. Successful publishers could own a score of newspapers, as E. W. Scripps already was proving before 1900, but the newspaper by its nature remained predominantly a home-owned enterprise. The competitive battles were to be fought out in each local publishing field and later in regional publishing areas.

The great corporations and industrial concentrations which were maturing between 1880 and 1900 were of vital significance, but they were only a part of the enormous changes in American life. Mechanization, industrialization, and urbanization brought swift and extensive social, cultural, and political developments. People were being uprooted physically and mentally by the effects of the economic revolution, and a new environment was evolving in which no social institution — least of all the newspaper — could remain static. Even a brief examination of the character of this new environment will indicate the basic causes of the tremendous changes which developed in the daily newspapers of American cities beginning in the 1880s. It was by no mere chance that the "new journalism" of Joseph Pulitzer's New York *World* dated from 1883 and that daily newspaper owners and managers decided to form a trade association in 1887.

Arthur M. Schlesinger has chosen the phrase "the rise of the city" to characterize the period from 1878 to 1898. Census figures show that the number of American towns and cities of 8000 or more population doubled between 1880 and 1900. The population of those urban places more than doubled, jumping from some 11 million to 25 million. In 1880 there were 50 million Americans, of whom 22.7 percent were living in towns and cities of more than 8000. By 1900 that figure had risen to 32.9 percent of a total population of 76 million.

The biggest percentage of these gains in urbanization occurred during the ten years between 1880 and 1890, which were the years of greatest ferment in the daily newspaper business. The rise of the city was particularly evident in the northeastern industrial states, where urban centers now predominated over declining rural areas, and in the Middlewest. New York City jumped in population from a million to a million and a half during the decade. Chicago, the rail and trade center of inland America, doubled its size, passing the million mark in 1890 to become the nation's second city. Next in line were Philadelphia, at the million mark; Brooklyn, at 800,000; and Boston, Baltimore, and St. Louis, in the half-million class. Altogether there were fifty-eight cities with more than 50,000 population. Eighty percent of them were in the East and Middlewest, and half of them were in the five states of New York, Massachusetts, Pennsylvania, New Jersey, and Ohio.

Into these cities was pouring an ever rising tide of immigration, which brought new blood and new problems for American society, as well as the problem of increasing readership appeal for the daily newspaper editors. Again the decade of 1880–90 stands out, since in those ten years more than five million immigrants came to America, double the number for any preceding decade. Altogether, approximately nine million foreign-born were added to the population in the twenty years between 1880 and 1900, as many as had come during the forty years preceding 1880. As a result the newspapers of New York City in 1890 served a population that was 80 percent foreign-born or of foreign parentage. Other major American cities had foreign-born residents numbering from 25 to 40 percent of their populations. To the older Irish, British, and German streams of migration were added great numbers of Scandinavians, French-Canadians, Poles, Italians, Russians, and Hungarians. Of these, the Germans and the Scandinavians particularly migrated into the Middlewest, while the other groups tended to remain in the Atlantic states.

While the East and the older parts of the Middlewest were the major centers of industrialization and urbanization, the rest of the country was advancing steadily, if less conspicuously. The South, slowly recovering from the Civil War, was redistributing its agricultural lands and establishing tobacco manufacturing, cotton mills, and iron furnaces. The western plains territories, pierced by the transcontinental railroads, doubled their populations between 1880 and 1890, as the line of the frontier disappeared from the map of the United States. In the Far West the great boom that was to become southern California was in the making. Major population centers were still scarce in the South and West in 1890, but the process of urbanization was under way.

The rise of the city meant a quickening of material progress. The new American cities paved their streets with asphalt and bricks after 1880, and they bridged their rivers with steel structures patterned after the famed Brooklyn bridge of 1883. Horsecars and cabs could no longer carry the throngs of city dwellers or serve adequately the vast suburbs which mushroomed about metropolitan centers. New York's elevated trains of the 1870s and San Francisco's cable cars were adopted by other large cities. Then came the electric railway and streetcar, perfected in 1887, to meet the urban transportation problem. By 1895 some 850 electric lines were in operation.

Electricity was becoming a great new servant, both as a source of power and as a source of light. American cities had barely begun to install arc lights in 1879 when Thomas A. Edison perfected the incandescent bulb. When the current flowed out from his Pearl Street generating station in 1882 to light the stock exchange and the offices of the New York *Times* and the New York *Herald,* a new era in living had begun.

America was being tied together by its industrial revolution, and its communications network kept pace with the sense of urgency which was characteristic of the new order. The telephone, invented in the 1870s, already had one user for every thousand persons in 1880. By 1900 there was one telephone for each hundred. Intercity lines multiplied during the 1880s, until by 1900 the Bell system covered the country. Western Union quadrupled its telegraph lines between 1880 and 1900. The railroads, with 93,000 miles of track in 1880, reached a near saturation point of 193,000 miles by 1900. The federal postal service, still the primary means of communication, greatly extended its free carrier service in cities during the two decades and instituted free rural delivery in 1897. In business offices the invention of the typewriter and adding machine speeded the work pace and simplified the handling of increased correspondence and records.

Each of these material advances and changes in the physical character of American society had its impact, large or small, upon the nation's journalism. The nationwide financial and industrial expansion which took the name of "big business" transformed the big city newspaper into a corporate enterprise rather than a personal venture. Increasing mechanization, spurred on by inventive genius, revolutionized the printing processes just as it had other industrial processes. The tremendous growth of the cities permitted larger newspaper circulations, which were in turn made necessary by larger investments and operating expenses. And a steady increase in the number of urban communities, as population expanded and the economic benefits of industrialization spread across the country, offered a host of new publishing opportunities which were seized upon quickly.

The most striking evidence of what was happening to the daily newspaper is to be found in a bare statistical summary. Between 1870 and 1900 the United States doubled its population and tripled the number of its urban residents. During the same thirty years the number of its daily newspapers quadrupled and the number of copies sold each day increased almost sixfold. Both in numbers and in total circulation the daily newspaper was rising even more rapidly than the city which spawned it.

There were many less tangible reasons why the daily newspaper was making such tremendous strides as an American social institution. The forces of social and economic interdependence, products of industrialization and urbanization, played a leading part in the creation of the lusty "new journalism." The peoples of the cities, being molded together as economic and cultural units, increasingly turned to the daily newspapers for the story of their urban life and their common interests. At the same time the country itself was being rapidly unified by the rush toward economic interdependence. Improved communications facilities were a manifestation of this nationalizing influence which pervaded all American life. And again, the daily newspaper was the chronicler of the national scene, the interpreter of the new environment. The city reader, whether he was seated in new-found comfort on a streetcar or in his better-lighted home, was the eager customer of the publisher who successfully met the new challenge to journalism.

As American social and economic life became more complex and as the national wealth accumulated, many cultural advances were possible which in turn promoted the new interest in the daily newspaper. The cities, with their concentrated populations and earning capacities, naturally led in expansion of social and intellectual activity. But they also set the pace for an increasing cultural development of the entire country. The percentage of children attending public schools in the United States jumped from 57 to 72 percent between 1870 and 1900, while illiteracy declined from 20 to 10.7 percent of the population. At higher educational levels growth of the state universities and of private colleges financed by America's new men of wealth resulted in notable advances in the social sciences, as well as progress in the physical sciences and the humanities. Millions shared in this new knowledge through the chautauquas and public study courses which became of major importance toward the close of the century as means of adult education. Free public libraries, spreading rapidly across the nation after 1880, found their great benefactor in Andrew Carnegie. In them were available both the literary achievements and the popular writings of American and British authors. The older literary magazines were joined in the 1890s by a group of popular ten-cent publications which revolutionized the periodical trade and spread their influence across the country with the advent of rural free delivery. It must be noted, however, that the general level of cultural attainment was still low. Even by 1900 the average American had received only five years of schooling in his lifetime. If the public bought encyclopedias galore from the book publishers because it wanted to know more, it also bought dime novels by the millions. If the chautauqua was a booming institution, so were horse racing, prize fighting, and baseball. Cultural and business organizations were expanding in number, but growing even faster were fraternal and social groups. In the newspaper world Adolph Ochs could find enough serious readers in the metropolis of New York to support the reborn New York *Times*, but the great mass of readers was attracted by the devices of yellow journalism, which sought a popular level as it both entertained and informed.

It should be noted briefly, too, that not everybody was successful or contented in this new economic and social environment, despite the general blessings that industrialization had bestowed upon the country. Political and economic events became of more than ordinary interest to masses of people whose new livelihoods in the cities and in the factories were immediately affected by financial panics, labor disturbances, and even political debates over the tariff and free silver. The newspaper reader of the 1880s and 1890s might devour all the details of the doings of America's new-rich society and its alliances with European nobility, or he might applaud the financial coups of a James J. Hill, but he also was disturbed by the excesses of economic individualism. Newspapers which attacked the traction company bosses of Chicago and Kansas City, or the manipulations of freight rates in favor of a great corporation, or the dangers of reckless market speculation, found widespread popular approval.

A running battle was being fought during the closing years of the nineteenth century between those who believed that government should not interfere with the course of economic development, except to protect business in its onward drive, and those who believed government regulation must be invoked to maintain an equitable society and economic freedom. In general the protests, while loud and widespread, served only to alleviate the worst features of excessive individualism. The drastic proposals of Marxian Socialism found but few adherents, even among the immigrant populations of the cities. And the idealistic writings of Edward Bellamy and Henry George stirred popular thinking, but did not result in the socialistic solution of economic ills which the authors advocated. The practical victories, such as they were, were won by the advocates of moderate regulation of economic affairs, who secured progressive state statutes and federal legislation restricting the abuses of the railroads and the trusts.

Sharp divisions began to appear between those who had gained wealth in the process of national economic upheaval, and those who had gained only a crowded room in a city tenement, a poverty-stricken tenant farm in the South, or a precarious existence on the dry plains of the West. Falling farm prices during the 1880s spurred the political activities of the discontented in the South and West. There the Grangers, the Greenbackers, the Farmers' Alliance, and the Populists rose to demand economic equality for agriculture. Their strongest plea was for an increase of money in circulation, and the merging of the forces of free silver, soft money, and economic reform under the banner of William Jennings Bryan in 1896 provided America with the most political excitement of a generation. But, despite the bitter experiences of the depression of 1893, the advocates of William McKinley and political and economic conservatism won the decision.

In the cities the rise of the labor movement on a nationally organized scale provided a much sharper clash than that between business and agriculture. The Knights of Labor, with a "one big union" plan, reached a peak membership of 700,000 during the two years of industrial turbulence which followed the panic of 1884. But the movement fell away because of poor planning and a belligerence which incurred public mistrust. The steadier American Federation of Labor, built in 1881 as a national organization of the various craft unions, became the principal voice of the labor movement. Its nationwide strikes in 1886 for a shortening of the ten-hour workday won a reduction to eight or nine hours for some

200,000 workers out of the 350,000 involved. The reaction in many industries was the formation of employers' associations which raised defense funds to fight the carefully planned demands and strikes of the individual craft unions. It should be observed, however, that the American Newspaper Publishers Association was never committed as an organization to such practices, even though it was founded during a peak of labor disturbances and its members had as employees workers from the powerful International Typographical Union.

In such a swiftly changing and exciting environment, then, the daily newspaper was coming of age. From 971 dailies in 1880 to 2226 in 1900; from 3.5 million circulation to 15 million; from 10 percent of the adult population as subscribers to 26 percent — these were the statistical evidences of its arrival as a major business. The enormous success of the New York *World*, which between 1883 and 1887 broke every publishing record in America, was evidence that a "new journalism" had been created by Joseph Pulitzer and his staff which would change the character and the appearance of the daily newspaper and enormously increase its mass influence.

Pulitzer found in the New York City of 1883 a chance to develop once again a people's newspaper which would satisfy the average city dweller and attract the immigrant group, of which he himself was one. He enlivened the *World's* significant news coverage to satisfy one set of changing conditions, and he achieved sensationalism both in news content and in newspaper appearance to satisfy another trend. He combined outstanding promotional ability with editorial aggressiveness and a crusading spirit to win a mass following. He utilized mechanical and format improvements and drove the circulation of the *World* from 20,000 in 1883 to 250,000 in 1887. He sold the biggest morning paper for the cut-rate price of two cents and filled its pages with more advertising than any newspaper had ever had.

These were the characteristics of the "new journalism," which was appearing to a less complete degree in other American cities. James W. Scott's Chicago *Herald* and William M. Singerly's Philadelphia *Record* were other examples of brightened, low-priced morning newspapers which successfully challenged the established older press. The biggest challenge, however, was coming from the evening newspaper field, which claimed seven eighths of the increase in numbers of dailies between 1880 and 1900 as reading habits of the city population changed and mechanical and news-gathering innovations favored the evening publications. James E. Scripps' Detroit *News*, E. W. Scripps' Cleveland *Press* and Cincinnati *Post*, Melville E. Stone's Chicago *Daily News*, and many other new leaders were low-priced, aggressive, easily read evening dailies. When the American Newspaper Publishers Association was formed in 1887, it was the owners and managers of the evening and new-style morning papers who took the lead.

Newspapers such as these were evolving into complex business institutions. Their installation of bigger presses, stereotyping equipment, and newly invented typesetting machines skyrocketed investment and operating costs. They required departmentalized editorial staffs for coverage of local news, business, and sports, and for the Sunday editions. They fought for reforms in press association coverage of national and international news and competed in that field at increased expense. Their business departments became more and more important as circulation promotion increased and competition for large advertising volume intensified. By the middle 1880s the managers of these daily newspapers were harassed by a host of new problems which smaller papers found of little concern. They were also conscious of the financial and business trends of the changing American economy and particularly of the increased advertising problems of the new industrial environment. A call for the formation of a daily newspaper trade association which would attempt to meet some of those problems in an organized fashion was the logical outcome. It was also only proper, and necessary under the American form of government, that such a trade association should be organized to speak for a segment of American business in the growing contest for political and economic power. Only by such organized means could the voices of business, labor, agriculture, and other groups be heard effectively in the free interchange of opinion which is necessary in a democracy.

CHAPTER II

The Founding

AT noon on February 16, 1887, at Powers' Hotel in the city of Rochester, New York, William H. Brearley of the Detroit *Evening News* addressed forty-five other daily newspaper publishers and managers in entirely traditional style: "The gentlemen will please come to order." The stenographer's report[1] continues with Brearley's opening words: "We have, of course, a little plan to suggest. . . ." And another group of Americans had begun the process of forming an organization.

This, however, was no ordinary occasion. The meeting in Rochester was the climax of six months of careful planning and campaigning by a small group representing the new leadership of the nation's daily newspapers. It marked a recognition of the fact that the newspaper publishing business of the United States was emerging into the modern era. The men who had come to Rochester were conscious of the need for an organization such as they proposed to create, even though they could not know the influence that organization would possess in future years.

Nineteen of the forty-six publishers, business managers, and advertising managers who signed the register on opening day represented daily newspapers of nearby New York towns and cities. The others were fairly well scattered: five each from Michigan and Ohio; three from Indiana; two each from Rhode Island, Massachusetts, and Pennsylvania; and one each from New Jersey, Delaware, Connecticut, Florida, Wisconsin, Iowa, the District of Columbia, and the province of Ontario. They had not traveled in

[1] "Proceedings of the Convention of Newspaper Proprietors held at the City of Rochester, New York, on Wednesday and Thursday, February 16, 17, 1887." This is a typewritten copy of the stenographic record of the convention, kept in the New York office of the American Newspaper Publishers Association. Unless otherwise noted, all details of the first meeting presented in this chapter are taken from this record.

midwinter without a serious purpose and they concluded their business with dispatch. Before nightfall of the following day they had founded the American Newspaper Publishers Association.[2] The names of the fifteen men who figure most prominently in the story of the ANPA's founding offer proof that this daily newspaper trade association was organized by journalists who understood the impact of current economic and social change upon the publishing business. Ten of the fifteen represented the dynamic evening newspapers of the "new journalism" or morning papers which had adopted the business techniques, news policies, and format of the new era. Such a listing also emphasizes the fact that the ANPA was to be interested almost exclusively in business problems of daily newspapers, rather than editorial policies, since ten of the fifteen were business or advertising managers of their papers, while only five were publishers or publisher-editors.

Most famous of the publishers present was Melville E. Stone, founder, editor, and copublisher until 1888 of the Chicago *Daily News*, which was presenting a bright new face in Illinois journalism. Stone later became the first general manager of the reorganized Associated Press. Colonel Charles H. Jones of the Jacksonville *Florida Times-Union* was another aggressive newspaper leader, who also served as second president of the National Editorial Association, an organization of the weeklies. In 1888 Jones took over the editorial direction of the St. Louis *Republic*, and from 1893 to 1895 he was publisher of Joseph Pulitzer's New York *World*. During the next two years he leased and edited Pulitzer's St. Louis *Post-Dispatch* until differences with Pulitzer and failing health forced his retirement. William M. Singerly, publisher of the Philadelphia *Record*, was a millionaire who bought the *Record* in 1877 and made it into a highly successful, crusading one-cent morning newspaper. Samuel H. Kauffmann was president and one of the owners, with the Noyes family, of the Washington *Evening Star*, while Joseph A. Dear was the editor of the Jersey City *Jersey Journal*.

Milton A. McRae, the brilliant business associate of E. W.

[2] The stenographer recorded the name as "American Newspaper Publisher's Association." For the next few years it was called "American Newspaper Publishers' Association." In 1897 the group was incorporated as "American Newspaper Publishers Association," without the wandering apostrophe. That form and its abbreviation, ANPA, will be used here.

Scripps, was the most famous of the group of business and advertising managers who strongly influenced the ANPA's organization. McRae, then business manager of the aggressive Cincinnati *Post* for Scripps, later became general manager and part owner of the Scripps-McRae League of Newspapers. Well known for their managerial abilities were other representatives of evening papers: Brearley of the Detroit *Evening News*, who in 1887 became publisher of the Detroit *Journal*;[3] W. J. Richards of the Indianapolis *News*; Herbert F. Gunnison, later publisher of the Brooklyn *Eagle*; and J. Ambrose Butler of the Buffalo *News* publishing family. From the highly competitive Boston field came Colonel William W. Clapp, manager of the sensationalized *Journal*, and Edward P. Call, advertising manager of the staid *Herald*. The other major participants, all from morning papers, were J. C. Briggs, advertising manager of the Columbus *Ohio State Journal*; George F. Prescott, advertising manager of the Cleveland *Plain Dealer*; and William Cullen Bryant, a namesake and distant relative of the famous poet-editor of the New York *Evening Post*, who was manager and later publisher of the Brooklyn *Times*.

The dynamic southern colonel, Jones, was unanimously chosen temporary president of the meeting and C. E. Ganz of the Albany *Evening Journal*, temporary secretary. The chair then appointed a business committee to consider plans for organization. Butler was named chairman. The members were McRae, Gunnison, Call, J. H. Farrell of the Albany *Press*, W. F. Balkam of the Rochester *Union and Advertiser*, and W. H. Welch of the Des Moines *Leader*. D. T. Hunt of the Rochester *Post Express* was made chairman of a committee to name permanent officers of the convention, and the two groups retired to transact their business.

Meanwhile the chair introduced again "the gentleman who originated the idea," Brearley, and he explained the background of the meeting while the convention awaited the action of its committees. From his rambling speech and from a memorial paper prepared by Gunnison in 1909 on the occasion of Brearley's death,[4] we may reconstruct the events which preceded the calling of the Rochester conference.

[3] Brearley's name is sometimes incorrectly spelled *Brearly*.
[4] Brearley died March 26, 1909, and Gunnison prepared a statement on the history of the association and Brearley's part in its founding for the *Report of the*

What bothered Brearley and prompted him to action, he explained to the convention, was that, although there were many editorial associations in the country, none was particularly interested in the business problems of daily newspapers. He referred to such early organizations as the Wisconsin Editorial Association, the Connecticut Newspaper Association, and the New York Press Association, all dating from 1853; and state associations in New Jersey, Indiana, Nebraska, Maine, Illinois, Missouri, Vermont, Minnesota, New Hampshire, Massachusetts, Alabama, Arkansas, Colorado, and Rhode Island, founded in that order before 1880.[5] When these groups started, there was no sharp differentiation between the persons or problems of editor and publisher. But by the 1880s problems of advertising, labor, circulation, mechanical innovations, and business procedures were more important to managers like Brearley than discussions of editorial problems. The processes of industrialization and urbanization were drawing a sharp line between the metropolitan and the small-town press.

The first attempt at national organization of publishers occurred at the 1884 convention of the Minnesota Editors' and Publishers' Association. Its president, B. B. Herbert of the Red Wing *Daily Republican,* sponsored a call for the organization of a National Editors' and Publishers' Association.[6] A group of publishers and editors met during the fair at New Orleans in February 1885 and a year later in Cincinnati. At the 1886 meeting they adopted a constitution for the National Editorial Association, of which Herbert was the first president.

Brearley attended the Cincinnati convention, but he found that the National Editorial Association was not the business-minded group he wished to see formed. He was asked to prepare

Twenty-third Annual Meeting of the American Newspaper Publishers Association. Not finding the single copy of the minutes of the first convention at that time, he gathered his material from scrapbooks and other sources of information and thus preserved some facts which complete Brearley's own account as given at the 1887 meeting. Gunnison commented at the 1909 meeting, "It seems to me the time has come when we ought to have a committee to prepare a complete history of the Association."

[5] Alfred McClung Lee, *The Daily Newspaper in America* (New York: Macmillan, 1937), pp. 223–24.

[6] B. B. Herbert, *The First Decennium of the National Editorial Association of the United States* (Chicago, 1896), pp. 39–41.

a paper on advertising, and in it he proposed the formation of a
National Publishers Business Association. "I felt pretty badly
squelched by the reception given me," he told the 1887 meeting
in Rochester. A committee formed by the National Editorial Association quietly put Brearley's suggestion to death.[7]
But Brearley was not to be denied. He was the ambitious advertising manager of the *News*, founded in 1873 by James E.
Scripps as an aggressive, popular evening newspaper and built
by the efforts of the Scripps family team into a leading Detroit
daily by the middle 1880s. To aid him in his work, Brearley
wanted "annual conventions of the business managers of the leading newspapers of the country, not to have a junketing spree, but
to discuss and direct their own business . . . the editorial conventions utterly fail to give any practical help on this subject;
their membership is largely composed of small country weeklies;
their exercises are impossible theories or denunciations of the
'metropolitan press'; and the end and aim most apparent is the
banquet or excursion." [8] He therefore definitely went to work on
his project in the summer of 1886.
A plea for the establishment of better business arrangements
by newspapers, made by Brearley June 2 before the Michigan
Press Association, was published in the June 23 issue of the
American Advertiser Reporter. During the next month a thousand
copies of the *Reporter* were sent through Brearley's efforts to the
leading newspapers of the country, along with a circular propos-
ing a publishers' business association and a return postal card for
comments. In his circular Brearley pointed out the need for full
exchange of information about advertising prospects and advertising agencies and about advertising space actually sold by the
larger dailies. He advocated the establishment of a New York
headquarters for publishers where files of their newspapers could
be kept, a collection agency maintained, and information on advertising matters assembled. Only the leading dailies of the country would be members of the organization and each would have

[7] H. F. Gunnison's statement in *Report of the Twenty-third Annual Meeting*
(1909), p. 34.
[8] Lincoln B. Palmer, "The A.N.P.A. — Past and Present," *Publishers' Guide*,
20:39 (May 1912). This article is a historical review by the then general manager
of ANPA.

one share of stock. Brearley suggested the future name of the group when he said, "I therefore want to see our American Publishers Association formed on a practical business basis." [9]

Brearley found three other members of the rising newspaper management class immediately responsive to his plan. They were McRae, the Scripps business manager, Briggs of the *Ohio State Journal,* and Butler of the Buffalo *News.* During the convention of the Western Associated Press in Detroit on November 17, Brearley called a meeting which was attended by McRae, Briggs, Butler, George F. Prescott of the Cleveland *Plain Dealer,* James H. Stone of the Detroit *Tribune,* and A. H. Finn of the Port Huron, Michigan, *Tribune.*[10] Brearley held proxies from twenty-two other publishers and business managers.

It was decided that Brearley, Briggs, and Butler should proceed as a committee of three to call a convention whenever they could obtain the signatures of 30 of the 211 publishers of dailies with more than 5000 circulation. Brearley sent out a circular announcing the formation of the committee November 27, followed by another mailing in December. On January 25 Brearley was able to announce that more than eighty newspapers had approved the plan, and his circular called for a meeting in Rochester three weeks later. Those who came were led by the representatives of the rapidly expanding popular evening newspapers, and the more spirited low-priced morning papers, although there was a fair sampling of attendance from the older established dailies. Noticeably missing were the New York City dailies, none of whom were represented in the founding of the organization, probably because they mistrusted the motives of the "provincial press" in urging cooperation on advertising problems.

In his talk to the 1887 convention Brearley made a side reference which established a permanent policy of the association, that of maintaining the privacy of association affairs. Referring to the presence of a stenographer, he said, "What reports he shall make shall be our reports and not go out generally. There has been a conference with the Rochester papers and it has been agreed that only brief reports shall go out. . . ." Brearley's main

[9] *Report of the Twenty-third Annual Meeting* (1909), p. 34.
[10] *Report of the Twenty-sixth Annual Meeting* (1912), p. 19, in a summary of ANPA history by Bruce Haldeman of the Louisville *Courier-Journal.*

concern was that the advertising agents who had come to the convention should not learn the details of the discussions regarding them. In later years the main concerns of the association were in maintaining privacy of membership discussions regarding advertising and labor policy and in protecting the use of the association's publications for the membership. Of this first convention a writer on the history of the ANPA in the "Golden Jubilee Number" of *Editor & Publisher* said in 1934: "With the exception of a brief 'open' session the first day, all proceedings were held behind closed doors, and their record is to be found only in the memories of those who were present." [11] The files of the newspaper trade publications, the *Journalist* and the *Fourth Estate,* show the effects of this policy of closed meetings in their incomplete reports of early ANPA conventions.

After Brearley's speech the committee on permanent organization brought in its report. The honor of being permanent president of the convention fell to a representative of the highly regarded Boston *Journal,* publisher David Winslow. Named to the five vice-presidencies were Stone, Gunnison, Richards, William McManus of the Philadelphia *Record,* and John H. Haldeman of the Louisville *Courier-Journal* publishing family. Brearley was assigned the post of secretary and Call was named treasurer. The report was adopted as read.

Now the crucial resolution of the convention was presented by Butler for the business committee: "Is it desireable to form an organization, under the laws of the State of New York, to include papers of five thousand circulation and over, to be called the American Publishers Association?" There was some discussion, during which Colonel Jones, the temporary president, moved an amendment making the name "American Newspaper Publishers Association." The resolution was adopted as amended. A debate then ensued as to whether the association should be a corporation or merely a mutual association, and that question was referred to a committee of three and an attorney.

Having thus cast the die in favor of an American Newspaper Publishers Association, the delegates turned to another resolution presented by Butler: "Resolved, That the object of this organiza-

[11] *Editor & Publisher,* 67:311 (July 21, 1934).

tion is to protect and advance the business and advertising interests of the members of the proposed association, and that it is the sense of the business committee that delegates will present their views for the advancement of said organization and its interests, fully and freely."

The discussion which followed, while neither full nor free, illustrated one of the major problems of the rapidly expanding daily newspapers — increasing advertising revenues through the establishment of businesslike procedures for dealing with advertisers and the growing number of advertising agencies. Two of the topics discussed dealt with rate cutting, four with commission payments to advertising agents, and ten with the value of advertising. There was little disagreement on the final ten topics.

The expansion of business upon a national scale, and the consequent necessity for increased national advertising and merchandising efforts, had brought about a rapid growth in the number of advertising agents and agencies after the Civil War. The business of being the go-between for advertisers and publications was a haphazard one. The agents confined their efforts to buying space in newspapers and magazines on behalf of their clients according to their scanty knowledge of the worth of such space. They found that publishers would pay them discounts on stated advertising rates, ranging from 15 to 30 percent, and even as high as 75 percent. The discount represented the agent's profit, since at that time he did not prepare copy for the advertiser. Larger metropolitan papers were able to deal fairly effectively with the agents and limit their discounts, but the agents often were able to play one publisher against another and obtain handsome commissions for extending the favors they had to offer. The field was crowded with all manner of agents, ranging from the businesslike and respected agencies of George P. Rowell, N. W. Ayer, and J. Walter Thompson to the sharp-dealing agents of the patent medicine trade. The modern practices of agency control of advertising accounts and of general payment of commissions at 15 percent plus 2 percent for cash discount were yet to be evolved. And the complaints of the publishers who found themselves at the mercy of the agents were many.

Milton McRae reported something that all those present prob-

ably knew when he said, "There are here today three different
advertising agents . . . to place for the Hop Bitters one hundred
thousand dollars worth of advertising in about 35 city dailies."
McRae charged that the agents were trying to find publishers
who would cut their advertising rates to obtain Hop Bitters advertisements, thus permitting the agent to rebate part of his commission to the advertiser. The convention resolved that such
practices must stop, and the members pledged themselves not to
deal with advertising agents who were known to divide their
commissions with advertisers.

The problem of the amount of commission which should be
paid to an advertising agent was discussed without any definite
conclusion being reached — except the conclusion that the advertising agent had become an essential man in the newspaper
publishing business. L. L. Morgan of the New Haven *Register,*
while approving of agents, suggested that their commissions be
limited to 10 percent "instead of 25, as some of the papers do."
W. J. Arkell of the Albany *Evening Journal* said flatly, "I make a
discount of 20 per cent." Richards of the Indianapolis *News* reported that ten years before all three Indianapolis papers had
established commissions at 15 percent "without one single kick."

When Richards made a motion that it be the sense of the convention that a maximum commission of 10 percent henceforth be
allowed advertising agencies, there were immediate protests.
Colonel Jones of the *Florida Times-Union* moved to substitute a
maximum rate of 20 percent. Dear of the *Jersey Journal* suggested a compromise of 10 percent for metropolitan papers and 15
percent for smaller dailies. No action was taken; the motion was
just forgotten since it was evident that those present feared that
adoption of a fixed commission rate by some newspapers would
upset local competitive situations. Prescott of the Cleveland *Plain
Dealer* and Brearley closed the afternoon's discussion by advocating the establishment of a New York office of the association,
which would keep members in close touch with all phases of the
advertising field.

The first injection of the question of labor relations into the affairs of the ANPA came during the evening session of the opening day. The business committee presented a resolution setting

forth the object of the new association, to which Joseph A. Dear of the *Jersey Journal*[12] moved an amendment. The resolution, with Dear's amendment italicized, read as follows:

Resolved, That it is the sense of this meeting that the object of this association when formed, shall not be the establishing of an advertising agency for the purpose of procuring of advertising; but for the protection of the business interests of the members by exposing irresponsible customers, the gathering and dissemination of information of value to publishers, the making of collections, *and the rendering to each other of such other assistance as may be within our power.*

The proposed addition of this "general welfare" clause brought the subject of labor relations onto the convention floor. Nothing had been said in Brearley's circulars about the possibility of joint action in meeting the wage and hour demands which the American Federation of Labor had begun to press actively in 1886. It would seem likely, however, that the rise of the International Typographical Union since 1852, its affiliation with other craft unions in the American Federation of Labor, and the growing use of mechanical equipment requiring specialized labor encouraged some publishers to look with favor upon the establishment of a trade association which might deal with the problem.

Dear added the final clause, he said, because "This is a time of great agitation, of great confusion in the labor world." Our employees, he said, are more or less organized, and their conduct in many cases has "placed newspapers in peculiarly unpleasant situations." Printers with a typographical union "who think they can move the world" should be met by an organization of American newspaper publishers. Such an organization, Dear declared, should meet oppressive actions of printers with the "combined resistance of the newspapers of the country." In addition, Dear warned, "we have the pressmen all over the country organizing — in New York they have pressmen who are making some very strange demands — we had a little fight and beat them, but that was just good luck. . . ."

Dear explained that his phrasing of the final clause, which would make the new association one concerned with all business problems of daily newspapers rather than just advertising prob-

[12] One of Joseph Dear's sons, Walter M. Dear, served as ANPA president from 1941 to 1943.

lems, was deliberately ambiguous. This was necessary, he said, so the world "would not think that we are contemplating disrupting present relations with our employees." But he insisted that relations with employees, as well as advertising contracts, should be ruled by the owners, not by the workers or the advertising agents, and that the latter two groups should be made to understand this fact.

When Dear had finished speaking, Brearley uttered a hope for more discussion, saying "This afternoon it looked as though no one wanted to discuss anything but advertising." But there was no more discussion forthcoming. Whatever the other delegates thought about this suggestion of a resolute attitude toward labor unions, they kept to themselves. The motion, however, was adopted as Dear had amended it.

While awaiting the report of the committee on incorporation, the delegates returned to the subject of advertising. The chair announced the question as: "What are the qualifications of an advertising agency?" And an anonymous publisher replied: "Cheek is the main thing." That the publishers were sensitive about this subject was made clear when two proposals concerning regulation of advertising agencies were voted down as "antagonistic to the agencies." One would have asked the agencies to form a protective association with minimum capital requirements and a seal of approval. The other would have pledged those present to deal only with honest agents. Prescott of the Cleveland *Plain Dealer* made one suggestion which was to bear fruit when he proposed that the association follow a recommendation by George P. Rowell, a leading advertising agent and newspaper directory publisher, and compile a list of reputable agents from among all those then doing business. It was agreed that a committee should compile such a list for the benefit of the membership.

When the second day's session began on the morning of February 17, Brearley reported that "there are at least eight different agents here this morning endeavoring to bring to bear all they can upon the point that this meeting is opposed to the best interests of the newspapers." They were afraid, he said, that commissions would be limited to 10 percent. Some cautious delegates offered an "appeasement resolution" pledging that the meeting was not in any way antagonistic to the advertising agencies, but the motion was defeated. The convention then discussed horse-car advertising as a rival of newspaper advertising; free publicity, especially in dramatic reports; and a charge by E. M. Hoopes of the Wilmington, Delaware, *Morning News* that there was a bureau in operation which was being paid for getting news stories into print.

Brearley finally took the floor to explain to the impatient members why the report on incorporation had been delayed. The committee had been unable to locate a lawyer during the night and had been using as the basis for its report the constitution and by-laws of the Gentlemen's Club of Detroit. Eventually the firm of Taylor and Shaffer aided the committee, and in the afternoon Brearley presented its recommendations.

The decision was that the association organize as a voluntary association and that the executive committee decide before the next annual meeting as to the advisability of incorporating under the laws of New York State. The articles of association were then proposed and adopted. They provided that the name of the organization be the American Newspaper Publishers Association and included the statement of purpose which had been approved the evening before. The administrative work of the association was to be handled by an executive committee composed of four officers and five other members elected at the annual meetings, which were to be held on the second Wednesday in February. The bylaws gave the executive committee authority to decide qualifications for membership and to establish and run an association office. The bylaws also set the initiation fee at $20 and the annual dues at $25 and otherwise defined the duties of the officers.

Singerly, the millionaire publisher of the Philadelphia *Record*, then was elected first president of the association. Colonel Clapp, manager of the Boston *Journal*, was named vice-president. Brearley again took the secretary's post and Bryant of the Brooklyn *Times* became treasurer. The five other members of the first executive committee were Butler, Richards, Call, Jones, and Kauffmann. The articles of association were signed by the delegates still present, and the first annual meeting of the American Newspaper Publishers Association adjourned.

In Brearley's diary there appears this notation under February 16 and 17, 1887: "American Newspaper Publishers Association formed at Rochester, N.Y. Well attended. Important meeting. I was elected its secretary. Office to be in New York City." And on the following day: "Went to New York and helped arrange an office and get it started." [13] The ANPA was now in business.

[13] As reported by his son, Harry Chase Brearley, in an article in *Editor & Publisher*, 70:6 (Apr. 17, 1937).

CHAPTER III

Formative Years

THE American Newspaper Publishers Association, launched in the years when the United States was becoming an industrial, urban country, could hardly fail to grow or to face new problems in its function as a national trade association. Each year the members met in convention after 1887 the increasing complexities of the daily newspaper publishing business made it more apparent that cooperative group action was essential.

In the larger cities the daily newspaper was becoming a business institution with departmentalized direction and complex financial operations. The modern, mass-circulation city daily was developing as the dominant journalistic pattern in the years around the turn of the century, years during which it was given great impetus by the clash between Joseph Pulitzer and William Randolph Hearst in New York City. If the initial success of the New York *World* in the 1880s had startled and stimulated the newspaper fraternity, the enormous struggle which began with Hearst's invasion of the New York field in 1895 left the onlookers breathless. In 1897 the combined morning and evening circulations of the *World* reached the awe-inspiring million mark, but Hearst's *Journal* pushed ahead during the Spanish-American War to set a new top figure of a million and a half combined circulation.

These two bitter contestants, whose excessive use of the techniques of sensationalism to win circulation brought the era of yellow journalism to the nation's press, represented the extreme in size and cost of operation. But just as many newspapers in other cities adopted the shrillness and the forced excitement which characterized the news presentation of the *World* and the *Journal*, so did they adopt also the new reader-winning policies which brought improved news coverage, pictures, comics, Sunday supplements, and color printing. As a result of the intensified effort to attract more readers in the growing cities, larger circulations became the general rule. During the first twenty-five years of ANPA history, the average circulation of daily newspapers doubled, while the number of papers which had reached the major circulation figure of 100,000 copies daily jumped from approximately ten to thirty.[1]

The sheer size of the business operations of these expanding daily papers made for increased attention to the problems of management. Census figures showing revenues of daily newspapers alone are not available except for the year 1879, but it was evident that the dailies kept pace with the rapid financial growth of the country. In 1879 total circulation revenues for daily newspapers amounted to 22 million dollars, while advertising brought in 21 million dollars. By 1909 the circulation revenue of all American newspapers totaled 84 million dollars and advertising revenue 148 million dollars. The great bulk of this revenue went to dailies. Granted that the New York *World* of the mid-nineties, with its reputed annual million-dollar profit on a valuation of 10 million dollars, was a more complex financial operation than was an E. W. Scripps $30,000 publishing venture, still each felt the pressures of the problems which had come with the new order in journalism.

These problems involved all phases of daily newspaper publishing. Advertising solicitation for the dailies had become big business, but so had the advertising agencies with which the papers dealt. Other media, particularly the magazines, were now recognized as keen competitors for the increasingly important advertising appropriations of American business. Expanding circulations meant that newsprint was becoming a major cost factor, and here the publishers found newsprint manufacturers obtaining tariff legislation to protect a near monopoly. Bigger and faster presses, typesetting machines, stereotyping, color printing, and photoengraving brought mechanical problems to papers large and small. Increased mechanization also resulted in an in-

[1] Frank Luther Mott, *American Journalism* (New York: Macmillan, 1941), p. 547.

crease of labor costs and brought a need for reaching settlements with the organized unions of the printing crafts. Distribution of papers over a widening area brought conflict with news companies and increased the attention given to second-class postal rates and service. Larger investments in newspapers meant new difficulties over copyright protections and libel law interpretations.

The changing American daily newspaper also had problems affecting editorial and news policies, but these were not considered to be within the province of a trade association established primarily to further the business interests of its members. The American Newspaper Publishers Association therefore seldom discussed or took action on questions of an editorial or news character, unless they also involved business considerations. The association turned its attention in the years before the end of the century, however, to all the business problems listed in the foregoing pages. In these formative years of the organization's history are to be found clearly indicated the major trends of its continuing activities. Before 1900 the ANPA was to become a firmly established trade association, promoting group actions in the fields of advertising, mechanical development, labor relations, newsprint supply, circulation, and copyright and libel law.

Detailed information about the ANPA's first year of operations and its second annual convention is scanty. Under Brearley's direction an office had been opened at 104 Temple Court in New York City. James S. Metcalfe, who later became editor of the humor magazine *Life*, was employed by the executive committee as the first office manager, and he issued twenty-four bulletins to members during the year.[2] It is also recorded that the membership met in Indianapolis, February 8–9, 1888,[3] but the full details of that convention probably will never be known since no copy of the minutes of the meeting seems to exist. William M. Singerly of the Philadelphia *Record* was reelected president. Colonel Charles H. Jones of the *Florida Times-Union* became vice-president, L. L. Morgan of the New Haven *Register* was elected secretary, and William Cullen Bryant of the Brooklyn *Times* con-

[2] *Minutes of the Third Annual Meeting* (1889), p. 4.
[3] *Journalist*, Feb. 18, 1888.

tinued as treasurer. William H. Brearley, the organizer of ANPA, was given a vote of thanks as he left the secretaryship,[4] and except for one mention of his name in the 1890 convention minutes he played no further part in the affairs of the association he had helped to create.[5]

The 1889 meeting was held in New York City, where ANPA conventions have met every year since. There Metcalfe reviewed office operations during the first two years. Despite the fact that the membership rolls had grown to include 128 newspapers, Metcalfe termed interest in the association "apathetic." Twenty percent of the members were not availing themselves of inquiry privileges in the conduct of their advertising business, he said, although 624 inquiries were answered the second year as compared to 376 the first year. Ten collections of accounts, totaling $551.70, were made, and twenty-four bulletins were sent to the members each year.

The ANPA office was moved to 206 Potter Building in May 1889, and in October Metcalfe resigned as manager "to go into more literary pursuits" with *Life*. G. M. Brennan became office manager; he received fifty dollars a week for his services in 1890 and his assistant, Mamie A. King, fifteen dollars.[6] ANPA records do not give the exact length of Brennan's service, but the 1892 association bulletins disclose that the ANPA secretary, L. L. Morgan of the New Haven *Register*, had also become manager of the New York office. When Morgan died later in 1892, William Cullen Bryant of the Brooklyn *Times* was named secretary and manager, positions which he held until his death in 1905. J. T. O. Canterbury served as office head assistant to Bryant during this period.[7]

Two editor-publishers held the presidency of the ANPA during the ten years following 1889. James W. Scott, a forceful and liberal publisher who founded the Chicago *Herald* in 1881, served

[4] H. F. Gunnison's historical review in *Report of the Twenty-third Annual Meeting* (1909), p. 34.

[5] Brearley was owner of the Detroit *Journal* from 1887 to 1892 and founder of the Detroit Museum of Art and the Detroit Chamber of Commerce. His fortunes then waned, and he did literary work in New York for fifteen years before dying there in 1909 at the age of sixty-two. *Fourth Estate*, Apr. 3, 1909.

[6] *Minutes of the Fourth Annual Meeting* (1890), p. 4.

[7] *Bulletin 1287*, May 20, 1905.

as president from 1889 to 1895. Well liked by the newspaper world, he had pushed the *Herald* to second place among Chicago papers and with his business associate had founded the Chicago *Evening Post*. In 1895, the year he retired as ANPA president, he had just assumed full financial control of the *Evening Post* and the consolidated *Times-Herald* when he died at the height of his career.[8]

Succeeding Scott as president was Charles W. Knapp of the St. Louis *Republic*, who held office from 1895 to 1899. The son of one of the principal owners of the *Missouri Republican*, Knapp had begun working for the paper in 1867 and was long in charge of its Washington bureau. He became president of the publishing corporation in 1887, a few months before the paper's name was changed to the St. Louis *Republic* and Colonel Charles H. Jones became editor. Knapp was an ANPA director or officer from 1890 to 1915.

The first New York City publisher to join the ANPA was William M. Laffan, who was in charge of the business management of the New York *Sun* during the later years of the editorship of Charles A. Dana. Laffan founded New York's first popular evening paper, the *Evening Sun*, and the Laffan News Bureau. He served as ANPA treasurer from 1889 to 1893. The first Pacific Coast representative was F. K. Misch of the San Francisco *Call*, secretary from 1889 to 1890. Other newcomers who took a major part in ANPA affairs before the turn of the century included Frederick Driscoll, business manager of the St. Paul *Pioneer Press*, who was a director from 1893 to 1900, and E. H. Woods of the Boston *Herald*, vice-president from 1891 to 1895.

Four of the ANPA founders remained as leaders throughout this period. They were J. Ambrose Butler of the Buffalo *News*, a director until 1895 and vice-president from 1895 to 1899; Samuel H. Kauffmann of the Washington *Evening Star*, a director or officer until 1899 and president from 1899 to 1902; Milton A. McRae of the Scripps-McRae League, a director from 1891 to 1899 and vice-president from 1899 to 1901; and Herbert F. Gunnison of the Brooklyn *Eagle*, treasurer from 1894 to 1899.[9] Two others, W.

[8] *Fourth Estate*, Apr. 18, 1895.
[9] See the Appendix for a complete listing of the officers and directors of the association, 1887–1949.

J. Richards of the Indianapolis *News* and Edward P. Call of the Boston *Herald*, were particularly influential members of the association.

{ Cooperation between the American Newspaper Publishers Association and the National Editorial Association was attempted from 1889 to 1892, with leading NEA papers having associate membership in the ANPA. The officers of both groups attended each other's conventions in 1890 and 1891, and in the latter year there were twenty-six associate members of ANPA from the older group. But in 1892, the New York *Times* reported, the ANPA terminated the associate memberships of the NEA papers, complaining that they were held chiefly by editors and owners of country papers who had no interest in larger affairs of the newspaper business.[10]

The importance attached by the ANPA to discussions of business problems was indicated in another way in 1890. The annual meeting that year voted to have an executive session "when newspapermen shall not be admitted, and when the stenographer shall not be employed" for "a little inside talking." Such a session was held on labor problems at the close of the 1890 meeting, and President Scott announced at the start of the 1891 meeting that the reports of the committees on labor and elevated railroad advertising would be held for "executive session." Said Scott, "We had so much success last year with what we term an Executive Session . . . there seems to be an inclination on the part of nearly all the members to have most of the proceedings conducted in that way. We will talk more freely, especially on questions relative to the various labor unions, the price of materials, and personal opinions of various advertising agents and agencies."

The reluctance of the members to include a record of the executive session discussions in the minutes deprives us of a firsthand account, but many evidences of the discussions and actions taken in executive sessions appear in minutes of subsequent annual meetings or in bulletins of the association. Within a few years a stenographer was again taking full notes on all discussions

[10] New York *Times*, Feb. 18, 1892, p. 3. The minutes of the 1892 annual meeting, like those of 1888, are missing from the files of the ANPA. Unless otherwise noted, references to events at ANPA annual meetings are from the official minutes and convention reports of the association.

at the annual meetings, although little was released for publication during this period.

Protection of the use of the association's published bulletins also has been an ANPA rule for understandable business reasons. The 1890 annual meeting, warned that the bulletins of the New York office were being read by outsiders, voted a $25 fine for divulging information to nonmembers, especially to advertising agents for nonmember papers. Both the use of association information by nonmembers and possible trouble from publication of credit references about advertisers and agents were the reasons for the effort to restrict circulation of the bulletins. *Bulletin 240*, issued in 1894, carried a code which was devised to protect publication of credit references.

Bulletins have been issued every year of the association's existence, though the first bulletin preserved in ANPA files is *Bulletin 237*, issued on January 4, 1894.[11] It contains six tips on new advertising business, fourteen credit evaluations of advertisers, a note on the annual meeting, and an item about a proposed tariff on wood pulp. Other bulletins issued during 1894 covered such diverse subjects as electric power for running presses; mass libel suits instituted by one Tyndale Palmer against newspapers; prices paid for hand composition; cold stereotyping; wage scales for printers; a report on a strike in a Brooklyn newspaper plant; second-class postage rates; copyright legislation; returned copies by news dealers; and mechanical tips. But the vast majority were devoted to credit ratings, warnings about advertisers and agents, tips for new advertising business, and information about agencies placing contracts.

The bulletins, printed on sheets about five inches wide by eight inches deep, were first divided into three main classifications. "A" bulletins were concerned mainly with credit ratings and reports on collections of bad accounts. "B" bulletins contained general news of the publishing business, notices asking for information, requests to trade or sell mechanical equipment, reports on libel suits, and summaries of new legislation and court decisions of interest to publishers. "C" bulletins gave tips on new advertising business, naming the companies or advertising agen-

---

[11] The bulletins for each year have been bound and indexed.

cies placing the accounts. After 1903 the designation "B Special" was used for bulletins concerning labor disputes and association labor news, and beginning in 1908 labor bulletins were issued as a separate series.[12] Several other separate series were begun in later years.

The publications of the New York office multiplied rapidly as the association became interested in more and more publishing problems. The number of bulletins issued jumped from 24 in 1888 to 70 in 1893. In 1906 there were 47 bulletins published in each of the A, B, and C series, as well as 32 B Specials. The separate items included in all these bulletins totaled 4306. In 1911 *Bulletins: Labor* alone covered more than 700 pages of fine type.

Typical examples of B bulletin notices are these, taken from *Bulletin 766*, October 3, 1900:

Any member having for sale a three or four-deck Goss press can hear of a purchaser by addressing New York office.

Some time ago we had a request for the address of Dr. Perin, the palmist. We understand that for the next few days he will be located at the Latonia Hotel, Covington, Ky.

A member would like to hear of any one having a good, second-hand stereotyping press for sale, one that will print four, six, eight, ten, twelve, or sixteen pages. Would prefer a Hoe or Goss press; must be in excellent condition, terms to be cash. To be used in a city of sixty thousand population by a newspaper with twelve thousand circulation. Address, with all particulars, Secty., New York office.

The bulletins on advertising subjects present a continuing picture of the American advertising business from 1887 to the present. Some examples of A bulletins, giving credit references, are these taken from *Bulletin 461*, October 2, 1897, and *Bulletin 634*, May 5, 1899:

DURGIN, W. B., & Co., Real Estate Agents, Rochester, N.Y. Status 12; strictly cash with order advised.

FANE, EDWARD F., 1307 F Street, N.W., Washington, D.C. Is a young married man doing a general advertising business and an advertisement writer. Credit X.

REVILO REMEDY COMPANY, Windfall, Ind. We learn the above is com-

[12] *Bulletin 1076*, Aug. 11, 1903, is the first B Special. *Bulletins: Labor 1* in the new series is dated Jan. 4, 1908.

posed of Oliver P. McCleary. The article being advertised is a cure for drunkenness. Strictly cash with the order advised.

CAPITAL CITY ADVERTISING AGENCY, 38 North Pearl Street, Albany, N.Y. From local report should advise cash in advance.

HONEST SERVICE ADVERTISING AGENCY, 44–48 Van Buren Street, Chicago, Ill. The concern is not incorporated; has been in business about one month and is not generally known as an advertising agency. Credit N.

SANDLASS, L. A., 302 West Lombard Street, Baltimore, Md. Places the advertising of Bromo Seltzer, Hunter Whiskey and that of several Baltimore houses. Regarded as worthy of credit to a fair amount.

C bulletins telling members of prospective new advertising business read like this listing in *Bulletin 651*, June 15, 1899:

AYER, N. W. & SON, Advertising Agents, Philadelphia, Pa. Asking rates on a 50-in., 13 times, weekly, and the same space daily. It is possible that the ad. may be that of Dr. Williams' "Pink Pills for Pale People."

BRANDENSTEIN & SON, "M. M. & Co., Japan Tea," San Francisco, Cal. Advertising of the above is being placed in western papers by E. C. Dake of San Francisco.

COLGATE & Co., "Colgate's Standard Flavoring Extracts," Boston, Mass. Are being advertised in New England papers and the business is being placed by the Snow-Mackay Adv. Agency, Boston.

DIAMOND CRYSTAL SALT Co., "Favorite Table Salt," St. Clair, Mich. N. W. Ayer & Son are placing the advertising of the above.

HY-JEN CHEMICAL Co., "Hy-Jen Breath Purifier," Detroit, Mich. A 1-in. ad. is being sent out to a few dailies by H. C. Hall, Detroit.

IMPERIAL MFG. Co., "Poudre de Fatigue," Kalamazoo, Mich. A small advertisement of the above is being sent out to western papers direct.

KENNEDY, DONALD, "Kennedy's Medical Discovery," Roxbury, Mass. A 64 line ad. of the above is being placed in a few papers.

KOCH'S LYMPH CURE, 155 West 15th St., N.Y. City. Are asking rates on a 5 or 6 inch ad. weekly and daily for six months.

OMEGA CHEMICAL Co., "Omega Oil," 25 Central St., Boston, Mass. It is rumored that Remington Bros., adv. agts., N.Y. Life Building, N.Y., have secured the contract to place this business.

During the first few years of ANPA history, the members discussed many advertising questions. The most constant problem was that of recognition of reputable agents and agreement upon the amount of commission they should be paid. The status of patent medicine advertising was another major topic, as was the competition for advertising revenues from other media — magazines, car cards, and outdoor billboards. Much of the discussion in the annual meetings ranged over such topics as the newspaper's responsibility for fraudulent advertising, theatrical advance notices, position of advertisements in newspapers, women advertising canvassers, free advertising for doctors, and "how can you find out the other fellow's true circulation?" The biggest battle was waged, however, over the matter of newspaper relations with advertising agencies, the prime topic in 1887.

At the 1889 annual meeting a resolution was adopted stating that the association "recommends" that the maximum commission paid by members to agencies be 15 percent, that commissions be paid only to those agents whose names were on the list approved by the executive committee, and that there be no preferred positions, except upon payment of an extra rate. The executive committee, meeting in May 1889, ordered a list of several thousand known advertisers and agents sent to newspaper publishers and appointed a subcommittee composed of L. L. Morgan, W. C. Bryant, and F. K. Misch to prepare a list of recognized agents. In October the list was approved and ordered sent out to members.[13] But since no part of these recommendations was binding on any member, publishers continued to be plagued by the problem of resisting pressure from large advertisers and agencies to pay special commissions and to give preferred position in the advertising columns.

Standardization in methods of computing advertising rates was forwarded by action of the 1893 annual meeting. The ANPA decided that "14 lines to the inch of agate, and 12 lines to the inch of nonpareil, be made the standard measure of the American Newspaper Publishers Association." The meeting also went on record against paying advertising agency commissions to advertisers placing their own copy.

An executive session was provoked a year later by a motion to reduce the commissions of advertising agents to 10 percent. The resolution was adopted, but its opponents emphasized that it was

[13] *Minutes of the Fourth Annual Meeting* (1890), p. 4.

not binding upon individual members. The following year W. C. Bryant commented: "When this organization was started some members paid thirty per cent commissions and even higher, and twenty-five per cent was the common rule. Now twenty per cent is the maximum, and fifteen per cent is common. Ten per cent is not yet much adopted. . . ."

The membership revived the effort to compile a list of recognized advertising agents in 1896, when a new committee on the problem was appointed, with General Charles H. Taylor of the Boston *Globe* as chairman. But the opponents of group action in regulating the agencies fought back once more in 1898, when, after a stormy discussion, the members voted that there was "no officially recognized ANPA advertising agents list." Finally, in 1899, opposition to the listing of approved agencies subsided. A resolution was passed setting up a committee from the board of directors (formerly the executive committee) "to make up an official list of general advertising agents, both cash and credit," and to pass on qualifications and financial resources of all new agents before ANPA members gave them credit. Appointed to the committee on advertising agents were C. M. Palmer, New York *Journal*, W. L. McLean, Philadelphia *Bulletin*, and A. A. McCormick, Chicago *Times-Herald* and *Evening Post*.[14] The committee, with changing membership, has functioned to the present day.

As the amount of advertising in daily newspapers increased in the 1890s, the variety and the quality of the content of advertising columns improved. Retail store advertising gained steadily, with the impetus given it by the early department store kings, John Wanamaker of Philadelphia, A. T. Stewart of New York, and Marshall Field of Chicago. National advertising of soaps and foods in the 1880s was supplemented in the next decade by the addition of campaigns for the Eastman Kodak, phonographs, bicycles, and other articles. But the patent medicine manufacturers were still the leading advertising clients of newspapers and magazines. Their copy extolling the virtues of Castoria, Scott's Emulsion, Peruna, or Lydia Pinkham's Female Compound still bulked large. More dangerous than these popular remedies were the

---

[14] *Bulletin 630*, Apr. 28, 1899.

cure-alls which were accepted as substitutes for doctoring in remote areas and in crowded cities. Some offered protection out of
medicine bottles against the dangers of tuberculosis or yellow
fever; some even contained poisons which brought death to in-
cautious users.

Increasing demands for restriction of sales of patent and proprietary medicines, to reach full expression during the Theodore
Roosevelt administration, were first noted by the American Newspaper Publishers Association in 1894. A bulletin called the attention of New York State publishers to the "old patent medicine
bill," up in the legislature again, "which would result in serious
injury to some of their most liberal advertisers." Members were
advised to write to their state assemblymen.[15] In 1897 another
bulletin called attention to Indiana and Kansas legislative proposals "which would seriously interfere with the sale of patent
medicines, etc., and thereby injure the advertising of the papers." [16] Again in 1899 New York State publishers were warned
against bills introduced in the state legislature requiring proper
labeling of medicinal preparations, particularly those containing
poisonous ingredients, and restricting their sale. Said the ANPA
bulletin: "All of these bills are against the interests of the proprietary article manufacturers who are large advertising patrons
of newspapers, and if passed would ruin their business. Members
of the Association should aid through influence with their local
senators and assemblymen in killing off these measures." [17]

Another, and more defensible, policy advanced by the association leadership was action against what was called the "evil of
substitution." On the day preceding the 1897 convention, a special meeting of ANPA members was called for a conference with
leading patent medicine manufacturers, to discuss the matter of
"substitution by druggists of local products for well-advertised
remedies. As can be readily seen, this is in the interests of the
newspapers as well as the patent medicine proprietors. . . ." [18]
Milton A. McRae of the Scripps-McRae League, W. J. Richards
of the Indianapolis *News*, and Fred E. Whiting of the Boston

[15] *Bulletin 244*, Feb. 9, 1894.
[16] *Bulletin 417*, Feb. 12, 1897.
[17] *Bulletin 603*, Feb. 24, 1899.
[18] *Bulletin 416*, Jan. 30, 1897.

Herald were named to confer with a committee of the Proprietary Medicine Association on this problem of substitution of
other products for advertised brands, a problem still important in
the national advertising field today.

As the muckrakers of the early twentieth century began their
work, the enthusiasm of the newspaper publishers for their patent medicine friends began to wane. In 1903 one discussion topic
publicly listed for the ANPA annual meeting was: "Why should
publishers secure testimonials for patent medicine advertisers?
Can this practice be stopped?" [19] The 1905 annual meeting
passed a "resolution of advice" to the association committee
meeting that year with a group from the Proprietary Association
of America, which stated that ANPA members individually were
observing the course of pure food and drugs legislation, that they
favored conservative and just measures, but opposed drastic and
unfair legislation.

Many factors combined to produce this change of policy. The
Ladies' Home Journal, owned by Cyrus H. K. Curtis and edited
by Edward W. Bok, had banned patent medicine advertising
from its columns in 1892. The Scripps-McRae League of Newspapers, under the influence of liberal E. W. Scripps and Robert
F. Paine, editor, established a policy of exclusion of unethical
advertising in 1903 and rejected hundreds of thousands of dollars' worth of censorable copy that year, to the annoyance of the
advertising agencies.[20] Attacks on the trusts and monopolies, on
adulterated foods and unsanitary packing practices, and on other
malpractices of "big business" were made by many newspapers,
and were rampant in the new popular ten-cent monthly magazines and nickel weeklies which had revolutionized magazine
publishing. The *Ladies' Home Journal* and *Collier's* particularly
delighted in exposés of the patent medicine trade. Taking advantage of this general spirit of reform were the scientists of the
Department of Agriculture, who exhibited at America's great
fairs proof of the dangers and shortcomings of the food and
drugs businesses. When the movement culminated in passage of

[19] *Editor & Publisher,* 3:1 (Feb. 21, 1903).

[20] Milton A. McRae, *Forty Years in Newspaperdom: The Autobiography of a
Newspaper Man* (New York: Brentano's, 1924), pp. 213–14. McRae says little
about his ANPA activities.

the federal Pure Food and Drugs Act of 1906, there was no resistance to this reform by the ANPA as an official body.

The growth of national magazines had worried newspaper publishers even before some of the magazines attacked the patent medicine trade. The general illustrated monthlies of high literary and artistic character, *Harper's*, *Century*, and *Scribner's*, were joined after 1893 by the popular, low-priced publications, headed by *Munsey's*, *McClure's*, and *Cosmopolitan*. At the 1894 ANPA convention A. J. Wilson of Chicago read a paper pointing out that newspapers were losing general advertising to magazines because newspaper advertising rates were too high, compared to the rates offered by the magazines which were rapidly expanding their circulation. An executive of N. W. Ayer and Son advertising agency was invited to speak at the same convention on the subject of cooperation with advertising agencies. A discussion topic at the 1895 convention put the problem succinctly in these words:

How can daily papers secure a larger proportion of the general mercantile advertising of the country as compared with patent medicine advertising? It is obvious that there is a very large amount of high grade general advertising appearing in the magazines and weekly and monthly publications, such as *Ladies' Home Journal, Youth's Companion*, etc., which never finds its way into the columns of the metropolitan papers. A very large proportion of the general advertising in daily papers is medical advertising. The cause for such conditions? Is a change possible? If so, how?

The answers suggested by members in the discussion included harder work on advertising solicitations, lower rates for general advertisers, and better promotion of newspapers as an advertising medium.

Outdoor and car-card advertising were discussed as competitors of the daily newspaper from 1890 on. A committee on elevated railroad advertising was named at the 1890 annual meeting (it also had horsecar advertising under its jurisdiction), and its report in 1891 was important enough to be considered in executive session, as we have seen. At the 1893 annual meeting J. A. Butler of the Buffalo *News*, chairman of the committee on legislation, reported that he believed a law restricting elevated railroad and horsecar advertising would be passed in New York State "after two years of effort." The grateful membership continued him in his job.

To promote the advertising space sales of its members, the executive committee decided in May 1889 to consider publication of the association's own newspaper. In October the committee voted to start the paper, named the *Newspaper Record*, before the 1890 convention met. One issue of five thousand copies was printed to be sent to advertising agents, to two thousand leading advertisers of the United States and Canada, and to association members.[21] The project lapsed after the first issue, however, and the growth of such trade publications as *Printers' Ink* (1888), *Newspaperdom* (1892), and the *Fourth Estate* (1894) made a special ANPA publication seem less necessary.

The growth in daily newspaper circulation in the late nineteenth century and the consequent expansion of advertising revenues were made possible by the development of new mechanical equipment in the pressrooms. In turn, the practitioners of the new journalism demanded new printing techniques to increase mass appeal and faster means of production to keep pace with circulation gains. These demands helped create a never ending process of advancement in the printing arts and in editorial practices. Discussion and study of new mechanical equipment was a major convention activity of the ANPA in its early years and one of its most constructive business activities. Typesetting machines, soon to be known by the trade name of Linotype, faster presses and stereotyping, photoengraving, dry mats and electrotyping, color printing in Sunday supplements, and typewriters for the front offices all claimed the attention of the publishers.

The first casting of a line of type for newspaper use was made in July 1886 in the New York *Tribune* plant on Ottmar Mergenthaler's new Linotype machine. The *Tribune*, the Louisville *Courier-Journal*, and the Chicago *Daily News* financed the Mergenthaler Linotype, which at the start had an output three times that of the traditional hand compositor. The Linotype was quickly adopted by the larger papers, particularly the evening dailies, who needed its time-saving performance in order to cover the day's news closer to press deadline time. Victor F. Lawson of the Chicago

---

[21] *Minutes of the Fourth Annual Meeting* (1890), pp. 4, 67.

Daily News reported to ANPA members at the 1889 annual meeting on his experiences with the Mergenthaler machine, which was seen in operation at the meeting along with the Thorne, Electro-Matrix, and Lagerman machines. A tournament for typesetting machines was sponsored by the ANPA committee on typesetting machines in Chicago during October 1891, and the committee reported to the 1892 annual meeting on the advantages and disadvantages of the various models.[22] The following year the various machines were discussed again, including Mark Twain's model, the Paige. This model was exhibited at the Chicago World's Fair, but it proved to be a financial failure for the author-promoter. In 1894 the president of the Mergenthaler Linotype Company addressed the ANPA convention on the history of the Linotype, which he reported was then selling for $3000. By 1907 Herman Ridder of the New York *Staats-Zeitung* could include in his presidential comments to the ANPA a notation that the Mergenthaler Linotype was the dominant machine in its field.

American pressmakers, under the leadership of R. Hoe and Company, had converted the presses of the leading newspapers from hand to steam power and from flat-bed to rotary printing before the Civil War. The next step was adaptation of the stereotyped plate to the newspaper press in 1861, permitting breaking of column rules for illustrations, headlines, and advertising — an advance not possible for users of type-revolving presses. The solid stereotyped plate, produced from the type form and curved to fit the cylinder of the rotary press, permitted an enormous speeding up of the hourly rate of newspaper printing. Equally necessary to this speed-up was the development of presses which used a web, or continuous roll of newsprint, and printed on both sides of the roll in one operation. Stereotyping was coming into widespread use around 1890, by which time automatic folders operating at press speed were also available to the big dailies. By 1890 a Hoe press could produce 48,000 twelve-page papers in an hour, but this figure was eclipsed during the circulation struggle between the *World* and the *Journal*. Hearst's mechanical genius, George Pancoast, made one major improvement when he per-

[22] New York *Times*, Feb. 18, 1892, p. 3.

fected the use of electric-powered presses in 1896. Color printing on rotary presses, first done regularly in America by the Chicago *Inter Ocean* in 1892, was adopted and advanced quickly by the New York newspapers to enhance their Sunday supplements and comic strips. The "Yellow Kid," dividing his allegiance between the *World* and the *Journal*, became New York's most famous character and inspired the critics of the new sensationalism to dub the mass-circulation newspapers as the "yellow press."[23]

From 1890 on, the American Newspaper Publishers Association devoted much convention discussion time to these mechanical improvements, particularly to the process of stereotyping. In 1902 the first elaborate bulletin on mechanical processes was issued, a ten-page affair with five illustrations, reporting a discussion by H. A. Cutler of the Minneapolis *Tribune* on "A System of Electric Drive for Large Newspaper Presses."[24] The attention of ANPA members was directed also to the progress being made in reproduction of printing plates by means of mats or electrotypes. Such reproductions of a master plate could be distributed by advertising agencies or feature syndicates to newspapers throughout the country.

Artists' drawings, reproduced by means of woodcuts and zinc etchings, began to give way to halftone reproductions of photographs in the closing years of the nineteenth century, as the photoengraving process became usable in newspapers. Pictures in the dailies multiplied after 1897, when it was demonstrated that photoengraved line cuts and halftones could be printed on high-speed presses. ANPA members held discussions in which the value of a newspaper having its own photoengraving plant was debated. There was growing recognition of the importance of speedy reproduction of news pictures, particularly those of local interest, but the cost involved was considerable. The Boston *Globe* reported in 1893 that it was spending $30,000 a year on its photoengraving plant.[25]

The ANPA annual meeting in 1892 authorized a committee to meet with all other interested groups to establish a standard method of type measurement, which was important because com-

[23] Mott, *American Journalism*, pp. 525–26.
[24] *Bulletin 921*, Apr. 4, 1902.
[25] *Minutes of the Seventh Annual Meeting* (1893), pp. 15–18.

positors were paid by the piece method — measuring the amount of type set each working day. The committee met in November 1892 with representatives of the United Typothetae of America (non-newspaper printers), the International Typographical Union, and the American Type Founders' Company, principal makers of type in the United States, and helped to establish a system of standard type measurement.[26]

The more extensive use of typewriters, which had been adopted in many newspaper offices in the 1880s to facilitate the faster composition which new typesetting machines permitted, claimed the attention of ANPA members in 1893. A committee of the association, appointed to consider the use of typewriters in news offices, told the annual meeting that the Remington machine was the best on the market. As a result five hundred machines were ordered in 1893 through the New York office of the association by individual members, and many more newspaper reporters began to learn to type.

The sweep of mechanical improvements in the publishing business, bringing with it labor specialization and larger working forces, gave the American Newspaper Publishers Association some concrete labor relations problems before 1900. The articles of association adopted in 1887 left the way open for the ANPA to represent newspaper publishers collectively in labor controversies, although the suggestion made in Rochester that the ANPA adopt a resolute labor policy was received in silence. Eight months after the founding of the ANPA, the United Typothetae of America was organized under the leadership of Chicago and New York typothetae. These "typeplacers" were master printers, proprietors, and printing firms other than newspaper publishers. They organized as an employers' association to oppose a demand by the International Typographical Union for a uniform nine-hour day and established a belligerent policy toward the union.[27] But the newspaper publishers sought another answer, one which would avoid strikes and work stoppages. In a highly competitive field, particularly in metropolitan areas, suspension of publication

[26] *Ibid.*, pp. 18–20.
[27] Clarence E. Bonnett, *Employers' Associations in the United States* (New York: Macmillan, 1922), pp. 226–88, a detailed study of the United Typothetae of America. Bonnett has a shorter study of ANPA labor relations (pp. 207–25).

meant perhaps fatal loss of circulation and advertising. Suspension also could jeopardize the status of a newspaper which published legal advertising. Such arguments were more compelling at the turn of the century than under present-day publishing conditions.

Danger of newspaper shutdowns through strike action brought an intensified concern with matters of labor policy as the ANPA developed its activities after 1887. One factor, however, definitely favored the publishers. The typographical union had grown steadily since its reorganization in 1852, but the craft union policy of the American Federation of Labor caused it to split as mechanical improvements and labor specialization rapidly transformed the publishing business. The International Printing Pressmen and Assistants' Union split off from the ITU in 1886, followed by the International Photo-Engravers' Union in 1900 and the International Stereotypers and Electrotypers' Union in 1901. Had the printing trades workers remained in one big union and maintained a unified bargaining policy, the entire history of newspaper labor relations would have been altered.

Manager James S. Metcalfe of the New York office of the association reported to the 1889 annual meeting that "one important work carried out by the New York office has been the publication of statistics concerning rates of pay and other matters of interest to publishers." The members voted to have the association report monthly on labor disputes and their settlement and discussed the effect of typesetting machines on labor relations. In 1890 the annual meeting received a communication from Edward T. Plank of the International Typographical Union that confirmed their worst fears. Plank stated that the union favored typesetting machines but only if they were operated by practical printers at the union scale. Said President James W. Scott of the Chicago *Herald,* "I suggest that this matter be brought up again in executive session." No record was kept of the discussion, but the membership recognized that the union was establishing a basic policy toward mechanical innovations. In this instance the ITU successfully insisted that its hand printers graduate to the new typesetting machines.

That the debate over this issue was a bitter one is apparent from later ANPA records showing that a committee on labor troubles was authorized during the closed session.[28] This committee reported to the ANPA executive committee in November 1890, stating that "the investigations of the committee demonstrated that the Association has resources sufficient to assist any member in the adjustment of labor trouble upon a few hours notice." [29] The committee, in other words, had investigated the possibilities of supplying replacements for striking printers. But a plan for such replacements was never put into effect, as is proved by an occurrence at the 1895 convention. That year W. M. M. Speer of the Albany, New York, *Argus* declared he would contribute to a fund if the ANPA, or an outsider with the sanction of ANPA, would maintain "a force of linotype operators for use when there is a sudden demand for them." Speer explained that his union had given him a three-hour notice of a strike call and that he was unable to procure replacements, else he would have told the union "to get out and stay out." There was no discussion of Speer's proposal, and the ANPA again avoided adoption of a belligerent labor policy.

Just before the executive session on labor troubles began in 1890, President Scott commented, "Local associations will be the principal labor of the coming year." By that he meant organizing associations of newspaper owners in cities having three or more daily papers to present a common front on wage and hour problems and during periods of strikes. In some cities these local associations antedated ANPA. At the 1893 annual meeting Chicago members explained the workings of their local association, founded in 1884, "in order to encourage a local association in New York particularly." Other than the fact that the Chicago association was a stock company, with one share for each Chicago paper, no specific details of the discussion were included in the minutes of the annual meeting. Local associations, however, commonly hired an executive to deal with the unions and attempted to obtain citywide labor contracts.

Labor discussions continued at ANPA conventions each year. In 1892 the *Journalist* reported: "The sessions were mostly execu-

[28] *Minutes of the Fifth Annual Meeting* (1891), p. 4.
[29] *Ibid.*

tive and while we know that the topics under discussion were machine composition, typographical unions, and allied matters, the deliberations will not be made public." [30] The question of starting a school for typesetting machine operators in New York City, in cooperation with the Mergenthaler Linotype Company, was advanced in 1893 but not acted upon. Wage scales for machine operators and agreements of local associations with unions in twenty cities were reported in an 1894 bulletin, which said that the usual scale for linotype operators was $3 to $3.50 for an eight-hour day. [31] Two months later another bulletin reported, "The demand on the part of publishers throughout the country for a reduction in the wage scale for both hand and machine composition seems to be spreading," and members were asked to send in information to be published. [32] The publishers were feeling the pinch of the depression of 1893.

In September 1894, when the advent of typesetting machines in Cincinnati threw a large number of printers out of work, they decided to start their own paper, the *Evening News*, to be set entirely by hand. An ANPA bulletin complained that the union was violating its trust by setting up a rival to the established dailies. [33] But Milton A. McRae was able to report to the 1895 convention that the printers' paper had failed after bankrupting the union treasury of $12,000. "I don't feel very kindly about it all," McRae said.

First references to arbitration contracts with the printing unions, soon to become a major ANPA activity, were made at the 1895 meeting. [34] Various members reported on local arbitration contracts with unions, among them publishers in Boston, Kansas City, St. Louis, and Denver. The Denver publisher pointed out that because of declining living costs the arbitration clause had been used to reduce wages from $30 to $26 a week, and he commended the processes of arbitration to the members.

The same commendation came from Colonel Frederick Dris-

[30] Feb. 20, 1892.
[31] *Bulletin 238*, Jan. 5, 1894.
[32] *Bulletin 248*, Mar. 14, 1894.
[33] *Bulletin 281*, Sept. 7, 1894.
[34] Frank B. Noyes of the Washington *Evening Star* told the 1913 ANPA convention that his paper made an arbitration agreement with the ITU in 1887, which he thought was the earliest such agreement made.

coll of the St. Paul *Pioneer Press*, who was a leading advocate of the policy of organized negotiation and arbitration. But Driscoll proved that he had an eye for the future when at the 1895 meeting he obtained adoption of a resolution establishing the policy that contracts should be signed only with individual unions — not with allied trade committees representing all mechanical unions and workers — "else a five-dollar feeder can stop your whole establishment." Driscoll warned that the nation's newspaper publishers soon would be forced to take unified action in establishing a labor relations policy, and his prediction was to come true in 1900.

The American Newspaper Publishers Association, as already demonstrated in the discussion of patent medicine advertising, early began to raise its voice whenever governmental regulation or legislation affected the business interests of publishers. This, of course, was the natural and legitimate function of a trade association operating under a democratic system of government, in which the interests of various groups must be advocated before legislative bodies and administrative officials so that a proper balance may be obtained among these interests in the public welfare. Libel and copyright legislation, the tariff on wood pulp for newsprint, the telegraph system, second-class postal rates, and the income tax law were all subjects of ANPA activity during the years from 1887 to 1897.

At the 1890 annual meeting William H. Brearley spoke on the value of securing uniform libel laws in the states, urging that state and city publishers' associations send men to the legislatures to promote new legislation. A committee on libel law headed by J. H. Farrell of the Albany, New York, *Times-Union* was authorized at the 1893 convention and served two years. It had as its duty the preparation of a model state libel law, using the Minnesota law as a guide. The need for cooperation by publishers to win changes in libel law procedures was illustrated by the complaint to the 1895 convention of K. G. Cooper, manager of the Denver *Republican*. Cooper declared that in the previous fourteen years his paper had been sued for a total of $1,200,000. It had paid out $650 after going to the Supreme Court on three different occasions. But it had also paid $25,000 in lawyers' fees and was forced to keep a lawyer employed nearly full time to handle libel cases. Since the libel problem was on the state level, it became one for the various state editorial associations, rather than for the ANPA.

The 1890 annual meeting also resolved that the members were "in hearty accord with the effort now being made by American authors to obtain from Congress a fuller security for literary property"— a reference to the Chace international copyright bill. But the major interest of the publishers was in winning modifications in federal copyright legislation. A committee on copyright law was appointed by the executive committee in December 1894, consisting of S. S. Carvalho of the New York *World* and W. C. Bryant of the Brooklyn *Times*, secretary-manager of the ANPA. Its aim, an ANPA bulletin reported, was to secure an amendment to the federal copyright law.[35] That law, the ANPA explained, originally was written to protect authors, photographers, and artists against book publishers and lithographers who infringed upon property rights. It provided that the penalty for infringement of any copyright by a publisher should be a payment of one dollar for each copy found in the possession of the violator, or in the case of a work of art, ten dollars a copy. But when this law was applied to publishers of mass-circulation newspapers, it resulted in undue punishment, the ANPA contended. Courts had held that all newspapers published were once in the possession of the publisher, and the penalty could be as large as the circulation of the paper. This, the ANPA bulletin declared, made possible suits for as much as $800,000, when the copyrighted material in question had only a $5 value. The bulletin requested members "NOT to publish anything about the matter prematurely" but to stand ready to request the aid of local congressmen, adding, "at the proper time it will be desirable for as large a delegation as possible to go to Washington to appear before the House committee. . . ."

During January 1895 eight ANPA members, headed by Carvalho and Bryant, went to Washington to aid in the passage of the ANPA-sponsored amendment to the copyright law. The House Committee on Patents, headed by Representative James

[35] *Bulletin 303*, Jan. 5, 1895.

W. Covert of New York, was agreeable to the publishers' request and initiated action, whereupon an ANPA bulletin urged members to "communicate at once with their congressmen." [36] Carvalho reported to the 1895 ANPA convention that a $100 minimum penalty for copyright violations had been agreed upon, subject to a later conference with representatives of the American Publishers' Copyright League and the Authors' Copyright League. This conference was held February 21, and it was agreed that the penalty for infringement of photographic copyrights should be a minimum payment of $100 and a maximum of $5000, while that for improper publication of a work of fine art should be $250 to $10,000.[37] Congress accepted the amendment to the copyright statute as thus stated and it became law. The American Newspaper Publishers Association expressed its thanks to Covert, chairman of the House Committee on Patents, in October 1895, when a bulletin urged that former Congressman James W. Covert receive the support of newspapers in his race for judge of the New York supreme court, saying, "members in New York and Brooklyn can do no less than say a good word for him. . . ." [38]

The association brought its fight to minimize the penalties for copyright infringement to a successful conclusion in 1909, when its copyright committee, under the chairmanship of Theodore W. Noyes of the Washington *Evening Star*, obtained a reduction in the maximum penalty for violation of a photographic copyright from $5000 to $200, and in the minimum from $100 to $50. Congress, however, made the willful violation of a photographic copyright a misdemeanor, punishable by a $100 to $1000 fine or one year in prison, or both. *Editor & Publisher* commended ANPA, saying it "is directly responsible for the new copyright law so far as it concerns newspapers." [39]

Official ANPA concern with second-class postal rates first became a matter of record in 1892. A committee on postal laws was appointed that year to submit to the Post Office Department and to Congress a statement of changes in the postal laws desired by publishers. Its members were J. S. Seymour, New York *Evening*

[36] *Bulletin 305*, Jan. 17, 1895.
[37] *Bulletin 313*, Mar. 12, 1895.
[38] *Bulletin 349*, Oct. 31, 1895.
[39] *Editor & Publisher*, 8:8 (Apr. 24, 1909).

Post, T. J. Keenan, Jr., Pittsburgh *Press,* and Frank B. Noyes, Washington *Evening Star.*[40] Chairman Keenan reported to the 1893 annual meeting that through the committee's efforts "two Congressional bills by Paddock and Henderson affecting the status of second-class postal material had been side-tracked." In 1896 and 1897 the ANPA backed the Loud bill, proposed to correct abuses of the use of second-class postal rates, which were intended to apply to legitimate newspaper and periodical publications, but which were being used by publishers of advertising sheets. The ANPA executive committee visited Washington to help push the bill and claimed that ANPA support got the legislation through the House of Representatives.[41] It failed of final passage, however. Thus the association was established as an interested party in consideration of second-class postal rates, as later chapters will show in detail.

The problem of tariffs on wood pulp and newsprint, also to be a major interest of the ANPA throughout its history, is first recorded in 1893, when a convention discussion was held on the subject of "abolition of duty on ground wood." The executive committee was authorized to secure the inclusion in the Wilson tariff bill of a clause taking all duties off importation of wood pulp and to adopt such measures as would be necessary to secure passage. An ANPA bulletin in 1894 urged every member to write his congressman at once, asking that wood pulp be admitted free; "if a majority are in concert there is but little doubt but that they can accomplish their object."[42] Evidently a majority were not in concert, for this activity failed.

Other brief activities indicate the interest of the ANPA in legislative fields before 1900. In 1894 resolutions were introduced concerning government maintenance of telegraph systems, but it was voted that "it was inexpedient for the Association to take any action in the matter."[43] The same year an ANPA bulletin suggested that newspaper publishers were in need of a fractional paper currency, to facilitate mailing of money to publishers in

[40] New York *Times,* Feb. 19, 1892, p. 3.
[41] *Report of Proceedings of the Eleventh Annual Convention* (1897), p. 3.
[42] *Bulletin 237,* Jan. 4, 1894.
[43] *Fourth Estate,* Mar. 1, 1894, p. 1.

payment of bills.[44] The 1895 convention discussed the 1894 federal income tax law, which the publishers decided was unconstitutional, as the Supreme Court later held. And, probably somewhat self-consciously, the 1899 convention debated the question, "Do the newspapers want another war?" The delegates unanimously decided in the negative but noted that all classes of papers had made and held circulation gains as a result of the Spanish-American War excitement.

Thus the American Newspaper Publishers Association developed its functions during its formative years, becoming a trade association of established reputation ready to joust with labor unions, newsprint manufacturers, advertising competitors, other businesses, and the government, whenever newspaper publishers' interests were at stake. And it was to find many jousting opportunities.

[44] *Bulletin 247*, Mar. 9, 1894.

CHAPTER IV

Association Affairs, 1900-1918

WITH the turn of the century the American Newspaper Publishers Association began a rapid growth which saw its 46 first-
day members of 1887 increased tenfold to 465 members in 1918.
As it grew the association formalized its methods, established an
official staff, and developed organized means of forwarding the
membership's aims.

During the years from 1900 to the end of World War I, many
forces were at work in American society which made an expansion of ANPA activities necessary. The United States was consolidating its position as an industrialized, urban country. Constructive relationships between publishers of newspapers and labor unions had to be shaped in accordance with changing socioeconomic attitudes. The power of government was being increased by the application of Theodore Roosevelt's "Square
Deal" and Woodrow Wilson's "New Freedom," two progressive
political programs which grew out of the changed national environment and represented efforts to advance the common welfare. Newspaper publishers, like other economic and social
groups, needed a voice which could speak in competition with
other voices in political and economic contests.

The material progress of the newspaper also insured the
growth of the trade association. The number of daily newspapers
rose from 2226 in 1899 to an all-time high of 2600 in 1909. Pressures of competition and of wartime operating costs reduced the
number of dailies to 2441 by 1919. But total daily newspaper circulation gained steadily, from 15 million copies in 1899 to 24 million in 1909 and 33 million in 1919. Advertising revenues of
newspapers, which had become more important than subscription revenues, more than doubled between 1900 and 1914, and

doubled again during the war years. Membership in a trade association devoted to the furthering of business interests of newspapers seemed both desirable and necessary to an increasing number of publishers whose complex business operations required constant attention.

The association had 128 members in 1889 and the next ten years saw little numerical increase. But the geographical influence of ANPA was widened as papers from all sections of the country became members, and its prestige was enhanced by the adherence of the New York City dailies. By 1901 membership stood at 165. The 250 mark was reached in 1906, and by 1911 the total stood at 304. In 1917 the ANPA boasted 400 members, and wartime publishing difficulties encouraged membership to the new high of 465 in 1918.

After 1898 the annual meetings of the association were held regularly at the old Waldorf-Astoria in New York City. The group met in late February each year until 1908, when the meeting date was changed to the fourth Thursday in April, so that the ANPA conclaves would take place immediately after those of the Associated Press, of which most ANPA publishers were members.

Incorporation of the association as a stock company under the laws of New York State was authorized by the 1897 annual convention. Two hundred shares of stock, each worth five dollars, were issued. The purposes of the incorporation were described as:

To provide a common agency for gathering and disseminating information of value to publishers of reputable newspapers; to protect them from irresponsible customers; to act as agent or attorney in fact for corporations and individuals in all transactions in which corporations or individuals may lawfully engage and employ an agent or attorney in fact, and to render such other assistance or service to its stockholders as may be within its corporate powers.

The final change in association organizational form came in 1913. Following the lead of the Associated Press, the ANPA incorporated under the membership corporation law of New York as a cooperative, nonprofit organization of limited membership.

The board of directors, as the executive committee was called after the 1897 incorporation, met three or four times a year during this period to decide association policies. Its membership was increased to seven directors and four officers in 1900, and in 1915 an additional director and the past president were added to the board.

With the death in February 1905 of William Cullen Bryant of the Brooklyn *Times,* who had been serving as secretary-manager since 1892, the board of directors voted to name a full-time general manager. On May 11 the directors elected to the post Lincoln B. Palmer, then thirty-nine years old. He was to serve until 1939 and play a large part in the affairs of the association. Palmer had learned the printing trade at an early age and then had spent four years studying in Europe. He was graduated from the Columbia University law school in 1887 and practiced law for eight years. In 1898 he became advertising manager of the New York *Commercial Advertiser,* and he held the same post with the New York *Globe* before becoming ANPA general manager. Palmer's name first appeared on the bulletins on May 20, when the association moved to its new offices in the *World* building on Park Row.

Under Palmer's direction the activities of the New York office were expanded considerably in the next few years. To the regular bulletins previously described were added other special bulletin series: *Bulletins: Labor* in 1908, free publicity bulletins in 1909 (bound separately after 1911), and extensive newsprint bulletins, bound separately after 1917.[1] By 1912 the New York office was handling annually twelve thousand inquiries from members and six thousand advertising collection claims. And that year the ANPA decided to form a fire insurance department for the benefit of the members, calling it the American Newspaper Publishers Reciprocal Exchange, with Victor F. Lawson of the. Chicago *Daily News* as chairman. In another service activity, Palmer reported to the 1907 convention that ANPA members had saved $20,000 in 1906 by buying typewriters wholesale through the New York office.

Detailed treasurer's reports, made to the annual meetings after 1908, show that ANPA was becoming a major enterprise. Receipts from dues and initiations totaled $40,000 in 1908 and rose to $75,000 by 1918. In the latter year total receipts reached the

[1] Only the labor bulletins were issued in a separately numbered series.

$100,000 mark. The expense of the general office rose from $37,-500 in 1908 to $65,000 in 1918. The annual appropriation for labor relations activity jumped from $14,400 in 1908 to $25,000 in 1918. The membership contributed from $10,000 to $25,000 a year during this period to a special newsprint fund for the Paper Bureau and in 1918 contributed $99,000 to an emergency paper fund.

Until the turn of the century the association had been led by only three presidents: William M. Singerly, publisher of the Philadelphia *Record*, James W. Scott, publisher of the Chicago *Herald*, and Charles W. Knapp, publisher of the St. Louis *Republic*. Eight more presidents were elected before 1918. Of these eleven men seven were owner-publishers and four were from the managerial staffs of their papers. Only three of the eleven — Scott, Knapp, Bruce Haldeman — can be classified as predominantly interested in the editorial function; the talents of the others were devoted mainly to management.

Samuel H. Kauffmann, one of the owners of the Washington *Evening Star*, served as president from 1899 to 1902. Charles H. Taylor, Jr., an owner and manager of the Boston *Globe*, advanced to become president from 1902 to 1905 and continued as a director until 1938, holding an influential position in the ANPA for forty-two years. Sherman S. Rogers, manager of the Chicago *Daily News*, held the presidency from 1905 to 1907.

In 1907 came an extremely rare event in ANPA history, an election contest on the floor of the convention. It brought to the presidency one of the association's most dynamic figures, Herman Ridder, owner-manager of the New York *Staats-Zeitung*.[2] Ridder, who had worked his way up to control of that influential foreign-language paper, served as president until 1911 and led the association's newsprint tariff battle. Bruce Haldeman, publisher-president of the Louisville *Courier-Journal*, was ANPA president from 1911 to 1912, and Elbert H. Baker, general manager of the Cleveland *Plain Dealer*, from 1912 to 1914. Two more business managers followed to the presidency: Herbert L. Bridgman of the

[2] Ridder received sixty-one votes to forty-seven for A. A. McCormick of the Indianapolis *Star*, former vice-president and chairman of the special standing committee on labor matters, of which Ridder was also a member. Edward P. Call received nine votes. *Report of the Twenty-first Annual Meeting* (1907), p. 38.

Brooklyn *Standard-Union* from 1914 to 1916 and Hopewell L. Rogers of the Chicago *Daily News* from 1916 to 1918.

There were twenty-one other men who were particularly active leaders of the association in this period, as directors or committee chairmen. Ten of them were publishers and eleven were managers of their newspapers. Eight can be classified as from the editorial side and thirteen from the advertising or management side. Again it is apparent that the ANPA in its leadership, as well as in its activities, was predominantly a daily newspaper business association.

Among the directors and officers was Hilton U. Brown, a director from 1904 until 1935, who had advanced from a reporter's job to the position of general manager of the Indianapolis *News*. Frank P. Glass, owner and editor of the Birmingham *News*, was a director after 1906 until he became ANPA president in 1918. Edward P. Call, a manager or publisher in turn of the New York *Evening Post, Mail & Express, Commercial*, and *Journal of Commerce*, was a long-time treasurer and chairman of the committee on advertising agents. Other officers included Herbert F. Gunnison, publisher of the Brooklyn *Eagle*; William J. Pattison, business manager of the New York *Evening Post*; John Stewart Bryan, publisher of the Richmond *News-Leader*; and Medill McCormick, editor of the Chicago *Tribune*. Leading directors were Condé Hamlin, business manager of the New York *Tribune*; Charles W. Hornick, manager of the St. Paul *Dispatch* and later publisher of the San Francisco *Call*; W. L. McLean, publisher of the Philadelphia *Bulletin*; H. H. Cabaniss, publisher of the Atlanta *Journal*; Joseph T. Nevin, publisher of the Pittsburgh *Leader*; S. P. Weston, business manager of the Seattle *Post-Intelligencer*; Jason Rogers, publisher of the New York *Globe*; John B. Townsend, manager of the Philadelphia *Press*; Harry Chandler, publisher of the Los Angeles *Times*; and John F. MacKay, business manager of the Toronto *Globe*.

Two of the most influential members of the ANPA before World War I were never officers or members of the board. They were John Norris, business manager of the New York *Times*, and Don C. Seitz, business manager of the New York *World*. They alternated as chairmen of the committee on paper after 1898, with Norris becoming a paid executive in charge of newsprint activities in 1908. Both served on the second-class mail committee for several years, and Seitz led the Free Publicity Department established in 1909, as well as being chairman of the committee on advertising agents after 1906.

The special standing committee on labor problems had as its chairman from 1900 to 1907 A. A. McCormick, then business manager of the Chicago *Record-Herald*. The association's first labor commissioner was Frederick Driscoll, former publisher and business manager of the St. Paul *Pioneer Press*, who served from 1900 until his death in 1907. He was succeeded by H. N. Kellogg, business manager of the New York *Tribune*.

This extensive listing of the men who controlled the policies of the ANPA before World War I clearly shows the dominance of the large daily newspapers published in metropolitan centers, as represented by their publishers and business managers. Missing are some of the more familiar names in journalism history, such as those of Adolph S. Ochs and Louis Wiley of the New York *Times*, Samuel Bowles IV of the Springfield *Republican*, Frank B. Noyes of the Washington *Evening Star*, E. W. Scripps and his editor, Robert F. Paine, and William Randolph Hearst. All these men except Scripps and Hearst took part in various ANPA annual sessions, but they were not active leaders.

As the association's prestige grew, prominent Americans found its annual meeting an important sounding board. Not only distinguished publishers and editors, but businessmen and public leaders appeared as guest speakers at the annual banquet which was the association's leading social activity. At the 1889 banquet in the Hoffman House, famed editor Henry Watterson of the Louisville *Courier-Journal* and George P. Rowell, dean of American advertising agents, shared the speaking honors. Charles A. Dana, the long-time editor of the New York *Sun*, spoke in 1892. Murat Halstead, famous editor of the Cincinnati *Commercial Gazette* who had come east to edit the Brooklyn *Standard-Union*, addressed the publishers on libel problems in 1895.[3]

The New York *Herald* reported in 1902 that the publishers banqueted in the Astor Room of the Waldorf-Astoria, the gal-

[3] *Fourth Estate*, Feb. 28, 1895, p. 1.

leries being crowded with ladies "who waited patiently while the publishers edited the elaborate menu." Thomas B. Reed, former Speaker of the House of Representatives, and Chinese Minister Wu Ting-Fang, both former newspapermen, were the speakers.[4] William Randolph Hearst appeared at the 1904 banquet, the only time his name enters ANPA annals.[5] Commodore Robert E. Peary with "First News from the Pole," George Harvey, Alfred Harmsworth (later Lord Northcliffe), and Uncle Billy Perkins made a diverse group of speakers in 1905.

William Jennings Bryan chided the publishers about the tariff in 1908, the first year the banquet was held jointly with the Associated Press.[6] President Woodrow Wilson of Princeton University spoke on the power of the editorial in 1910, two years before his first presidential campaign. Mayor Gaynor of New York City created a stir that year by calling William Randolph Hearst a forger in connection with the publication in the New York *American* of photostats damaging to Gaynor, but George Ade brought a lighter touch to the banquet.[7]

President William Howard Taft spoke on the Canadian reciprocity agreement in 1911. War gave the 1918 banquet a governmental tone, with Secretary of the Navy Josephus Daniels, Secretary of War Newton D. Baker, and Charles Evans Hughes as speakers.

ANPA annual meetings considered many problems, and the group was small enough to have general debate and comment on both important and unimportant details. For example, the topics committee suggested these items, among others, in 1905: joint fire insurance, insurance for employees, serial stories, labor disputes, newsprint economies, railway time tables (advertising or news), trading stamps, retail merchants' associations, circulation premiums (soup plates, pickle forks, and Bibles), second-class mail rates, copyright law, testimonials for patent medicine advertising, and copyrighting of news. In 1906: editorial matter — what kind helps advertising pull? And in 1907: simplified spelling? To the last question the ANPA answered "No," despite Theodore Roosevelt's campaign.

[4] New York *Herald*, Feb. 21, 1902, p. 6.
[5] New York *Times*, Feb. 19, 1904, p. 5.
[6] *Ibid.*, Apr. 23, 1908, p. 1.   [7] *Ibid.*, Apr. 29, 1910, p. 1.

As the association carried out its major aims in increasing measure, it began to have need of legal services for legislative and courtroom appearances. In 1897 a bulletin reported that "L. W. Stotesbury of Shaw, Baldwin & Stotesbury is the attorney of the Association, currently engaged in handling mass libel suits brought by the Union Associated Press against many American newspapers." [8] In 1905 the committee on paper announced it had retained James M. Beck as counsel.[9] In 1909 Robert C. Morris and Guthrie B. Plante of Morris and Plante, described as attorneys for the association, advised the membership that they believed the Federal Corporation Tax Law of 1909 was unconstitutional and suggested that members should protest all payments made under the law.[10] Morris and Plante represented the protesters against the Newspaper Publicity Law of 1912 as ANPA counsel, and Beck also offered arguments before the United States Supreme Court in an unsuccessful attack upon the law.[11]

A reconstituted legislative committee, with Elbert H. Baker of the Cleveland *Plain Dealer* as chairman, considered relations with the government during the war years. It reported to the 1917 annual meeting that the committee had interviewed the Secretaries of War and Navy on matters of wartime censorship. Baker stated that the committee considered the press censorship provisions of the Espionage Act unduly severe. The membership voted in favor of strict but voluntary press censorship, such as became, for the most part, the policy of the government. In 1918 the annual meeting voted, amid references to the public information activities of George Creel, to send a committee to Washington "to see about editing of the flood of material sent out by the government and other national organizations issuing wartime publicity."

As was apparent from the listing of committee chairmen, the principal problems of the ANPA from the turn of the century to 1918 were four in number: labor relations, newsprint prices, second-class mail rates, and advertising and free publicity. Each of these topics will be taken up in turn in the following chapters.

[8] *Bulletin 483*, Dec. 18, 1897.
[9] *Report of the Nineteenth Annual Meeting* (1905), p. 3.
[10] *Bulletin 2119*, Jan. 8, 1910.
[11] *Bulletin 2672*, Oct. 9, 1912; *Bulletin 2803*, Dec. 7, 1912.

CHAPTER V

Arbitration with Labor

EACH year after the organization of the American Newspaper Publishers Association, problems of labor relations with mechanical trade unions were a subject of constantly growing discussion and association action.[1] And in 1899 the ANPA embarked upon the formulation of a comprehensive labor policy that was to be one of the most important actions ever taken by the publishers.

Increasing mechanization of newspaper publishing in the closing years of the nineteenth century had required larger labor forces performing more specialized tasks. The publishers had formed local associations in major cities to deal collectively with the unions and had, through the ANPA, begun to study current wage scales and the outcome of labor disputes in various parts of the country. They had toyed with the idea of offering belligerent opposition to the unions, but compelling arguments against interruption of continuous newspaper publication made such a solution unfeasible. Instead, local publishers' associations had begun to sign arbitration agreements with their printers which would minimize the danger of labor disputes.

When the publishers met for their 1899 sessions, they were in a troubled frame of mind. The International Typographical Union, which had grown out of local unions established after 1800 and had become a national union in 1852, had just won a battle for a nine-hour workday throughout the printing industry. Newspaper publishers had not opposed this aim of the ITU and two other American Federation of Labor affiliates, the International Printing Pressmen and Assistants' Union (which separated from the typographers in 1886) and the International Brotherhood of Bookbinders. They had watched the other printing proprietors,

[1] For earlier details, see pages 23–25, 45–49.

organized as the United Typothetae of America, fight against the
nine-hour day until 1898, when it was grudgingly accepted.[2]
Then the newspaper publishers had seen the breaking out of
printers' strikes in several metropolitan centers. A particular sore
point was the suspension of publication of Chicago daily newspapers for four days in 1898 because of difficulties with stereotypers.

At the 1899 annual meeting the following topic was presented
for discussion: "Has the time arrived for newspaper publishers to
lend assistance to those publications which seek freedom from
labor dictation? The growing burdens, particularly to one-cent
papers in big cities, of composing room pay-rolls." Whatever was
said by the members was ordered stricken from the published
proceedings. But a little later the same day, during a discussion
on the advisability of establishing schools of instruction for mechanical employees, A. A. McCormick, general manager of the
Chicago *Times-Herald* and *Evening Post*, reopened the discussion on labor policy. The convention proceedings reported:

Mr. McCormick made a long and earnest speech advocating a certain
course toward labor unions, which was warmly endorsed by Colonel
Driscoll [Frederick Driscoll, St. Paul *Pioneer Press*]. Mr. Lawrence
[M. J. Lawrence, *Ohio Farmer*, Cleveland] moved that a committee
be appointed to make arrangements for the plan suggested by Mr.
McCormick and submit definite plans before the close of the convention.

McCormick's address, unreported in the minutes, thus brought
the ANPA membership to a decision on the question of association labor policy. It set off a chain of events which led to the
adoption of international arbitration agreements with the printing trade unions and the establishment of a negotiatory trend in
daily newspaper labor-management relations. As a result the
daily newspaper publishers, as a national group, became pioneers
in the fields of collective bargaining, conciliation, and arbitration. The position they established contrasted sharply with the
belligerent attitude of many contemporary industries.

Carrying out the resolution on labor policy, the chair appointed McCormick, Driscoll, Herman Ridder of the New York *Staats-*

[2] Bonnett, *Employers' Associations*, p. 233.

Zeitung, M. J. Lowenstein of the St. Louis *Star,* and Charles H. Taylor, Jr., of the Boston *Globe* as a committee to consider Mc-Cormick's plan. McCormick reported back to the convention later in the day that all action on the matter had been referred to the board of directors for intensive study. A resolution ordering the formation of local publishers' associations in all cities then unionized and the hiring of an organizer by the ANPA was also referred to the board for consideration of the costs involved.

In December 1899 the board of directors appointed a committee to report to the next annual meeting on the subject of labor relations. It consisted of McCormick, Taylor, J. Ambrose Butler of the Buffalo *News,* W. H. Seif of the Pittsburgh *Times,* Don C. Seitz of the New York *World,* Charles W. Knapp of the St. Louis *Republic,* and Charles H. Grasty of the Baltimore *News.* This committee drafted a number of resolutions, which were presented to the 1900 annual meeting.

The climax came with the unanimous adoption, after long and unreported discussion, of the following enabling resolution:

Resolved, That the president of the American Newspaper Publishers Association appoint a national labor committee of three members to take up labor questions affecting generally the members of the Association, and that said committee is hereby empowered to take all measures necessary in its judgment to protect the interests of members of this Association who may be in trouble with labor unions, subject to the direction of the Board of Directors.

This action definitely committed the association to the establishment of a national labor policy for the daily newspaper publishing business. It was immediately followed by the adoption of a series of supporting resolutions which set the pattern for the work of the labor committee.

The most important of these resolutions authorized the labor committee to proceed with negotiations for national arbitration agreements with the labor unions. Another authorized the hiring of an organizer-manager, whose salary and mileage expenses would be paid by voluntary contributions from interested members. The membership also voted that the labor committee should be supreme over local associations in questions involving national unions and ordered that local associations should be chartered by the labor committee. A final resolution touched upon a point of tremendous importance for the future by declaring that no new operating rule of a labor union which affected a publisher's property was to be recognized unless approved by the labor committee.

It should be noted that the enabling resolution which put the ANPA into the labor relations field was worded in terms which would permit the association to adopt a belligerent policy toward the printing unions if attempts at securing arbitration contracts failed. For this reason, perhaps, the membership shied away from the name "labor committee" as it proceeded to implement the resolutions. The name of the labor committee was changed to "Special Standing Committee" and the title of the organizer-manager became "Special Commissioner."[3] For purposes of clarity the commissioner will be called labor commissioner here.

The biggest argument over the forming of the special standing committee and the hiring of a commissioner involved the question of cost. At the 1900 meeting various local associations and individual publishers who were desirous of seeing the new plan given a trial guaranteed the expenses. At the next annual meeting a regular subscription, still on a voluntary basis, was established at fifty cents a month for each typesetting or typecasting machine. A list of 57 papers subscribing to the fund was published in 1902, and the number of participants rose to 147 in 1903 and 157 in 1904.[4] This voluntary arrangement continued through 1907.

One month after the passage of the momentous resolutions the special standing committee announced that it had chosen the first labor commissioner.[5] He was Frederick Driscoll, ANPA director who had just retired from publishing activities. The team of Driscoll and Joseph A. Wheelock had begun in 1863 to build the St. Paul *Pioneer Press*, with Wheelock as editor and Driscoll as general manager, but the association had ended in December 1899. *Editor & Publisher* in 1903 referred to Driscoll as "probably one of the best authorities on labor matters in connection

[3] *Report of the Fifteenth Annual Meeting* (1901), p. 3.
[4] *Bulletin 908*, Mar. 12, 1902; *Bulletin 1139*, Mar. 2, 1904; *Bulletin 1260*, Mar. 6, 1905.
[5] *Bulletin 711*, Mar. 23, 1900.

with the newspaper publishing business in the world." [6] Certainly he worked religiously to promote the negotiatory labor policy embarked upon by the association.

Upon his appointment Driscoll announced his policies. He declared that the special standing committee and the commissioner would serve as an arbitration committee, settling labor disputes through national arbitration; that they would obtain data concerning wages in various cities and labor conditions in plants of ANPA members; and that his headquarters would be in Chicago. He emphasized particularly that he and the committee were "not appointed to provoke controversies or antagonize labor. . . ." [7]

With that announcement Commissioner Driscoll and the special standing committee went to work. Alfred Cowles of the Chicago *Tribune,* original chairman of the committee, shortly became ill, and A. A. McCormick of the Chicago *Times-Herald* took his place, serving as chairman until 1907. Committee members were Herman Ridder of the New York *Staats-Zeitung* and M. J. Lowenstein of the St. Louis *Star.*

In December 1900 the commissioner and special standing committee reported to the board of directors on an arbitration agreement in course of negotiation with the International Typographical Union which would provide machinery for settlement of disputes arising over terms of existing contracts. [8] At the 1901 annual meeting the agreement was ratified by the ANPA membership, after unreported discussion, by a margin of fifty-nine votes. Many of the members still had misgivings and the agreement was voted a one-year trial. The typographical union referred the agreement to a membership referendum, which favored ratification by 12,-544 to 3530. [9] The first hurdle had been cleared.

When the 1902 ANPA annual meeting convened, Driscoll was able to announce jubilantly that there had been no strikes during 1901 in mechanical plants of ANPA member publishers. He presented the texts of five-year arbitration agreements with the International Typographical Union and the International Printing Pressmen and Assistants' Union and asked for unanimous ap-

[6] *Editor & Publisher,* 3:1 (Feb. 21, 1903).
[7] *Bulletin 714,* Mar. 31, 1900.
[8] *Report of the Fifteenth Annual Meeting* (1901), p. 3.
[9] *Bulletin 816,* Apr. 13, 1901.

proval. The only dissenting vote was cast by Harry Chandler of the Los Angeles *Times*.[10]

Driscoll announced in May 1902 that the two five-year agreements had been formally executed in April and would extend until April 30, 1907. The leaders of the unions, he said, "have a proper respect for employers, when *organized*. . . ."[11] The agreements, practically identical, included the following parts:

1. An international arbitration agreement between the ANPA and the international union involved;

2. A code of procedure agreed upon by those two bodies;

3. Provision for individual arbitration contracts to be made by publishers and local unions, binding them to terms of the international agreement and undersigned by the chairman of the special standing committee and the international union president involved. These contracts prohibited strikes, boycotts, and lockouts and provided for continuous service. They called for settlement of disputes under existing contracts and also for arbitration of proposed new scales of wages and hours.

The code of procedure urged that parties to a dispute resort first to conference and conciliation and then to local arbitration, with possible final appeal to an international arbitration board. Local arbitration boards were to have three members agreed upon by the two parties. The international board was to be composed of the chairman of the ANPA special standing committee, the president of the international union involved, and a third disinterested person if deemed necessary.

The first agreements covered typographers and pressmen and the stereotypers and photoengravers who were still members of the ITU. As the latter two groups won autonomy from the ITU, their separate unions were included in the arbitration plan.

There were many difficulties in carrying out the arbitration procedure. Local boards satisfactory to both sides were hard to

[10] General Harrison Gray Otis of the *Times*, Chandler's father-in-law, protested sharply to Driscoll in May 1901 (*Bulletin 837*, June 7, 1901) about the ANPA cooperating with labor unions. The *Times* had replaced ITU printers in 1890 with members of the International Printers' Protective Fraternity, a group labeled as "scabs" by the ITU. In 1901 the ITU attempted again to unionize the *Times'* mechanical staff, and in 1903 the ITU cooperated with William Randolph Hearst when Hearst started an opposition paper, the Los Angeles *Examiner*. The dispute was climaxed in 1910 with the famous McNamara dynamiting case.

[11] *Bulletin 936*, May 2, 1902, containing the text of the agreements.

find; too many cases were appealed to the international board; and in some instances local unions spurned unfavorable decisions. In general the decisions followed current economic trends. A prosperous year meant wage advances, while a recession brought publisher victories.

The program succeeded largely because of the earnest effort and cooperative spirit of the leaders from the ANPA and from the unions. Driscoll, McCormick, Ridder, Lowenstein, Bruce Haldeman of the Louisville *Courier-Journal*, and other interested publishers kept the ANPA membership in line during periods of doubt as to the value of negotiation and arbitration. On the other side President James M. Lynch of the typographers, President George L. Berry of the pressmen, President James J. Freel of the stereotypers, and President Matthew Woll of the photoengravers gave full support to the movement, cooperating actively with Driscoll within the bounds of their union responsibilities and disciplining any recalcitrant locals.

The first arbitration case involved a technical issue of jurisdiction in the plant of the Akron *Beacon-Journal*. After a local board consisting of a representative of the paper, a union leader, and an attorney had failed to agree, the international board decided the case in favor of the union.[12]

The second case resulted in a compromise decision. The Toronto *Globe* called Commissioner Driscoll and President Lynch of the typographers to Toronto on May 1, 1902, to arbitrate a dispute. The paper was paying $14 a week for an 8½-hour workday; the men wanted $18 for an eight-hour day. Under the decision they got $16 for eight hours' work. Driscoll took the opportunity to form a local publishers' association among the six Toronto papers.[13]

President Lynch of the ITU addressed the 1902 ANPA convention for two hours, answering numerous questions, and Driscoll reciprocated by speaking at the ITU convention and the pressmen's gathering the same year. He also reported attending in August the first convention of the International Stereotypers and Electrotypers' Union, which had won autonomy from the

[12] *Bulletin 968*, Aug. 23, 1902.
[13] *Bulletin 941*, May 22, 1902.

ITU in 1901 as a new American Federation of Labor affiliate, but which was bound to the arbitration agreement made with the ANPA by the parent union.[14] The fourth of the great newspaper printing unions, the International Photo-Engravers' Union, which seceded from the ITU in 1900, was chartered by the American Federation of Labor in 1904 and held its first convention in October, with Driscoll attending in order to obtain an arbitration agreement.[15] The agreement was completed in November 1905 and was set to expire with the others on April 30, 1907.[16] In 1903 the printing unions formed the Allied Printing Trades Council at a meeting in Indianapolis, to settle interunion matters and attempt to present a solid front to employers. To Driscoll's dissatisfaction, they also set about forming local allied printing trades councils to offset the local associations of the publishers.[17] Interunion cooperation, however, was far less effective than a "one big union" policy would have been.

Meanwhile the New York City publishers tried the arbitration method and found it practical. The powerful Typographical Union No. 6 presented demands in June 1903 for either an increase in wages or a decrease from eight to seven hours' work a day at the same pay. With Bishop Frederick Burgess of the Episcopal diocese of Long Island serving as the public member, the local arbitration board decided that there should be no change at all in wages or hours. The decision, Driscoll asserted, saved New York publishers $200,000 a year and "illustrates forcibly the advantages of arbitration."[18] In December 1903 the Publishers Association of New York City and the local pressmen's union agreed to arbitrate a 20 percent wage increase demand. H. N. Kellogg of the New York *Tribune*, the union president, and the Reverend T. R. Slicer composed the local board, which gave the union a 10 percent increase after lengthy hearings ending in May 1905.[19]

Labor trouble in the Pacific Northwest almost wrecked the arbitration agreements in the summer of 1903. Had it done so, the

[14] *Bulletin 952*, June 26, 1902; *Bulletin 968*, Aug. 23, 1902.
[15] *Bulletin 1189*, July 18, 1904.
[16] *Bulletin 1394*, Jan. 22, 1906.
[17] *Bulletin 1021*, Feb. 16, 1903.
[18] *Bulletin 1066*, July 3, 1903.
[19] *Bulletin 1298*, June 3, 1905.

ANPA almost surely would have become a belligerent antilabor organization in 1904. The trouble began in February 1903 when a typographers' local requested a new wage scale from the Seattle *Post-Intelligencer.* The publisher made counterdemands, which he insisted should be arbitrated, but which the union held were not subject to negotiation. Meanwhile the Spokane *Spokesman-Review* and its ITU local were engaged in arbitration, with the Reverend William M. Jones as third arbitrator. The men were getting $4 a day for a 7½-hour day and had asked for a raise of fifty cents a day. Instead the arbitration award cut them to $3.50 for an eight-hour day.[20]

With this example before them, the Seattle typographers refused to arbitrate their dispute, demanded that the *Post-Intelligencer* accept their terms, and went on strike July 7 when the publisher refused to yield. The Spokane union struck on July 27, and Driscoll charged President Lynch of the ITU with responsibility for violation of the arbitration agreement.[21] Lynch ordered the two unions to return to work but refused to accept the local Spokane decision.[22]

Relations between the American Newspaper Publishers Association and the International Typographical Union were strained to the breaking point. Then in October top officials of the two organizations got together in New York and later in Indianapolis to restore harmony and settle the Seattle and Spokane cases. In November the ANPA and ITU announced that friendly relations had been fully restored and the two cases settled, but both sides agreed not to divulge the terms of settlement.[23]

It was well for the International Typographical Union that it had mended its relations with the ANPA, for in January 1904 it began a crusade for the eight-hour day throughout the printing industry. The belligerent United Typothetae of America began raising a fund to battle the typographers and, with the Citizens' Industrial Association of America, urged the ANPA to join the ranks of fighting employers.[24]

[20] *Bulletin 1056,* May 29, 1903.
[21] *Bulletin 1076,* Aug 11, 1903.
[22] *Editor & Publisher,* 3:1 (Aug. 8, 1903).
[23] *Bulletin 1104,* Nov. 7, 1903; *Editor & Publisher,* 3:1 (Nov. 7, 1903).
[24] Bonnett, *Employers' Associations,* pp. 218–19.

The 1904 ANPA annual meeting decided to raise a labor fund on a voluntary basis, interested publishers to pay $40 a typesetting machine for three years. But events proved that the ANPA membership was sticking by the negotiatory policy. Driscoll reported to the 1906 convention that only sixty-four members had subscribed to the special fund. He further commented that the eight-hour day controversy had brought strikes to all union printing shops except those of newspapers and that the ITU and the United Typothetae were prepared to spend more than a million and a half dollars a year on the fight. The 255 members of the ANPA, he said, were 90 percent union and 10 percent nonunion, and most of them recognized the eight-hour day and the closed shop. Their wisdom in not fighting the typographers on the eight-hour day issue was demonstrated in 1908 when the long, costly battle waged by the United Typothetae came to an end with the union winning the decision.[25]

Renewal of the arbitration agreements now became the main activity of Commissioner Driscoll and committee members McCormick, Ridder, and Haldeman. They met with the ITU executive committee in April and June 1906 and reached an agreement which was published in August.[26] It contained three major changes. Both sides agreed that working conditions, as well as wages and hours, were to be arbitrable. The union, disappointed with the performance of disinterested third persons on arbitration boards, asked that they be eliminated, and this was done. In 1912, however, provision was again made for the addition of a third man to the boards when necessary.

By the third change the union obtained a clause which quickly became a major point of contention between publishers and unions and eventually brought about an impasse between the ANPA and ITU. This clause stipulated that provisions of international union law — ex parte statements by the unions — were to be exempt from arbitration procedures, even though such statements of union practices affected the publishers' business. The full implications of this union victory were not immediately realized by the ANPA, however.

[25] *Ibid.*, p. 234.
[26] *Bulletin 1473*, June 16, 1906; *Bulletin 1495*, Aug. 10, 1906.

The stereotypers, the photoengravers, and the Mailers' Union affiliate of the ITU all agreed to use the arbitration agreement worked out by the typographers. A slightly different version was negotiated with the pressmen. All were approved by the 1907 annual meeting of the ANPA, to run until April 30, 1912.

A month after he had seen the policy of negotiation reaffirmed, Commissioner Driscoll resigned for reasons of health. Ridder, now president of the ANPA, asked Driscoll to reconsider, but death took the first labor commissioner on March 23. H. N. Kellogg, business manager of the New York *Tribune*, was immediately appointed as Driscoll's successor, at a yearly salary of $10,-000.[27] Chairman McCormick of the special standing committee moved from Chicago later in the year, to become publisher of the Indianapolis *Star*, and resigned his post. Ridder then made Kellogg both commissioner and chairman of the special standing committee, with Bruce Haldeman of the Louisville *Courier-Journal* and Charles H. Taylor, Jr., of the Boston *Globe* as his committee members.

Financing the work of the special standing committee was put on a permanent basis at the 1908 annual meeting. Kellogg reported that the committee had spent $16,816 during the past year, but that voluntary contributions received from 167 members had totaled only $11,508. The members voted to make compulsory an assessment of $6 a year for each typesetting machine owned by a publisher. The committee's expenditures rose regularly each year until they totaled $25,000 in 1918. The office of the commissioner was moved to Indianapolis in 1911.

The spirit of cooperation between publishers and unions which now existed was demonstrated by the reciprocal appearances of their leaders before the various national conventions. The presidents of the four big unions issued a public statement in behalf of eighty thousand workers praising the publishers for the successful development of the arbitration agreements.[28] The climax came in November 1908, when Chairman John Norris of the ANPA committee on paper presented officials of the four unions to the Committee on Ways and Means of the House of Represen-

[27] *Bulletin 1597*, Mar. 30, 1907.
[28] New York *Times*, Apr. 24, 1908, p. 7.

tatives, then holding hearings on the tariff bill of 1909. The union men presented resolutions seconding Norris' request for removal of all duties on wood pulp and newsprint, contending that the tariff did not aid workers in the American newsprint manufacturing industry but did curtail the amount of newsprint available and raised its price to the detriment of the printing unions.[29] Relations between the unions and their employers seemingly were well cemented indeed.

But while Kellogg could report to the 1909 ANPA convention that only twelve national arbitrations had been necessary during the past year, he also had to list strikes by pressmen in Milwaukee, New Orleans, Houston, and Fort Worth. President Berry of the pressmen's union assured the convention that he was disciplining the striking locals, but labor trouble spread to Chicago and Denver pressmen in 1910.

A picture of the trend in mechanical department labor costs was given members at the 1910 annual meeting. Commissioner Kellogg presented figures showing the increase in number of men employed and wages paid from 1905 to 1909 in 148 ANPA members' shops. His report included the accompanying table.

The payroll increase for the 148 newspapers reporting, due both to additional workers and to higher wages, amounted to $1,818,000 a year, Kellogg said. For the total ANPA membership, he estimated, wages were up $3,600,000 a year. The commissioner glumly said that of ninety-five new arbitration contracts signed by local publishers from April 1909 to March 1910 all except one gave some increase to the unions, "who believe prosperity is with us again." [30]

But the figures cited by Kellogg do not support a contention that newspaper labor was overpaid. Figures from the Bureau of Labor Statistics show the following indexes for the year 1910 (1914 = 100): compositors, 92.7; all newspaper labor, 94.0; all labor, 94.4.

The figures show that the printing unions had been justified in seeking wage increases. The pressmen, even though they were

[29] *Tariff Hearings before the Committee on Ways and Means of the House of Representatives*, 60th Cong., 2d sess., H. Doc. 1505 (1909), pp. 5925–27.
[30] *Report of the Twenty-fourth Annual Meeting* (1910), pp. 35–37.

INCREASE IN EMPLOYEES AND WAGES IN NEWSPAPER MECHANICAL
DEPARTMENTS, 1905–1909

	Composing Room	Press Room	Stereo-typing	Photo-engraving	Mailing	Total
Number of papers reporting........	148	144	143	51	119	148
Number of men						
1905..........	5,069	1,412	735	285	1,268	8,769
1909..........	5,702	1,721	790	314	1,497	10,024
Percent of increase.......	12.4	21.8	7.6	10.0	18.1	14.3
Weekly Payroll						
1905..........	$108,333	$24,859	$15,217	$6,262	$13,279	$167,950
1909..........	$128,638	$33,475	$17,533	$7,418	$15,863	$202,927
Percent of increase.......	18.7	34.6	15.2	18.3	19.4	20.8
Weekly average per man						
1905..........	$21.37	$17.61	$22.06	$21.97	$10.47	$19.14
1909..........	$22.56	$19.50	$22.18	$23.62	$10.59	$20.24
Percent of increase.......	5.57	10.71	0.54	7.50	1.10	5.70

getting increases, were still below the average of the other major printing unions, a fact which contributed to the difficulties between the pressmen and the publishers. But the figures also show that the publishers, from their own point of view, were doing a good job of negotiating — despite their growing resentment of the situation. They were going to do an even better job in the years from 1910 to 1920, for the Bureau of Labor Statistics reported in the latter year that the index for compositors' wages stood at 160.7, while that for all labor was 199.0.

A committee on codification of typographical scales was appointed by the ANPA in 1910, with Henry N. Cary of the St. Louis *Republic* as chairman. It asked publishers in seventy-four cities to aid in its work, but only twenty-three responded, bringing a comment by Cary at the 1911 annual meeting that "we are losing out to the unions because we don't care." In San Francisco, Cary reported, the publishers had hired a man to handle all their labor negotiations and problems, and he announced that he was being employed by Chicago publishers in the same capacity.

The rumbles of discontent which were being heard from sections of the ANPA membership became louder at the 1911 annual meeting. A group of publishers headed by Victor F. Lawson of the Chicago *Daily News* revolted against the proviso that international union laws were not subject to arbitration.

These laws, among other things, required that all local advertising be set by machine or by hand in each newspaper shop in the city, even though the advertiser supplied mats requiring only casting; that foremen be union members; that promotion of personnel be controlled by the union; and that the union regulate the training of apprentices. These union laws, Lawson and others contended, cost the publisher a great deal of money and deprived him of some control of his operations. Lawson accused the special standing committee of failing to protect the publishers in negotiating the arbitration agreements.

As a result the ANPA appointed a committee of ten to negotiate for renewal of the arbitration agreements in 1912. To it were named the five members of the special standing committee: Kellogg, Haldeman, Taylor, George C. Hitt of the Indianapolis *Star*, and G. J. Palmer of the Houston *Post*. The other five were Lawson, Ridder, Charles W. Knapp of the St. Louis *Republic*, Don C. Seitz of the New York *World*, and S. S. Carvalho of the *World*. The ten ANPA representatives did their best during the next year to win Lawson's point against the ITU and the other three unions, but in February 1912 they were forced to admit defeat. Lawson himself explained the reason — there would be no arbitration agreements at all if the publishers insisted upon altering the international union law situation.[31] As President Bruce Haldeman commented at the 1912 annual meeting, the International Typographical Union was more intelligently organized and better disciplined than the American Newspaper Publishers Association, and the publishers had found out that they had to take what agreement the printers were willing to give.

New arbitration agreements with all four unions were approved at the 1912 meeting by the ANPA membership. But the International Printing Pressmen and Assistants' Union voted in a national referendum to turn down the new agreement with the

[31] *Bulletins: Labor 428*, Feb. 17, 1912.

publishers.[32] The old agreement with the pressmen expired May 1, 1912, and only local agreements remained in effect until a new national contract was signed in 1920. In addition twenty-four locals of the other three printing unions refused to make local agreements with publishers, and forty publishers, mostly in Cincinnati, Chicago, and New York, also vetoed new local contracts containing arbitration clauses.[33]

The refusal of the pressmen to sign a new national arbitration contract resulted from an arbitration decision of September 1911 giving William Randolph Hearst's Chicago *Examiner* and Chicago *American* a victory over their pressmen. Hearst contended that for five years he had paid higher wages and employed more pressmen than any of his Chicago competitors. A national arbitration board gave him the same terms as his competitors and, after a union protest, reaffirmed the decision.[34] Hearst consolidated his position by signing an agreement with his stereotypers which involved $3000 in back pay and then posted a notice that the *Examiner* and *American* pressrooms would operate under the same contract as other Chicago papers.[35] The men did not strike, however, until the crews on the various presses were cut 20 percent on the evening of May 1, 1912. On the following day the Chicago publishers' association canceled its contract with all the pressmen in the city, and the pressmen immediately went on strike against all the papers. The stereotypers attempted a sympathy strike, which President Freel of the international union quashed, and President Lynch of the typographers stopped a possible sympathy strike by his men. But pressmen in other cities staged sympathy walkouts, and the resentment over the whole affair doomed the new ANPA-IPP&AU arbitration agreement to defeat.

An ANPA publicity pamphlet issued in 1915 described the functions of the special standing committee during the period in this manner:

A Special Standing Committee, of which Mr. H. N. Kellogg is chairman, with offices in Indianapolis, has for many years maintained ami-

[32] *Bulletins: Labor 448*, Apr. 13, 1912.
[33] *Report of the Twenty-sixth Annual Meeting* (1912), p. 34.
[34] *Bulletins: Labor 376*, Sept. 9, 1911; *Bulletins: Labor 414*, Jan. 6, 1912.
[35] *Report of the Twenty-seventh Annual Meeting* (1913), pp. 36–53.

cable relations between the members of the Association and the various labor unions through arbitration agreements which preclude the possibility of strikes, and have proved to be a great factor in the maintenance of industrial peace in the newspaper offices. All active members are entitled to the protection these contracts afford provided they make individual arbitration agreements with the union, application for which must be made to the chairman of the Special Standing Committee. A list of men desiring employment is kept in the Indianapolis office and the chairman endeavors to supply competent help to members when they need it. He also keeps on file the contracts and scales of the labor unions in the various cities and will furnish copies of these scales when desired to members who wish them; they are often found very useful to members who are considering new propositions. The chairman is always ready and willing to answer questions on all phases of the labor situation, and to take up matters at issue with the International Presidents of the several labor organizations. In this way many serious disagreements are avoided and settlements reached without the danger of strikes or the necessity of going through arbitration proceedings.[36]

The reference in this statement to supplying men for members desiring them brings up an issue which almost caused trouble between the ANPA and the ITU in 1913 and 1914. Publishers and typographers in San Francisco were at loggerheads over their local contract, and the union asked permission of ITU President Lynch to call a strike in September 1913. H. W. Norton, manager of the San Francisco Newspaper Publishers' Association, requested Kellogg to obtain a replacement force for the San Francisco newspapers and, according to Kellogg, "an adequate force was secured."[37] Thereupon President Lynch charged Kellogg and the San Francisco papers with planning to break the local unions, and only after denials by Kellogg was peace restored. An arbitration agreement announced in 1915 was largely in favor of the publishers.[38] In May 1914 Lynch became labor commissioner of New York State and Marsden G. Scott became ITU head.

Sacramento, California, pressmen struck in 1912 and were ousted in favor of open-shop workers, a situation which survived an attempted boycott during 1913.[39] In New Orleans in 1915 a

[36] *American Newspaper Publishers Association, Its Works and Purposes* (pamphlet, 1915).
[37] *Report of the Twenty-eighth Annual Meeting* (1914), p. 19.
[38] *Bulletins: Labor 958*, Feb. 13, 1915.
[39] *Bulletins: Labor 758*, Oct. 4, 1913.

typographers' strike was answered by the establishment of an open-shop policy.[40] The publishers were getting tougher, and the ANPA membership in 1915 again voted to institute a voluntary defense fund, to be raised by payments of one dollar a month for each typesetting machine. The fund was dropped in 1917, however, after only $9000 had been accumulated.[41]

Despite these indications of discontent the ANPA special standing committee renewed its arbitration agreements with all the unions except the pressmen for the period from May 1917 to April 1922, and the 1917 annual meeting voted its approval. In the renewals was the heartily disliked clause: "International laws of the union in effect January 1, 1916, shall not be subject to the provisions of the arbitration agreement." In 1919 the pressmen asked for a new national arbitration agreement, which was signed January 1, 1920, to be in effect until April 30, 1922.[42]

The number of local arbitration agreements was rising steadily, from 140 in 1905 to 260 in 1913, 429 in 1918, and 605 in 1920. But despite this record of increasing use of arbitration procedures, the report of the special standing committee to the 1920 annual meeting held ominous news: in 1919 there had been forty-one illegal strikes and twenty-two near strikes in ANPA member plants. This rise in labor-management disputes played into the hands of those ANPA members who wished to take a firmer stand against the unions. They were to win their victory in 1922, and the story of this new phase in ANPA labor affairs will be told in Chapter XII.

[40] *Bulletins: Labor 968*, Mar. 27, 1915.
[41] *Report of the Thirty-first Annual Meeting* (1917), p. 3.
[42] *Report of the Thirty-fourth Annual Meeting* (1920), p. 222.

CHAPTER VI

The Newsprint Tariff

MAN'S ability to make low-cost newsprint from wood pulp, by a process introduced into America from Germany in 1867, has been a basic factor in the rapid growth of the daily newspaper. As Thomas B. Reed, once a publisher and more famous as Speaker of the House of Representatives, told the banqueting members of the American Newspaper Publishers Association in 1902:

Power and circulation of the newspapers has grown tremendously. You may flatter yourselves, gentlemen, that you know the reason why. This tremendous circulation is not because of your superior ability, but is due to the absurdedly cheap price of white paper. When it cost ten cents a pound instead of two cents a pound, even an editor hesitated when he took his pen in hand. . . .[1]

By 1900 the stage had been set for a battle between American newspaper publishers and newsprint manufacturers over the problems of cost and supply of "white paper." The circumstances involved were many. A new manufacturing process had been developed, revolutionizing the newsprint industry. Growing American newspapers needed greatly increased amounts of newsprint and found the cost of print paper a significant item in their annual budgets. Newsprint manufacturers, plagued by overly enthusiastic expansion, sought to protect the price of their product by monopolistic practices and by securing protective tariff legislation. The publishers, as consumers, fought to get unimpeded access to all sources of newsprint at the lowest possible price.

Newsprint made by hand from rag stock was expensive even during normal times. And when the New York *Tribune* had to pay $442 a ton for newsprint during the Civil War, and was still paying $340 a ton in 1866, the time was ripe for the introduction

[1] New York *Herald*, Feb. 21, 1902, p. 6.

of a new manufacturing process. Using water power this process ground spruce logs until the wood fibers were separated and a wood pulp remained. The wood pulp, combined with a small amount of rag stock, could be made into a usable print paper. By the 1890s a chemically produced wood pulp, called chemical pulp or sulphite pulp to distinguish it from mechanical or ground wood pulp, replaced rag pulp as the toughening element in newsprint.

These manufacturing advances, coupled with the increased productive efficiency of the Fourdrinier papermaking machine, brought the price of newsprint tumbling downward. Paper manufacturers, seeking the combination of spruce and nearby water, slashed into the forests of Maine, Michigan, Wisconsin, and Minnesota, to produce an ever growing supply of print paper. Newsprint cost $246 a ton in 1870, $138 a ton in 1880, $76 a ton in 1890, and reached a low of $42 a ton in 1899, the bottom price until 1933.[2]

In view of these statistics, it would seem that American newspaper publishers should have been quite content with the price of newsprint at the turn of the century. But such was not the case. The publishers were happy, of course, that they could obtain adequate supplies of moderately priced newsprint. They were, however, acutely conscious of the price of this raw material, which bulked larger and larger in their operating costs. As the tonnage of newsprint used increased, slight price fluctuations meant sizable differences in expenditures for mass-circulation dailies.

In 1880, on the eve of the introduction of Pulitzer's new journalism, the United States had 971 dailies and 9810 newspapers of all kinds. Twenty years later there were 2226 dailies and a total of 15,904 newspapers. In 1880 American newspapers used about 100,000 tons of newsprint, or about two thirds of the amount produced domestically, according to census data. In 1900 domestic newsprint consumption equaled domestic supply, both figures standing at 569,000 tons. Spirited competition to improve news

[2] Lee, *The Daily Newspaper in America*, pp. 743–45. Prices to 1880 are those paid by the New York *Tribune*; those later are average wholesale prices in New York City.

coverage and rapidly growing advertising volume had brought an increased number of pages to nearly all dailies. The metropolitan leaders, such as the New York *World* and the Hearst chain, doubled or tripled the size of their daily editions, which were sold in the hundreds of thousands of copies. Selling their product at competitive one- and two-cent prices, they were particularly concerned — as consumers — with the price of their basic raw material, newsprint. The 1909 census figures indicate that 21 percent of the total revenue of American newspapers was spent in buying newsprint. As leaders in the American Newspaper Publishers Association, the larger publishers used the strength of that organization to meet what they considered unfair price tactics on the part of the newsprint manufacturers.

The ANPA, coming on the scene in 1887, found the paper manufacturers already organized as a trade association. The American Paper Makers' Association, forerunner of the American Paper and Pulp Association, first met in 1878 to discuss industry problems. The papermakers complained throughout the 1880s that too many new companies were rushing into the business to harvest the quick profits presaged by increased demand for newsprint and higher grade magazine and book paper.[3] To meet the twin problems of overproduction and declining prices which were intensified in the 1890s, the manufacturers adopted the tactics of many other American businesses and effected a combination which the publishers declared amounted to a monopoly. This was the organization in 1898 of the International Paper Company, which won control of most of the mills east of the Mississippi River, with two thirds to three fourths of the domestic output of newsprint.[4] In self-defense twenty-six paper mills in Wisconsin, Michigan, and Minnesota two years later formed the General Paper Company to sell for all of them at a single price and thus compete with International.[5] The fears of monopoly expressed by the publishers seemed justified when the price of

[3] L. Ethan Ellis, *Print Paper Pendulum: Group Pressures and the Price of Newsprint* (New Brunswick: Rutgers University Press, 1948), p. 14, reflecting the comments of the *Paper Trade Journal.*
[4] *Report of the Federal Trade Commission on the News-print Paper Industry, June 13, 1917* (Washington: Government Printing Office, 1917), p. 23.
[5] Ellis, *Print Paper Pendulum,* p. 29.

newsprint in New York jumped from $42 a ton in 1899 to $56 a ton in 1900 — a 33 percent increase.

As the publishers formed their lines to battle against the "newsprint combine," they also found the tariff situation not to their liking. The newsprint manufacturers, given sizable protection against imported newsprint and wood pulp through the workings of the general American tariff policy, did not propose to surrender their advantage.

Under the Morrill Act of 1861 the Republican party had achieved a tariff policy of moderate protection. But as wartime internal taxes mounted on manufactures and incomes, upward tariff adjustments were made in order that American businesses could be protected at the 1861 levels. After the Civil War the taxes were dropped, but even a 10 percent horizontal tariff cut in 1872 failed to return tariff levies to the prewar levels. The Republican party during the 1880s defended the policy of full protection, while the two Cleveland administrations failed to produce tariff-cutting legislation. By the 1890s the protective features of the tariff had become a dominant political issue, and the McKinley Tariff of 1890 and the Dingley Tariff of 1897 strengthened the policy of thoroughgoing protection.

Newsprint had been protected by the tariff since the Civil War, and the Treasury Department had ruled that wood pulp fell under the protection of a general clause in the tariff regulations. The tariff of 1883 put pulp logs on the free list, reduced the protection afforded wood pulp from a 20 percent ad valorem duty to 10 percent, and cut the duty on newsprint from 20 percent to 15 percent ad valorem. The McKinley Tariff of 1890 continued these provisions, except that it changed the ad valorem duty on wood pulp to a specific duty of $2.50 a ton, a slight increase. The Wilson-Gorman Tariff of 1894 left newsprint under a 15 percent ad valorem duty and returned wood pulp to a 10 percent ad valorem duty.[6]

The ANPA had urged mildly in 1894 that the tariff on wood pulp be abolished.[7] When Congress began to consider the provi-

[6] *Tariff Acts Passed by the Congress of the United States from 1789 to 1897*, 55th Cong., 2d sess., H. Doc. 562 (1898).
[7] *Minutes of the Seventh Annual Meeting* (1893), p. 12; *Bulletin 237*, Jan. 4, 1894.

sions of what was to become the Dingley Tariff of 1897, one of
the ANPA's members appeared to lead the fight against the tariff
protections afforded the newsprint manufacturers. He was John
Norris, business manager of the New York *World,* who later was
to become business manager of the New York *Times,* later still
the paid chairman of the ANPA committee on paper and the
nemesis of the papermakers.

Norris made the first of his many appearances before congressional committees as the business manager of the *World* and not
as an official ANPA representative. But he gave the House Committee on Ways and Means its first exposure to an argument
which rapidly became the official position of the ANPA. He declared that the *World* used one thirteenth of the total newsprint
consumed in the United States. It and other newspapers were
threatened, Norris warned, by a proposed combination of newsprint manufacturers which would raise the price of paper "and
thereby tax knowledge and diminish the educational possibilities
of the newspaper." Norris argued that the tariff on newsprint
should be abolished, so that the domestic manufacturers of newsprint could be challenged by imports from Canada. When opponents of such a move asserted that the newsprint industry
would then become a Canadian business, because of the abund-
ance of wood, water power, and lower salaried labor there, Norris insisted that such would not be the case.[8]

The effect of Norris' argument upon the committee was not
great, as he himself warned the ANPA annual convention when
it met two months later in 1897. Norris told the convention that
the House committee would recommend a duty on wood pulp
which would increase the cost of newsprint a dollar a ton. He
moved that a committee of three be appointed to seek the abolition of the duty on pulp and paper. William Cullen Bryant of the
Brooklyn *Times* and L. E. Holden of the Cleveland *Plain Dealer*
objected that some newspapers which had supported the Republican party's position on the protective tariff would consider themselves seekers of "special privilege" should the ANPA engage in
such lobbying activity. Norris' resolution was adopted, however,
and he was appointed to head the committee.

[8] *Tariff Hearings before the Committee on Ways and Means,* 54th Cong., 2d
sess., H. Doc. 338 (1897), pp. 1753–67.

When the Dingley bill received final approval, the fears which Norris had expressed were fully justified. The new act placed a specific duty of $6 a ton on newsprint valued at not more than $40 a ton, a levy equal to the previous 15 percent ad valorem duty. Paper valued at $40 to $50 a ton carried an $8 duty, and the scale thus increased, although most newsprint fell in the lowest category. Ground wood pulp was assigned a duty of $1.67 a ton and chemical wood pulp $3.33 to $5 a ton.[9]

The Dingley Tariff, however, added a qualification that was to be highly important in United States–Canadian affairs and one that brought out into the open the growing competition between the two countries for control of the newsprint manufacturing industry. This qualification read, in connection with the duty on paper:

Provided, That if any country or dependency shall impose an export duty upon pulpwood exported to the United States, there shall be imposed upon printing paper when imported from such country or dependency, an additional duty of one-tenth of one cent per pound [$2 per ton] for each dollar of export duty per cord so imposed, and proportionately for fractions of a dollar of such export duty.[10]

This provision was aimed at Canadian efforts to prevent the exportation of pulpwood to the United States for manufacture into newsprint. The penalty would be an added duty on newsprint coming from the Canadian province which imposed an export duty on pulpwood. In the case of wood pulp, the tariff provided that the American government would collect as a penalty duty the same amount which had been charged as an export duty in Canada.

The timberland policy of the federal government of Canada and of all the provinces except Nova Scotia and New Brunswick had been not to sell timber stands but to lease the land, retaining control of the cutting and charging protective fees and dues for cutting rights. As a result, the amount of privately owned timberland in Ontario, Quebec, Manitoba, and British Columbia ranged from only 3.3 percent of the total in Ontario to 9.1 percent in Manitoba, the remainder being crown lands. In 1891 British Co-

[9] *Report of the Federal Trade Commission on the News-print Paper Industry,* June 13, 1917, compilation of tariff provisions on paper and pulp, pp. 148–51.
[10] *Ibid.,* p. 149.

lumbia prohibited the export of pulpwood cut from crown lands, and it was this, as well as rumors of restrictive action in Quebec and Ontario, that promp d Congress in 1897 to penalize such action.[11]

It seemed foolish to the Canadians to permit their pulp logs to be transported to the United States for manufacturing into newsprint. Canada, they knew, possessed most of the available timber for the making of wood pulp. The Dominion also had the water power necessary for the grinding of wood into pulp. Why should she not also manufacture the paper?

This was a logical argument in Canada, and it became more logical each year as the United States paper manufacturers tore through the accessible stands of spruce and balsam on their side of the border and imported increasing amounts of Canadian pulp logs to meet the rapidly growing demand for newsprint. Canadians could see that if they held firm and restricted the exportation of pulp logs, the papermaking industry inevitably would cross the border. Quebec province in 1900 reduced the dues on pulpwood cut on crown lands from 65 cents a cord to 40 cents a cord if the wood was not shipped from the province. This amounted to an export duty of 25 cents a cord, which, under the 1897 American tariff law, called for an additional penalty duty on newsprint from Quebec of 50 cents a ton.[12] In 1902 Ontario entirely prohibited the export of pulpwood cut on crown lands.[13] Eventually the embattled Canadians were to find that the American Newspaper Publishers Association was a major ally in this international controversy.

In 1898, however, John Norris was finding the conversion of some ANPA members to his point of view a major task. During the annual ANPA convention that year, Norris was shocked to discover that five ANPA officers had held a preconvention "social gathering" with five newsprint company executives, headed by Hugh J. Chisholm, vice-president of the newly formed International Paper Company. The five ANPA representatives were

[11] John A. Guthrie, *The Newsprint Paper Industry: An Economic Analysis* (Cambridge: Harvard University Press, 1941), pp. 31–41.
[12] Frank W. Taussig, *The Tariff History of the United States* (8th ed.; New York: Putnam's, 1931), p. 382.
[13] Guthrie, *The Newsprint Paper Industry*, p. 41.

President Charles W. Knapp, St. Louis *Republic*; Vice-president J. A. Butler, Buffalo *News*; Secretary William Cullen Bryant, Brooklyn *Times*; Treasurer Herbert F. Gunnison, Brooklyn *Eagle*; and Director Frederick Driscoll, St. Paul *Pioneer Press*. When Bryant disclosed during a convention session that the meeting had taken place, Norris was obviously irritated because he had not been informed of the meeting, since he had headed the committee sent to Washington the previous year to speak against the Dingley bill.

Norris told the convention that he had tried to win lower duties on paper and pulp during the Dingley bill hearings, but the paper manufacturers had overwhelmed him. He also warned the membership that the "white tariff combine is a sure go." The International Paper Company, he charged, would be a terrible threat to publishers, with its capitalization of $55,000,000 ($10,-000,000 in bonds, $25,000,000 in 6 percent preferred stock, and $20,000,000 in common stock) and its control of eighteen paper mills which produced the bulk of the nation's supply of newsprint.

Bryant and Butler disagreed with him, contending that the International Paper Company would deal with the publishers in a completely friendly way and that there should be no fear of monopoly. But as the debate progressed the five officers who had attended the "social gathering" were placed more and more on the defensive. Milton A. McRae, business manager of the Scripps-McRae newspapers, came to Norris' defense and urged that the *World*'s business manager be chosen to head an ANPA committee on paper. Driscoll also declared that the ANPA membership should look out for its business interests, regardless of the promises of the newsprint company executives. At the close of the debate a committee on paper was authorized and charged "to take such steps on behalf of this Association as they may deem expedient in dealing with the question of paper supply." Norris was named chairman, with Knapp, McRae, Samuel H. Kauffmann of the Washington *Evening Star*, and C. M. Palmer of the New York *Journal and Advertiser* as the other members.

Norris reported to the 1899 annual meeting that no progress had been made during the year on the question of newsprint. A

Joint High Commission had sought to reconcile the differences between Canada and the American paper manufacturers, without avail. The ANPA committee on paper had utilized the commission hearings to urge again free entry of paper and pulp. It also had prepared a brief for Congress and the newspapers, Norris continued, which advanced a new argument for the ANPA's position. Their slogan was: Preserve United States forests by using Canada's for a newsprint supply. Some Republican papers, Norris said, "could not contradict the teachings of a lifetime" by urging repeal of the paper and pulp tariffs merely as a benefit to the publishers, but they could do so in the name of forest conservation. Norris added that he believed a price of $30 a ton for newsprint was possible if tariff duties were abolished and the overcapitalized International Paper Company was defeated. International, he thought, should be capitalized at $15,000,000, not $55,000,000.

The 1900 ANPA convention, stirred by a rise in paper prices, passed a resolution asking Congress to investigate newsprint prices and the "paper trust." Members gave a new argument for the drive to repeal tariff duties on paper and pulp by asserting that Republican editors could support such a move because it was aimed at breaking up a trust. This, like forest conservation, was a legitimate reason, they contended, for newspaper publishers to ask Congress to make an exception in its general high tariff policy. The *Florida Times-Union and Citizen*, published in Democratic Jacksonville, caustically criticized these efforts to rationalize this attitude toward the newsprint tariff, saying that newspaper appeals for cheaper newsprint — while editors at the same time supported oppressive protective tariffs on woolen cloth, machinery, and the like —"furnished much amusement for the average American." [14]

ANPA action on the newsprint problem was still far from vigorous. In May 1900 an association committee headed by Samuel H. Kauffmann of the Washington *Evening Star* called on the House Committee on Ways and Means and the Senate Finance Committee to present copies of the resolution against the paper trust. Seven ANPA members, of the twenty who promised to do

[14] *Bulletin 910*, Mar. 13, 1902.

the job, were present.[15] But again in 1902 the annual convention called for reduced duty on newsprint and free entry of wood pulp. Charges of monopoly in the paper business were renewed in 1903, when many paper mills simultaneously arrived at a decision to curtail production at a moment when decreased production would tend to keep the price of newsprint firm.[16]

The first great explosion in the battle against the newsprint manufacturers came at the 1904 ANPA convention. There a "white paper crusade" was launched with full fanfare. John Norris, now business manager of the New York *Times*, denounced the International Paper Company and the General Paper Company, which he accused of plotting to divide the nation's newsprint sales business into exclusive eastern and western territories. Don C. Seitz, new business manager of the New York *World*, announced on behalf of Joseph Pulitzer that the *World* was contributing $10,000 to a fund to fight the paper trust. Herman Ridder of the New York *Staats-Zeitung* added a $1000 donation.

During this barrage Condé Hamlin of the St. Paul *Pioneer Press* proposed a resolution, which the membership approved, asking the President and Attorney General of the United States to institute a suit against one of the paper combinations, to test the legality of its existence. Seitz, Norris, and Hamlin were appointed as a committee on paper and empowered to raise $100,-000 from the ANPA membership on a voluntary basis to carry on the prosecution of the paper trusts. Seitz immediately retained James M. Beck as lawyer for the committee[17] and began to collect evidence from the nation's publishers. After a congressional hearing in which the ANPA leadership participated, the Department of Justice opened an investigation of the General Paper Company. Two years later the "white paper crusade" scored its first major victory. On May 11, 1906, a judgment was entered in the circuit court for the district of Minnesota dissolving the General Paper Company as a combination in restraint of trade.

Prices of newsprint fell after 1904, because of overproduction as well as the return of unrestricted competition among companies fearful of the "white paper crusade" and the government's

---

[15] *Bulletin* 730, May 11, 1900.
[16] *Editor & Publisher*, 3:1 (Dec. 12, 1903).
[17] *Report of the Nineteenth Annual Meeting* (1905), p. 3.

antitrust suit. But in 1907 the price of newsprint again became a burning question for the ANPA. A seller's market had developed in the newsprint business by the summer of 1907, as domestic production continued barely to equal domestic consumption, and a tight paper supply was reported in some areas.[18] The International Paper Company claimed that its profits had been cut from $3,961,657 in 1901 to $1,623,616 in 1907, because it was maintaining an average newsprint price of $40 a ton in the face of rising production costs.[19] International therefore decided to raise the price to $50 a ton and to restrict its usual long-term contracts to one-year periods.[20] Other companies followed International's lead and the battle was on.

Herman Ridder, publisher of the New York *Staats-Zeitung* and newly elected president of the ANPA, found his cost per ton had advanced from $35 to $49.[21] Perhaps because of this he called a special stockholders meeting of the ANPA in New York on September 18, 1907. There Felix Agnus of the Baltimore *American* claimed that International was going to raise his contract price from $38 a ton to $50, which he said would increase his expenses $50,000 a year. Josephus Daniels of the Raleigh *News* reported International was raising his price from $46 to $53 a ton. Some publishers contended that they could not get paper at any price. A resolution was adopted urging another federal investigation of the "paper trust" and repeal of all the tariffs that affected newsprint.[22]

A new stirring of the Attorney General's office to investigate the paper combine was one result and eventually led to the prosecution of some paper manufacturers. Another, and more important, result was attracting the interest of President Theodore Roosevelt to the newsprint and wood pulp tariff questions. The ANPA's story was told to the President, and it apparently had some effect. Roosevelt's annual message to Congress, sent De-

[18] Ellis, *Print Paper Pendulum*, pp. 34–35.
[19] *Report of the Federal Trade Commission on the News-print Paper Industry*, June 13, 1917, p. 24.
[20] *Pulp and Paper Investigation Hearings*, 60th Cong., 2d sess., H. Doc. 1502 (1909), pp. 1026ff.
[21] *Ibid.*, p. 53.
[22] *Report of the Twenty-second Annual Meeting* (1908) contains the record of the special meeting.

cember 3, recommended that general action on the tariff be post-
poned until after the 1908 presidential election, but it cheered
the ANPA by declaring that the tariff on wood pulp should be
repealed.

Armed with Roosevelt's recommendation on wood pulp, Ridder and the ANPA committee on paper clamored at the door of
the House Committee on Ways and Means, seeking action on
various bills which eliminated tariffs on paper and pulp and trying to prove that the paper manufacturers were profiteering.
With Norris and Seitz, Ridder tried to line up votes for a bill proposed by Representative Frederick C. Stevens, Republican from
Minnesota, which would eliminate the newsprint and wood pulp
duties if Canada removed its export restrictions. Ridder sent a
letter to publishers of all American newspapers and magazines
asking them to put pressure on congressmen and senators.[23] The
pressure on Congress was increased further when President
Roosevelt, in a special message sent on March 25 urging action
on a specific list of bills, recommended again that wood pulp be
placed on the free list as a conservation measure and suggested
a reduction in the tariff on newsprint from areas which did not
impose export restrictions.

Norris, reporting to the annual ANPA convention which convened on April 22, asserted that he had persuaded a majority of
the House — practically all the Democrats and eighty-one Republicans — to give him pledges that they would support the Stevens
bill. But, he complained bitterly, House Speaker Joseph G. Cannon had thwarted all the ANPA's hard work. Cannon, fearful
that passage of the Stevens bill would encourage further attempts to revolt against his leadership of the House, had cleverly
maneuvered the legislative situation to bring an end to any hope
of immediate action on the paper and pulp tariff bill.

On April 20 Cannon introduced a resolution "for the appointment of a select committee to investigate as to wood pulp and
print paper, and for other purposes."[24] The resolution was referred to the Committee on Rules, of which Cannon was chairman. The following day the resolution was presented to the

[23] *Bulletin 1793*, Mar. 21, 1908.
[24] House Resolution 344. *Congressional Record*, 60th Cong., 1st sess., Apr. 20,
1908, p. 4994.

House by Representative John Dalzell of Pennsylvania as a privileged report from the Committee on Rules.

The resolution recited the ANPA's charges that the cost of paper to users was 60 million dollars more a year than two years previously, that the price of newsprint had advanced 35 to 50 percent in the past few months, that the increase was due to a combination and conspiracy of wood pulp and paper makers, and that the present tariff was oppressive. The pulp and paper manufacturers, the resolution continued, had denied these allegations and had declared that price increases were due to increased costs of raw materials and labor. Therefore, the resolution concluded, a select committee of six members of the House should investigate charges of monopoly and the status of the tariff on wood pulp and newsprint.

The debate which followed, mainly between the Democratic minority leader, John Sharp Williams of Mississippi, and Representatives Dalzell and Sereno E. Payne of New York, chairman of the Committee on Ways and Means, was a general one.[25] It revolved around a filibuster on technical points of order which Williams had been carrying on for the past three weeks, and dealt with general tariff policies, as well as the resolution at hand.

Dalzell opened the debate by complimenting the ANPA on its energetic legislative activity, saying, "I suppose there is no gentleman in this House who has ever known in his experience such an agitation as has been aroused by the newspapers of this country within the past two or three weeks. I suppose there is no gentleman who has had as many telegrams and letters on any particular subject as he has had upon the necessity for legislation with respect to the price of paper." But whether or not new tariff legislation was needed, or a monopoly existed, or anything at all was amiss, Dalzell did not know.

Williams answered that "the rise in the price of paper is due both to a tariff and a combination, and the combination to the tariff." Declaring that Cannon's resolution was intended to whitewash the tariff, he said, "Its object also is to delay action and circumvent this man, Herman Ridder, at the head of this great association of publishers — this 'old German devil,' as some people

[25] *Congressional Record*, 60th Cong., 1st sess., Apr. 21, 1908, pp. 5024–33.

are beginning to call him at this time." Adoption of the resolution would preclude action on the Stevens bill or any other free paper and pulp legislation, the Democratic leader complained.

On the subject of Herman Ridder, Williams drew a reply from Payne, who said, "Mr. Williams seems to take as gospel truth the statements of Herman Ridder, and yet of all the men who have submitted statistics to Congress I know of no one who makes more mistakes than this same Herman Ridder." Payne declared that Ridder had originally implied that newsprint alone had risen in cost 60 million dollars over a two-year period, although that figure included all paper manufactured in the country. Newsprint had risen 24 million dollars in cost at most, and in Payne's opinion, far less.

The House approved Cannon's resolution by a vote of 156 to 112, and the Speaker immediately appointed the select committee: Chairman James R. Mann of Illinois, James M. Miller of Kansas, William H. Stafford of Wisconsin, and Henry Bannon of Ohio, all Republicans; and Thetus W. Sims of Tennessee and William H. Ryan of New York, Democrats. During the debate Williams and Representative David A. de Armond of Missouri had criticized the 4-2 split in favor of the Republicans, and the New York *Times* correspondent covering the story reported that the papermakers were pleased, since they expected the four "Cannon men" on the select committee to whitewash the paper trust.[26]

The American Newspaper Publishers Association, meeting from April 22 to 24 in New York City, viewed Cannon's maneuver with much distrust, to put it mildly. President Ridder accused Cannon, Dalzell, and Payne of blocking the passage of the Stevens bill through a subterfuge and declared that Republican members of the ANPA must go to Washington and force Cannon and Payne to release the Stevens bill from committee.

The publishers, in their anger at Cannon, ignored a prophetic warning from a Canadian member of the ANPA, John MacKay of the Toronto *Globe*. MacKay declared that the Stevens bill was futile in any event because it would not remove the duty on newsprint coming from countries charging duty on logs. Export

[26] New York *Times*, Apr. 22, 1908, p. 1.

duties on pulpwood were now the settled policy of the Canadian government and its provincial governments, MacKay warned, because Canada meant to get the papermaking business as well as the pulpmaking industry. But MacKay's words were lost in the debate.

Things were made no happier for the publishers when William Jennings Bryan, the prospective Democratic candidate for President, jibed at the first annual AP-ANPA banquet: "I am glad I am getting closer to the newspaper publishers — at least with regard to one matter. You are working for a let-up of the tariff on paper and pulp. I am working for a let-up of the tariff all along the line. You newspaper makers have not always been with me unanimously even on one point."[27]

When Chairman Mann of the House select committee telegraphed the ANPA convention April 24 inviting members to appear before his committee, Norris, Seitz, and Ridder said a group of fifty publishers ought to descend on Washington, and Ridder appointed Medill McCormick of the Chicago *Tribune* as their chairman. The next day Ridder, Norris, and the committee (which numbered far less than fifty) were in Washington. Mann, surprised at the publishers' speed, convened his committee to hear Norris' statement for the ANPA.[28] Norris, who spoke bombastically, used figures sweepingly, and was quick to call an opponent "deliberately untruthful" or a "liar," testified until May 5, and through five hundred pages of the committee's record.

Speaking of the increase in newsprint prices, Norris introduced answers to an inquiry made by the ANPA committee on paper among all the country's 2600 daily newspapers. The results showed what might be expected — that only the larger dailies with sizable newsprint costs were excited to action. Repeated urgings had brought in 450 replies to the questionnaire, some of them indefinite as to precise figures. Price increases from $2 to $17 a ton were reported by 203 publishers during the twelve months ending in October 1907. The average increase was $9.50 a ton. Some publishers reported no difficulties, like Friend W. Richardson of the Berkeley *Daily Gazette,* later Republican gov-

[27] New York *Times,* Apr. 23, 1908, p. 5.
[28] *Pulp and Paper Investigation Hearings,* p. 3.

ernor of California, who curtly replied, "I can get all the newsprint I want at a fair price." It later developed in the committee
hearings that William Randolph Hearst was happy too, for he
had a price of $37.60 a ton from the International Paper Com-
pany for his big eastern newspapers, instead of the market price
of $50.[29]

The Mann committee criticized Norris sharply for some of his
general assertions about the paper manufacturers. It also demonstrated its determination to get all the facts of the situation when
it cross-examined the representatives of the American Paper and
Pulp Association who appeared before it, particularly on the subject of paper manufacturers' meetings in New York before the
price increase of 1907. In general it may be said that both sides
retired from the committee hearings with full respect for the
committee members' ability. It was also obvious, as the Mann
committee called new groups of witnesses to Washington and
planned trips covering thousands of miles in the United States
and Canada to see at first hand pulp and paper industry centers,
that the battle would be a long one.

At Ridder's suggestion, therefore, the ANPA board of directors
decided in June to engage John Norris as paid director of association newsprint activities, the directors leaving his salary to
Ridder's discretion. Norris thereupon resigned as business manager of the New York *Times*.[30] The annual reports of the treasurer
of the association show that from 1908 to 1913 the committee on
paper collected voluntary contributions from members for its activities averaging $20,000 yearly. Norris received a salary of $15,-
000 annually.

Norris immediately began issuing bulletins of the committee
on paper, reporting on the travels of the Mann committee around
the paper and pulp regions and on newsprint conditions generally. As he reported, it became increasingly evident that the committee was doing a comprehensive job and would give Congress
for the first time an accurate picture of conditions in the industry.

Before the Mann committee was ready to make its report, however, the Committee on Ways and Means began hearings on the

[29] *Ibid.*, pp. 50–55, 1346.
[30] New York *Times*, June 12, 1908, p. 7.

tariff bill which was to become the Payne-Aldrich Tariff of 1909. Norris appeared before the committee on November 21, 1908, and took with him representatives of the four big printing unions — typographers, pressmen, stereotypers, and photoengravers — who supported his plea for free paper and pulp.[31] Norris repeated all the arguments he had given before the Mann committee in favor of free paper and pulp and against the "paper trust," and drew from smooth-talking Arthur C. Hastings, president of the American Paper and Pulp Association, the comment: "I have been listening this afternoon to the paper by Mr. Norris. I never did like that paper, and this is the third or fourth time I have heard the most of it."[32] If Norris' free use of statistics aroused distrust, Hastings also fared badly with the committee. He was grilled by Democratic members on charges that the paper companies were overcapitalized until he was forced to admit that some of the allegations were true.

The report of the Mann committee was presented to the House on February 19, 1909, by the chairman.[33] Mann declared the committee had collected a vast amount of testimony and information, had personally visited many pulp and paper mills and forest areas, had heard the publishers and the manufacturers, and had investigated labor conditions in the mills — and was making a unanimous report. Democrat Sims concurred, saying that during the investigation he could not tell whether Mann was a protectionist or free trader, Republican or Democrat, and that he, Sims, had never seen such a hard-working committee.[34]

The report left the doubting Thomases of the ANPA ready and willing to eat their earlier words of anger. The paper manufacturers, in turn, were stunned. Summarizing the different processes of producing wood pulp and estimating the amount of spruce wood in the United States used for newsprint, the Mann committee came to the conclusion that there was not enough spruce in the country to insure a continued supply of cheap paper. It found that imports of newsprint since 1900 had been al-

[31] *Tariff Hearings before the Committee on Ways and Means of the House of Representatives*, 60th Cong., 2d sess., H. Doc. 1505 (1909), pp. 5925–27.
[32] *Ibid.*, p. 5927.
[33] *Pulp and Paper Investigation*, 60th Cong., 2d sess., H. Rept. 2206 (1909).
[34] *Congressional Record*, 60th Cong., 2d sess., Feb. 19, 1909, pp. 2700–2.

most nil and had been outweighed by exports of the International Paper Company. In the meantime domestic production was barely keeping up with demand, either because of inability or lack of desire to manufacture more newsprint, and this condition kept prices in a precarious state. It found the cost of production of newsprint (excluding administration, sales costs, interest payments, and profits) to be from $29 to $34 a ton in the United States, lower figures than those claimed by the manufacturers. Therefore the committee recommended that wood pulp be put on the free list and that the tariff on newsprint valued at not more than 2¼ cents a pound (nearly all newsprint) be reduced from $6 to $2 a ton. The retention of this amount of duty, the committee said, was justified "both on the principle of a tariff for revenue and a tariff for protection."

There was a catch, however, in these recommendations. The committee had noted that much Canadian spruce was fit only for papermaking, and it had recognized that Canadian policy was to encourage paper manufacturing in Canada. Nevertheless, the committee urged that penalty duties be continued on newsprint and pulp coming from areas where export duties or restrictions were put on forest products, if those restrictions were not lifted. Mechanically ground pulp from these restricted areas would carry a duty of $1.67 a ton, and chemical wood pulp, duties of $3.33 to $5 a ton, as under the tariff of 1897. Newsprint from a restricted area would carry an additional duty of $4 a ton, nullifying the recommended tariff reduction.

The committee's idea was that the Canadians would lift their export restrictions on pulpwood in return for the concessions granted on the entry of wood pulp and paper. But the admissions of the Mann committee that the United States was now dependent upon Canadian sources for its newsprint only stiffened Canadian determination to hold firm and secure complete freedom of newsprint entry into the United States. Norris had advocated full reciprocity between the two countries on export and import of pulpwood, wood pulp, and paper when he appeared before the Committee on Ways and Means the previous year, and this eventually was to become the ANPA goal, as the only solution to its problem of securing sufficient quantities of low-priced newsprint for the expanding newspaper press.

For the time being, however, the ANPA committee on paper was quite satisfied with the Mann committee report. It had never seriously hoped to wring from the Republican Congress the concession of free entry of newsprint, and it was content with the recommendations which had been made. The ANPA leadership had done its best before the Committee on Ways and Means, which was readying the Payne-Aldrich bill in advance of the meeting of the new Sixty-first Congress.

President William Howard Taft announced in his inaugural address that he was calling Congress into special session on March 15, 1909, to consider tariff legislation, thus carrying out the promise of the Republican platform for downward tariff revision. On March 18 Chairman Payne of the Committee on Ways and Means introduced a bill which was better than the tariff revisionists had hoped for, but its provisions did not matter very much because Senator Nelson W. Aldrich of Rhode Island and his Committee on Finance were already planning a rewriting of the House bill which was to turn the legislation into a tariff with high protective provisions.

Congressman Mann made a lengthy statement to the House on March 31, defending the conclusions his committee had reached on paper and pulp duties, and he had the satisfaction of seeing his recommendations incorporated into the tariff bill as it passed the House on April 9. But the following day John Norris of the ANPA committee on paper ominously reported that paper manufacturers were active in the "several secret hearings the Senate Finance Committee has held in the past week." [35] When the tariff bill reached the floor of the Senate a few days later, the publishers found that the duty on newsprint had been upped from the House figure of $2 a ton to $4 a ton. The addition of a penalty of $4 a ton on newsprint coming from restricted Canadian areas would bring the total duties to $8 a ton — more than the existing $6 rate.[36]

[35] *Bulletin 1984*, Apr. 10, 1909.
[36] *H. R. 1438*, 61st Cong., 1st sess., H. Doc. 92 (1909), showing all changes in the tariff bill as it progressed through the Congress.

This action by Aldrich's Senate committee slightly soured a celebration planned for the 1909 annual meeting of the American Newspaper Publishers Association on April 21 in New York City. But at the joint AP-ANPA banquet a silver centerpiece was given to President Herman Ridder of the ANPA "in recognition of his work to obtain a reduction of the duties on wood pulp and print paper." [37] John Norris and Don C. Seitz were praised also. The toastmaster, Major J. C. Hemphill of Charleston, said that Speaker Cannon had declined an invitation to attend the banquet and bragged that ". . . he would not recognize us or the justice of our cause until we had run the steam roller over him, and then he pleaded that we had not been fair to him or his Committee on Rules." If the toastmaster referred to the growing revolt against Cannon's dictatorial powers in the House, any ANPA "steam roller" was being helped by many interested individuals and groups indeed, and particularly by the midwestern insurgents of the Republican party.

The publishers voted in convention (with three dissenting on a rising vote) to send telegrams to all United States senators, asking that the House rates be restored, and then settled back to hear Ridder, Seitz, and Norris explain what had happened to the tariff bill in the Senate Committee on Finance. Norris prefaced his remarks by saying that Ridder had been in Washington for three months in 1908, and that "not many would care to put up with the treatment he did." A member interrupted from the floor: "Who is the United States Senate?" Seitz answered: "Senator Aldrich." Following a burst of laughter Norris opened his statement on Aldrich's part in the raising of the duties recommended by the Mann committee and accepted by the House.

When he had visited Washington five weeks before, Norris said, things were not going too smoothly. With Ridder and Seitz he met Aldrich in his private office. The Rhode Island senator maintained that the ANPA representatives spoke for only a few big papers, not the whole field, and cited the Boston *Herald* as being against reduced duties on newsprint. That night, Norris said, he attended a meeting at which were present Senators Aldrich and Reed Smoot of the Committee on Finance, President

[37] New York *Times,* Apr. 23, 1909, p. 5.

Arthur C. Hastings of the American Paper and Pulp Association, and three officers of the International Paper Company.

Aldrich, Norris reported, was fair and candid, saying that he was a protectionist who wanted to know only two figures — the cost of producing a ton of newsprint in the United States and the cost in Canada. However, he would not use the Mann committee figures, which showed the American cost to be from $29 to $34 a ton. Instead, Norris complained, Aldrich took the word of the paper men that their cost was $37.15 a ton, $8 higher than that of Canadian manufacturers. Norris ended by denouncing Senator Eugene Hale of Maine as being a backer of the paper and pulp manufacturers, who were of course important in Maine.

Norris' report to the 1909 convention also disclosed that the committee on paper and the ANPA membership were interested in other factors involving newsprint besides the paper and pulp duties. Norris reviewed the newsprint price situation, which had been eased by the financial panic of late 1907. The International Paper Company had cut its $50-a-ton contracts to a $45 rate and was selling paper on big contracts at rates of $41 to $42 a ton delivered. The Mann committee investigation had broken up price-fixing plots and had frightened the manufacturers, he said.

When Norris told the convention that William Randolph Hearst had a ten-year contract with International, running from 1904 to 1914, which called for the delivery of 300 tons of newsprint a day to his New York, Chicago, and Boston papers at a rate of $37.60 a ton delivered, publishers of smaller daily papers proposed that the ANPA organize a buying agency for them to take advantage of lower rates on large purchases. Norris replied that the paper companies would not sell that way and that delivery of small lots would be a problem, but said he was willing to try if anyone was interested. Nothing came of the proposal.

The paper committee chairman also recounted how during the past year he had used the ANPA bulletin service to promote a campaign to reduce waste of newsprint, by eliminating excessive returns of unsold papers by dealers and by standardizing the width of newsprint rolls.[38] At Norris' suggestion the convention voted that the standard width of newsprint rolls should be 67

[38] *Bulletin 1873*, Sept. 12, 1908.

inches and the standard weight of the rolls 30 pounds. A survey by the committee on paper had shown that the 285 ANPA member papers used rolls of 165 different widths, forcing the paper manufacturers to make newsprint on order and adding to the cost. Standardization at the 67-inch figure would cut prices, allow manufacturers to maintain reserves of paper, and encourage standard prices to all publishers. Now, Norris said, different widths allowed manufacturers to bargain with each publisher and encouraged the policy of discrimination and "secret prices" which penalized the smaller papers.

The committee on paper also surveyed retail prices charged by daily papers in 1909 and found that of 862 papers, 235 were selling at one cent, 343 at two cents, 73 at three cents, and 211 at five cents, the latter being mainly morning papers with little street business.[39]

The tariff debate continued to simmer through the spring and early summer of 1909. In July the Senate passed its version of the tariff bill, with the $4-a-ton duty on newsprint still included. The legislation then went to conference with the House. Norris claimed that the conferees had agreed substantially on a rate of $3 a ton, midway between the House and Senate provisions, "when President Taft announced to Congressional callers on or about Saturday July 24, that a $4 rate was necessary for the application of the protection principle to print paper. The President made this ex parte decision without that full and impartial ascertainment of cost to which the consumers were entitled, and in disregard of numerous assurances volunteered by him in favor of the lower rate. In accordance with that intimation from the President, the conferees reported $3.75 a ton which probably will be adopted."[40] The conference report of July 30 was accepted by the House and the Senate by August 5, and Taft signed the Payne-Aldrich Tariff of 1909.

The bill had two features which were to cause more trouble with Canada and affect the newspaper publishers. One was an extension of the retaliatory principle, first adopted in 1897, aimed at Canadian provinces which restricted the exportation of pulp

[39] *Bulletin 1988*, Apr. 22, 1909.
[40] *Bulletin 2037*, Aug. 3, 1909.

logs to American paper mills. To the regular $3.75 duty on news-
print was added an additional $2-a-ton penalty duty (reduced
from $4 by the conferees) whenever the newsprint was imported
from a country or province which restricted or charged export
fees on the exportation of paper, pulp, or wood. In addition the
amount of any export fees charged was to be added to the duty
on newsprint. Wood pulp was to be admitted free of duty, unless
it came from a restricted area. Then mechanical pulp would carry a penalty duty of $1.67 a ton, unbleached chemical pulp $3.33
a ton, and bleached chemical pulp $5 a ton. The amount of any
export fee would also be added. This meant that newsprint coming from most of Canada would be assessed a tariff duty of $5.75,
and that from Quebec $6.10. The 1897 rate had been $6. Since
all wood pulp coming from Canada would also pay the 1897 rate,
there was little solace for the publishers.

Canada was expected to yield in the matter of export fees, but
the Dominion government and the provincial governments refused to give ground. Instead, the Dominion government joined
Ontario province in 1908 in prohibiting the export of pulpwood
from crown lands in the prairie provinces and British Columbia.
Quebec completely prohibited export of pulpwood from crown
lands in 1910, and New Brunswick followed in 1911.[41] When the
Treasury Department ruled on August 26, 1909, that the penalty
duties were in effect against most imports of newsprint and wood
pulp from Canada, Norris again struck out at President Taft in
an ANPA bulletin: "President Taft was fully advised of this situation and shouldered the responsibility for it. . . . Newspaper
publishers who are not protected by paper contracts for 1910
await the outcome of President Taft's action and Canada's retali-
ation with deep concern. . . ."[42]

The other provision of the tariff of 1909 which worried the
publishers and was to cause trouble with Canada called for the
addition after March 31, 1910, of a 25 percent ad valorem duty
to regular duties on imports from any country or province which,
in the opinion of the President, discriminated against the United
States in tariff matters. Canada in 1907 had passed a three-way

[41] Guthrie, *The Newsprint Paper Industry*, p. 44.
[42] *Bulletin 2053*, Sept. 3, 1909.

tariff which set maximum rates, rates one third lower for British preference, and intermediate rates to be granted to those countries favorably treating Canadian trade. France subsequently obtained the intermediate rates through a commercial treaty, but the United States remained at the maximum levels. As a result imports from Canada seemed to be subject to the added 25 percent ad valorem duty. Norris pointed out in horrified words that this would add a prohibitive additional duty of $8.50 a ton on newsprint coming from Canada.[43]

Meanwhile President Taft made a famous address at Winona, Minnesota, on September 17, which was a thoroughgoing defense of the Payne-Aldrich Tariff. He denied the charges of the midwestern insurgents that the new tariff violated the 1908 Republican platform pledges and persecuted the farmer. He also defended the paper and pulp section. In reply ANPA President Herman Ridder wrote Taft on October 16:

> The full text of your address at Winona, Minn., on the Tariff Bill has just come to hand. With the utmost respect we submit that your statement respecting the paper schedules shows that you could not have correctly read or understood what the print paper paragraph contained, as it passed the House of Representatives.
>
> You were apparently misled by designing men into a serious blunder, when, in the closing days of the tariff conference, they induced you to reverse your previous attitude upon print paper and changed your notions of what the Mann Committee recommended and the House of Representatives had approved. The Mann Committee, after a ten months' investigation, marked by unusual thoroughness, reported a $2 rate to cover the difference in cost of production at home and abroad. The draft proposed by it absolutely safeguarded American paper mills against the serious Canadian tangle which your advice to the tariff conferees has since precipitated.
>
> The fixing of the rate on print paper at $3.75 per ton, which you advised, has decided the Province of Quebec to prohibit the exportation of its pulpwood, and many American paper mills must close or move to Canada to obtain their supplies of raw material. The country is now in a fair way for a trade war with Canada because of your apparent failure to read carefully the Mann Committee's recommendations. We are threatened with an industrial disturbance which will involve business exchanges with Canada amounting to $285,000,000 per annum.

[43] *Bulletin 2066*, Sept. 27, 1909.

We sincerely trust that you can find some method of rectifying the mistake into which you were led. We fully appreciate the difficulties and responsibilities of your exalted office, and believe you are trying to do the best you can. We know that you must rely upon others for your information. We feel every citizen is under obligation to help you. Therefore we write this letter to you.[44]

The ANPA took another swipe at the President early in 1910, when it reprinted in an official bulletin an editorial appearing in the New York *World* referring critically to "President Taft's remarks about 'subsidies' to newspapers" in connection with the postal deficit.[45] But on February 2, while talking before the meeting of the Associated Ohio Dailies, John Norris put part of the blame for the high rate on newsprint imports at the door of Senator Robert M. La Follette of Wisconsin.[46] Thus La Follette joined Taft, Aldrich, and Hale in receiving the blame from Norris and the ANPA for the failure to carry out the recommendations of the Mann committee. Taft wrote to Theodore Roosevelt on May 26, 1910, that the 1909 tariff "did not cut low enough the rate on print paper and so we have had a hostile press, and this whether Republican or Democrat."[47]

The anxious President then took a step which was to put him back into the good graces of the American Newspaper Publishers Association. Seeking to avoid a trade war with Canada, which he knew the imposition of the 25 percent ad valorem penalty duty would bring, and yet convinced that he would have to declare the penalty on March 31, 1910, unless something was done in the meantime, the President decided to send negotiators to Canada. The American delegation to Ottawa set forth their country's viewpoint on matters at issue between the two countries and proposed a reciprocity agreement. When no understanding was forthcoming, Taft himself journeyed to Albany, New York, to confer with the Canadian minister of finance, William H. Fielding. On March 20 Taft and Fielding reached an agreement that

[44] *Bulletin 2083*, Oct. 30, 1909.
[45] *Bulletin 2131*, Feb. 5, 1910.
[46] *Reciprocity with Canada: Hearings*, 61st Cong., 3d sess., S. Doc. 834 (1911), p. 175.
[47] L. Ethan Ellis, *Reciprocity 1911: A Study in Canadian-American Relations* (New Haven: Yale University Press, 1939), p. 13, quoting from the Taft papers in the Library of Congress. Ellis tells the full story of the reciprocity negotiations.

the two countries should negotiate on a list of United States products which would be granted intermediate tariff duties by Canada, in return for nonapplication of the 25 percent ad valorem penalty duty. Taft thereupon announced that Canada was not discriminating against the United States, and Fielding and Secretary of State Philander C. Knox exchanged notes outlining the agreement to negotiate on reciprocal terms. The ANPA decided that "President Taft's grant of the minimum tariff to Canada should induce lower prices for print paper." [48]

At the 1910 ANPA convention the publishers plumped in favor of reciprocity, recognizing that only by settling trade differences with Canada could the United States hope to get imports of wood pulp and newsprint at the terms the publishers wished. The convention passed a resolution urging the adoption of a bill introduced by Congressman Mann which would allow free entry of Canadian pulp and paper if the export restrictions were removed. John Norris then went to President Taft with a suggestion that a special treaty on pulp and paper be negotiated with Canada, which would involve only Senate action. Charles M. Pepper, one of the American negotiators with the Canadians, vetoed this suggestion as impractical. From this time on, however, until the end of the reciprocity negotiations, Norris cooperated closely with Taft, and Pepper supplied him with information which was disseminated through the newsprint bulletins published by the association. [49]

Norris reported to the ANPA membership in December 1910 that while Pepper was advocating the retention of a $2-a-ton duty on newsprint, the Canadians would insist upon "free paper for free wood." [50] But when the final round of negotiations on a reciprocity agreement got under way, it was pointed out that the restrictions on the export of pulpwood were imposed by the provinces, for whom the Dominion government could not speak. The American negotiators then decided to include in their proposed legislation a section on pulp and paper which would not require reciprocal action by Canada.

The text of the reciprocity agreement, announced in January

[48] *Ibid.*, pp. 38–44; *Bulletin 2169*, Apr. 7, 1910.
[49] Ellis, *Reciprocity 1911*, p. 141, from evidence in the Taft papers.
[50] *Bulletin 2338*, Dec. 24, 1910.

1911,[51] provided that the two governments would seek to pass legislation containing four categories of tariff changes. One was an identical free list, containing mostly agricultural products. The second list, of manufactured and agricultural articles, provided for similar tariff reductions by both countries. Two smaller lists named articles on which the two countries would not have similar rates, but on which reductions would apply.

In addition a special paragraph (section two of the free list) was proposed for the American legislation. It provided that wood pulp of all kinds and paper valued at not more than four cents a pound (including all newsprint) would be admitted free of duty from Canada, provided no export charge or license fee had been imposed on the paper, the pulp, or the wood used in its manufacture.

There was a vital change in the penalty provision as worded in this new proposal. Previously all newsprint or wood pulp coming from a province had been subject to retaliatory duties if export restrictions had been placed on any paper, pulp, or wood coming from that province. Now paper or pulp made from wood cut on private lands could enter duty free, even though there were still restrictions on exporting wood cut from crown lands. The ANPA committee on paper announced that the pulp and paper clause in the reciprocity bill was entirely satisfactory to the publishers, and Norris estimated that about half the imports of newsprint from Canada would come in free of duty under that proposal. Eventually, Norris thought, the reciprocity bill would mean removal of all American-Canadian pulp and paper tariffs and restrictions, and would result in Canada's having the pulp business and the United States the paper business.[52] This was just what the Canadians feared, of course, as ANPA member John MacKay of the Toronto *Globe* could have told the paper chairman. Norris' unfortunate prediction, reported to the Dominion parliament in March,[53] contributed to the opposition growing in Canada against reciprocity.

Norris and Seitz defended the pulp and paper clause of the rec-

[51] *Congressional Record*, 61st Cong., 3d sess., Jan. 26, 1911, pp. 1515–19.
[52] *Bulletin 2361*, Jan. 28, 1911.
[53] U.S. Tariff Commission, *Reciprocity with Canada: A Study of the Arrangement of 1911* (Washington: Government Printing Office, 1920), p. 82.

iprocity bill before the Committee on Ways and Means of the House.[54] Norris then appeared before the Senate Committee on Finance, where he reviewed the story of price increases on newsprint and insisted that newspapers needed cheaper and larger supplies of paper. President Hastings of the American Paper and Pulp Association warned again that free entry of Canadian newsprint would mean that American manufacturers would be unable to compete.[55] However, the congressional session ended on March 4, and only the House of Representatives had approved the bill.

President Taft called a special session of the new Congress, which contained a Democratic lower chamber, and the reciprocity bill again passed the House on April 21. Taft then went to New York to help the publishers celebrate by speaking at the annual AP-ANPA banquet April 27. Animosity created by the tariff fight of 1909 apparently had been forgotten in the publishers' enthusiasm for the reciprocity bill, and Taft was cheered when he made a "now-or-never" speech for the legislation. He uttered an unfortunate phrase that was to plague him later, however, when he said: ". . . the bond uniting the Dominion with the mother country is light and almost imperceptible." Champ Clark, new Democratic Speaker of the House, had said in February that he hoped to see the American flag floating all the way to the North Pole, and these and other "annexation" statements were widely quoted in Canada during the fight against reciprocity which mushroomed there.[56]

The ANPA membership went on record in favor of the reciprocity bill and asked for speedy Senate action. Norris appeared again before the Committee on Finance in support of the bill and accused Maine's Senator Hale of trying to bulldoze the Canadian provinces on the matter of pulpwood.[57] The Tariff Board had reported to the Senate that the cost of newsprint production was $5.35 a ton lower in Canada than in the United States, owing

[54] *Reciprocity with Canada*, Hearings, 61st Cong., 3d sess., on H. R. 32216 (1911).

[55] *Reciprocity with Canada: Hearings*, 61st Cong., 3d sess., S. Doc. 834 (1911), pp. 166, 217–29.

[56] Ellis, *Reciprocity 1911*, p. 114.

[57] *Reciprocity with Canada: Hearings*, 62d Cong., 1st sess., S. Doc. 56 (1911), pp. 1137–63.

chiefly to the lower cost of pulpwood there.[58] Norris maintained, however, that the biggest American producer, International Paper Company, owned obsolescent mills which could not compete with more modern mills built in the late 1890s and therefore had to maintain an artificially controlled price on newsprint. The publishers were embarrassed during the Senate hearings when it was disclosed that ANPA President Herman Ridder had persuaded the Associated Press on February 17 to carry the following private message to its members: "By request, private to editors. It is of vital importance to the newspapers that their Washington correspondents be instructed to treat favorably the Canadian reciprocity agreement because print paper and wood pulp are made free of duty."[59] Needless to say, there were hasty disavowals of the message by all concerned.

The reciprocity bill passed the Senate and was signed by Taft on July 26. But three days later Sir Wilfrid Laurier, the Liberal party premier of Canada, was forced to dissolve the Dominion parliament, and in the national elections on September 21 the Conservative party came to power. The Conservatives chose to interpret the election as a mandate to let the reciprocity bill die through inaction, and thus all but the paper and pulp section of the American legislation was killed.

Under that section pulp and paper made from wood cut on privately owned land in Canada could enter the United States duty free. Germany, Norway, and Sweden, all exporters of wood pulp and some newsprint to the United States, received the same benefits as favored nations.[60] As it worked out, not much more pulp and paper came into the United States than before, but more than half the newsprint was now free of duty. The ANPA estimated in January 1912 that about 1000 tons a day of new production of print paper in the United States and Canada should be marketed in 1912. Domestic consumption was 4000 tons a day, and growing at the rate of 200 tons a day each year. A paper the size of the Kansas City *Star*, which used 18,000 tons a year, stood

[58] *Report by the Tariff Board Relative to Pulp and News-print Industry*, 62d Cong., 1st sess., S. Doc. 31 (1911).
[59] *Reciprocity with Canada: Hearings*, 62d Cong., 1st sess., S. Doc. 56 (1911), p. 1224.
[60] *Bulletin 2568*, Dec. 15, 1911.

to gain or lose $90,000 a year on a $5 shift in the price of news-print, the ANPA pointed out.[61]

Congressional acceptance of reciprocity had been an advance for the publishers' fortunes, but the ANPA scented a complete victory in the long fight for free pulp and paper when the election of 1912 turned Washington over to the Democratic party with the Woodrow Wilson administration. Early in 1913 the paper manufacturers and the publishers' representatives made their last stand before the Committee on Ways and Means. Norris claimed once again that the tariff on paper and pulp protected only those "who had monopolized the limited timber resources of the country," and that, tariff or no tariff, the paper industry was moving to Canada.[62] The framers of the Underwood Tariff of 1913 agreed with the publishers, and Norris was able to report to the ANPA annual meeting in April 1913 that the tariff bill if passed would remove all duties on pulp and newsprint, and that "prices will soften." The convention, with some members intimating that the election and not Norris had won the final round of the fight for free pulp and paper, voted to discontinue many of the committee on paper's activities after the passage of the tariff bill. Former President Herman Ridder pleaded that Norris be retained by the ANPA in some capacity, but the publishers were tired of paying special assessments to support Norris' activities and refused to make further contributions. When Norris died later in the year, the ANPA membership decided to reward him posthumously and made a donation of $12,000 to his family.[63]

The Underwood Tariff, when it was approved in October, placed all wood pulp on the free list, along with all paper valued at not more than 2¼ cents a pound (including virtually all newsprint). The retaliatory provisions against Canada were forgotten, and the publishers' victory was complete. Newsprint prices went downward slightly until the war crisis of 1917 intervened. Imports of newsprint from Canada shot from 55,563 tons in 1912 to 438,212 tons in 1916.[64] American newsprint production remained

[61] *Bulletin 2598,* Jan. 27, 1912.

[62] *Tariff Schedules: Hearings before the Committee on Ways and Means,* 62d Cong., 3d sess., H. Doc. 1447 (1913), pp. 4774–89.

[63] *Report of the Twenty-ninth Annual Meeting* (1915), p. 10.

[64] *Report of the Federal Trade Commission on the News-print Paper Industry,* June 13, 1917, p. 44.

at approximately the same level during the prewar period, but American paper manufacturers began moving across the border to cheaper supplies of pulp. If the tariff had been maintained, American manufacturers of newsprint might have resisted the competition of Canada for a longer period of time, but the coming of World War I and the greatly increased demand for newsprint in the United States which accompanied it undoubtedly would have forced their capitulation to the publishers in any event.

CHAPTER VII

The Second-Class Mail

FROM the time of Benjamin Franklin newspapers have been granted special rates by the United States postal service. One student of this policy, Simeon N. D. North, said that the government "assumed somewhat of the attitude of a patron of the newspaper press, and avowedly undertook to encourage its growth as the most important disseminator of intelligence among the people." [1] Another, Charles Evans Hughes, spoke of "the historic policy of encouraging by low postal rates the dissemination of current intelligence." [2] Some critics of the newspapers, however, have called the granting of special rates a subsidy. More often it has been called a privilege. The American Newspaper Publishers Association has denied that the second-class rate is either a subsidy or a privilege, defining it instead as a service and claiming that the newspapers have paid a fair rate for such postal service. The ANPA has opposed increased postal rates for newspapers on this basis, using only as a secondary argument the fact that the publishing business grew up in a period of low postal rates and geared itself to their continuance.

Although Franklin had legalized the delivery of newspapers by postriders in 1758, the Post Office Act of 1792 and an amendment in 1794 provided the first national legislation giving newspaper publishers a rate advantage. Congress declared that newspapers should be carried for one cent each inside the state of publication and for one and a half cents elsewhere. Exchanges between publishers were to be carried free, so that news could circulate around the country. Subscribers were to pay the postal

[1] *History and Present Condition of the Newspaper and Periodical Press of the United States* (Washington: Government Printing Office, 1884), p. 137.
[2] In the report of the Hughes Commission to Congress in 1912, cited later.

fees, which were only a fraction of the graduated scale for letters. These newspaper postal rates remained substantially unchanged until 1851, when Congress further aided newspaper circulation by providing free-in-county delivery for weeklies and cutting other delivery rates in half when payment was made in advance. Division of postal matter into definite classes was begun in 1863, when a second class for printed publications issued at stated periods was established, as well as a miscellaneous third class. Growing competition from express companies brought a major policy change in 1874, when the second-class rate was set at two cents a pound, with the publisher to pay the fees. A fuller definition of what constituted second-class matter was made by Congress in 1879, and the rate was reduced to one cent a pound in 1885. This contrasts with the letter rate of two cents established in 1883. In this way the pattern of the second-class postal rate was set, to last until World War I.[3]

Second-class matter, as defined by Congress in 1879, embraced all newspapers, magazines, and other periodical publications which were regularly issued at stated intervals as frequently as four times a year; which bore the date of issue, were numbered consecutively, and were issued from a known office of publication, which were formed of printed paper sheets without binding or permanent cover; and which disseminated information of a public character to a legitimate list of subscribers. Publications primarily for advertising purposes or without paid circulation could not qualify for the minimum postal rate allowed second-class matter.

After the charge for delivery of second-class matter had been reduced to one cent a pound in 1885, the Postmaster General declared that newspapers and periodicals constituted one third of the weight and bulk of the mail but returned only one fortieth of the revenue.[4] Part of the trouble lay in attempts by publishers of "borderline" periodicals, primarily advertising sheets, to take

[3] *Postage Rates 1789–1930, Abstract of Laws Passed Between 1789 and 1930 Fixing Rates of Postage and According Free Mail Privileges* (Washington: Government Printing Office, 1930).

[4] James H. Shideler, "Second-Class Matter: The American Press and the Subsidy, 1879–1933" (unpublished M.A. thesis, University of California, 1938), p. 51.

advantage of the extremely low postal rate through technical compliance with the 1879 rulings. Excessive mailing of sample and free copies, return of unsold publications by second-class mail through subterfuge, and attempts by book publishers to issue "libraries" technically complying with the second-class mail definition all added to the cost of the service to the government.

The American Newspaper Publishers Association saw the value of restricting the second-class mail to legitimate publications and in 1892 appointed a committee on postal laws to watch legislation being proposed to correct these abuses.[5] With T. J. Keenan, Jr., of the Pittsburgh *Press* as chairman, the committee helped block measures which it considered unsatisfactory in 1893[6] and then decided to back a bill introduced in 1896 by Congressman George A. Loud of Michigan to correct abuses of the second-class rates. Despite considerable backing from the ANPA, the Loud bill failed of passage.[7]

Another opportunity for ANPA action came in 1896 when the express companies, led by the American News Company, attempted to raise their rate on bulk deliveries of newspapers to the one-cent figure maintained by the government. An ANPA committee headed by Milton A. McRae of the Scripps-McRae newspapers was authorized by the 1896 convention to negotiate with the companies, and it obtained a maximum rate of half a cent a pound. The committee reported to the 1897 convention that its expenses for performing this service had been $522.

Another great impetus was given to newspaper and magazine publishing in 1897, when Congress established rural free delivery service. This was a particular boon to daily newspaper publishers, who now could get rapid delivery in rural areas, and to the low-priced magazines, which were running their circulations into the hundreds of thousands. The Postmaster General reported in 1901 that second-class matter had increased from an estimated 78 million pounds in 1882 to 450 million pounds in 1900.[8] The ANPA committee on postal laws enthusiastically endorsed the rural free delivery program and urged its extension.

[5] New York *Times*, Feb. 19, 1892, p. 3.
[6] *Minutes of the Seventh Annual Meeting* (1893), pp. 9–10.
[7] *Bulletin 412*, Jan. 21, 1897.
[8] Shideler, "Second-Class Matter," p. 46.

Worried over what he maintained were deficits incurred in the handling of second-class matter, the Postmaster General issued administrative regulations in 1901 correcting some of the abuses of the rates. In its second issue *Editor & Publisher* approved these restrictions and inveighed against the "journalistic fakirs," [9] and the ANPA convention of 1902 endorsed the action of the Postmaster General "in his efforts to confine second-class mail privileges to the publications legitimately entitled to such privileges." [10] *Editor & Publisher*, however, reported that some members with large job departments objected to the resolution. [11]

The ANPA committee on postal laws during these years and for the next decade was led by Don C. Seitz of the New York *World*, John Norris of the New York *Times*, Herbert F. Gunnison of the Brooklyn *Eagle*, Charles W. Knapp of the St. Louis *Republic*, and Harry Chandler of the Los Angeles *Times*. A critic of the second-class mail privilege complained in 1901 that this ANPA committee was too efficient, saying: "No lobby ever sent to Washington in furtherance of the most corrupt legislation has ever been more persistent or dealt less fairly with both legislators and public than the lobby that has worked for the retention of the second-class mail graft." [12] Magazines, represented by the Periodical Publishers' Association, were part of the "lobby" too, of course.

At the turn of the century, as newspapers and magazines boomed in size and circulation, the Post Office Department continued to question the cent-a-pound rate on second-class matter, insisting that such matter constituted 60 percent of the total weight of the mail while paying only 4 percent of the cost of service. The department estimated a deficit of more than 25 million dollars annually in the handling of second-class mail. It cost the government from seven to nine cents a pound to deliver the newspapers and magazines, while the publishers paid only one cent, the Postmaster General claimed. [13] Congress inquired into

[9] *Editor & Publisher*, 1:1 (July 6, 1901).
[10] *Report of the Sixteenth Annual Meeting* (1902), p. 8. Note that this ANPA resolution referred to the second-class mail as a "privilege."
[11] *Editor & Publisher*, 2:1 (Feb. 22, 1902).
[12] C. W. Burrows, *One Cent Postage* (1901), as quoted by Shideler, "Second-Class Matter," p. 49.
[13] Shideler, "Second-Class Matter," pp. 51–52.

the matter from 1906 on, but the ANPA and others interested denied the accuracy of the government's figures. After inconclusive debate, Congress in 1911 appointed a commission headed by Associate Justice Charles Evans Hughes of the United States Supreme Court to make an intensive investigation of postal rates.

The Hughes Commission made its report in 1912,[14] arriving at the figure of 7½ cents a pound as the cost to the Post Office Department for the handling and transporting of second-class matter. The commission recommended an increase in the second-class rates of only one cent to two cents a pound, however, stating that many publishers' businesses were established upon the assumption that low postal rates would continue to prevail. The commission's argument was based upon this key statement: "The historic policy of encouraging by low postal rates the dissemination of current intelligence, and the extent to which it has proved successful, should not be overlooked." [15]

President Taft, in transmitting the Hughes Commission report to Congress, declared that an increase in the second-class rate was both justified and desirable.[16] Taft had angered the press and the ANPA in 1910 by calling the one-cent rate a subsidy to publishers,[17] and his support of a rate increase now did not help his relations with the newspapers.

Nothing came of the recommendation for an increase in the second-class mail rate, but a rider attached to the Post Office Appropriation Act of August 24, 1912, known as the Newspaper Publicity Law, caused the American Newspaper Publishers Association to carry a legal fight to the Supreme Court. This law made it mandatory for publishers of newspapers and periodicals using the second-class mails to file twice a year (on April 1 and October 1) a sworn statement listing the names of the editor, managing editor, publisher, business manager, owner, stockholders, bondholders, mortgagees, or other security holders; and in the case of daily newspapers, giving the average circulation for the past six months. The statement was also to be published.

[14] *Report of the Special Commission on Second-Class Postal Rates*, 62d Cong., 2d sess., H. Doc. 559 (1912).
[15] *Ibid.*, p. 137.
[16] *Congressional Record*, 62d Cong., 2d sess., Feb. 22, 1912, p. 2317.
[17] *Bulletin 2131*, Feb. 5, 1910.

Furthermore, the law corrected a long-standing but dubious practice of some newspaper publishers by providing that all editorial or other reading matter published for money or other valuable consideration should be marked "Advertisement." A fine of $50 to $500 was set for violations of this clause.

Postmaster General Frank H. Hitchcock was reluctant to enforce the statute, which he thought served no useful purpose.[18] Quite possibly he also did not wish to fight with the press during the presidential campaign of 1912, already a most difficult one for the Taft administration. Chairman Don Seitz of the ANPA committee on second-class postage announced on September 27 that "at the request of a great majority of our members our counsel are arranging to test the constitutionality of the law."[19] Hitchcock then gladly agreed not to press for enforcement of the statute until the case had been settled in the courts and arranged for the New York City postmaster to attempt enforcement as a test.

As a result the Lewis Publishing Company, publishers of the New York *Morning Telegraph*, the *Journal of Commerce*, and the *Commercial Bulletin*, instituted proceedings on October 9 in the district court for the southern district of New York against Postmaster Edward M. Morgan of New York City, Postmaster General Hitchcock, Attorney General George W. Wickersham, and United States District Attorney Henry A. Wise. Robert Morris and Guthrie B. Plante, counsel for the ANPA, represented the publishing company.[20]

Hitchcock waived the question of court jurisdiction over Cabinet officers to expedite the action,[21] and on October 15 the defendants filed a demurrer to the publishing company's bill of complaint. The court granted a decree sustaining the demurrer. It then allowed an appeal to the Supreme Court on grounds that the Newspaper Publicity Law abridged the guarantee of freedom of the press contained in the First Amendment and constituted a denial of the due process of law clause of the Fifth Amendment. These proceedings allowed the case to go to the Supreme Court immediately.[22]

[18] *Editor & Publisher*, 12:1 (Sept. 14, 1912).
[19] *Bulletin* 2753, Sept. 27, 1912.
[20] *Bulletin* 2762, Oct. 9, 1912.
[21] *Bulletin* 2763, Oct. 11, 1912.   [22] *Bulletin* 2768, Oct. 17, 1912.

The arguments were made before the high tribunal on December 2 and 3, 1912, with James M. Beck joining the firm of Morris and Plante in representing the Lewis Publishing Company.[23] Beck previously had served the committee on paper of the ANPA in 1905. Although the Lewis Publishing Company had brought the suit, the ANPA was actively interested in the proceedings and was the real complainant.

The ANPA counsel representing the publishing company contended that the Newspaper Publicity Law was in no way a measure to regulate carrying of the mails. Rather, the counsel argued, it was an act to regulate journalism, and fire was particularly centered on the section requiring identification of paid reading matter as advertising. The argument ran that the Constitution did not give Congress authority to legislate in this manner under the post roads clause. Furthermore, the First Amendment forbade any law abridging the freedom of the press. The disclosures of ownership control insisted upon deprived newspapers of liberty and property without due process of law in violation of the Fifth Amendment, the counsel argued.[24]

In reply the government contended that since the law affected only those publications using the second-class mails, it clearly was not an act to regulate journalism. The power to regulate the mails had been used by Congress to confer the second-class mail privilege, and it was within the powers of Congress to say who should use that privilege, the government continued. And in any event, Congress had long exercised its constitutional authority in the postal field to decide who should use the mails and who should not.

While the Supreme Court considered the case, the national administration changed hands, and President Woodrow Wilson appointed Albert S. Burleson as Postmaster General. Deciding that the Newspaper Publicity Law should be enforced without awaiting the court decision, Burleson started sending notices to publishers. The ANPA intervened, and as Seitz reported later to the 1913 annual convention, "We sent Colonel Morris of our legal

---

[23] *Bulletin 2803*, Dec. 7, 1912.
[24] *Lewis* v. *Morgan*, 229 U. S. 288 (1912).

staff to Washington and got a restraining order, now in effect." [25]
The New York *Times* denounced Burleson and the act which he
proposed to enforce immediately, saying editorially: "It is mon-
strous to threaten the withdrawal of the privilege of the United
States mails against one class of business concerns for refusing to
make disclosures required from no others of a similar character." [26]

But the United States Supreme Court disagreed, and in its decision, handed down on June 10, 1913, unanimously sustained
the provisions of the Newspaper Publicity Law and ordered their
enforcement. The court decided that use of second-class mail
constituted a privilege and not a right, and that Congress, having
conferred the privilege, had indirect power to prescribe the conditions of its use. Chief Justice Edward D. White upheld the
viewpoint of the Hughes Commission that as a result of "the historic policy of encouraging by low postal rates the dissemination
of current intelligence," publishers of newspapers received great
pecuniary advantages through the second-class rate, and ruled
that Congress in thus acting for the public good could make such
restrictions as the Newspaper Publicity Law prescribed. The
New York *Times*, bowing respectfully to the court's decision, still
contended that the law did not benefit the public in any respect
and had been passed through the desire of "certain radical and
populistic legislators to punish the newspapers for their plain
speech." [27]

Thus the American Newspaper Publishers Association lost in
its first appearance before the Supreme Court. The membership
soon acknowledged that the labeling of "paid readers" as advertising was a good thing and that publication of circulation figures
was a good business practice. There were still doubts about the
requirement of disclosing true owners. But in 1914 the ANPA
membership agreed that the Newspaper Publicity Law could not
be repealed without making the publishers look dishonest, and
the convention that year requested the government to enforce

[25] *Report of the Twenty-seventh Annual Meeting* (1913), p. 25. The restraining
order formed the basis of a second case which was decided in conjunction with
Lewis v. *Morgan.*
[26] New York *Times*, Mar. 14, 1913, p. 8.
[27] *Ibid.*, June 11, 1913, p. 3.

rigidly all the provisions of the law, so that those who were complying honestly would not be placed at a disadvantage by the less honest. At the 1915 annual meeting various members demanded government prosecution of publishers who made perjured circulation statements, and others wanted an investigation of all sworn statements.

"The Post Office Department has trimmed us every time," an overly pessimistic ANPA member told the 1913 annual convention. He was not worrying so much about lost causes as he was about the proposal of zone rates on second-class matter. In the discussion which followed, the publishers decided that they could see the principle of increasing rates for geographic zones coming into the picture, upsetting the long-established one-cent-a-pound rate over any distance. The committee on second-class postage fought zone rates successfully in 1916, but the coming of World War I to America in 1917 brought government demands for additional revenue that could not be denied. The second-class mail was forced to provide some of this new revenue, as Chapter XI will show.

CHAPTER VIII

Advertising and Publicity

THE most constant and most important single activity of the American Newspaper Publishers Association, as a business trade organization, has been in the field of advertising. The ANPA was founded because the publishers and managers of daily newspapers were aware, by 1887, of the importance of three basic problems: the necessity of improving advertising solicitation techniques; the necessity of establishing workable relationships between advertisers, advertising agencies, and daily newspapers; and the necessity of promoting the daily newspaper as an advertising medium in competition with other media.

Each year that the ANPA has met in annual session since 1887, the technical problems of advertising have been discussed by the publishers and managers with emphasis on mechanical improvements in the production process. Because of the pressure of competition, individual newspapers have preferred to develop their own selling techniques, and their managers have been reluctant to discuss techniques that have attracted an above-average volume of advertising. After some hesitation, the publishers united to deal with advertisers and advertising agencies, who were themselves organized into trade groups. And by hard experience, the publishers found it advantageous to work together to promote the daily newspaper against competing media — magazines, billboards, car cards, and in later years, radio.

During the first two decades of the twentieth century, newspaper publishers received steadily increasing revenues from both local and national advertising. Retail store and nationwide brand-name advertising continued to push the traditional patent medicine advertisements into the background, and advertising agencies utilized scientific practices in the fields of media selection,

119

copywriting, and art work.[1] The number of national advertisers using newspapers or magazines rose from approximately 6000 in 1900 to some 13,000 in 1914, and then leveled off, so that the 1914 figure remained a record high until 1947.[2] This expansion of advertising volume not only made possible a record growth in the number of newspapers and magazines published, but also returned to the average publisher tremendously increased revenues. The profits, together with those resulting from circulation gains, were used both to improve the product and to build publishing empires.

How important advertising revenue was to become to the newspaper publishers is illustrated by comparing revenue from subscriptions and street sales with that from advertising. In 1879 daily newspapers received an equal amount from both sources. The next available census figures show that in 1909 advertising accounted for 63.8 percent of the revenues of all newspapers, daily and weekly. In 1914 this percentage stood at 64.9 and by 1919 it had reached 66. A postwar boom shot advertising revenue to 71 percent of the total in 1921.[3]

The distribution of total advertising revenue between the two major competitors, newspapers and magazines, remained fairly constant during this period. Census figures give the totals (in millions of dollars) shown in the following tabulation.[4] Accurate figures for billboard and car-card advertising totals are not available for this period, but the revenue involved was comparatively small.

Year	Newspaper Revenue	Magazine Revenue	Percentage of Total Revenue to Newspapers
1909	$148.5	$ 54.0	73
1914	184.0	71.4	72
1919	373.5	154.8	70
1921	521.7	155.3	77

The ANPA, after debating the question of publisher relations with advertising agencies, established its committee on advertising agents in 1899, as a continuing activity of the association. In

[1] See Chapter II and Chapter III, pp. 35–42, for earlier details.
[2] *Printers' Ink*, Oct. 29, 1948, p. 102.
[3] ANPA, *The Newspaper as an Advertising Medium* (New York, 1940), p. 74.
[4] Tabulated in Lee, *Daily Newspaper in America*, p. 749.

1901 the ANPA and the American Association of Advertising Agents (which had evolved out of organizational efforts of the agencies dating back to the 1870s) were meeting simultaneously in the same hotel and cooperated in discussing subjects of common interest.[5] The following year the ANPA membership discussed ways and means of sustaining financially embarrassed agencies during temporary periods of trouble.[6] The committee on advertising agents bowed to the power of the agencies when it reported to the 1905 ANPA annual meeting, without comment, that a system of allowing a 2 percent discount to agencies for cash payment of accounts was becoming widespread. This, the committee said, made the common commission to advertising agencies 15 percent plus 2 percent for cash — a commission which continued to 1949. Don C. Seitz of the New York *World*, committee chairman, reported to the 1907 meeting that the work of the committee was increasing. During the preceding year 30 of 76 applications for recognition as ANPA-approved agencies had been granted, and 43 recognized agents had been removed from the list for objectionable practices or for failure to cooperate with the committee.

The ANPA also considered problems of publisher relations with advertisers. In 1905 the American Advertisers Association, the International Advertising Association, and the Proprietary Association of America all met simultaneously with the ANPA, and committees were appointed to confer on problems of mutual interest. The ANPA membership that year looked askance, however, at organizational activities of local retail merchants. The publishers discussed ways of preventing the organization of retail merchants in various cities for the purpose of limiting retail advertising and reducing newspaper advertising rates. The membership also questioned the news value of the free publication of railroad timetables. The following year it was noted that granting free editorial space to news of automobile production was hurting the procurement of automobile advertising.

The rapid growth of general magazines, whose combined circulations more than quadrupled between 1890 and 1905, con-

[5] New York *Herald*, Feb. 21, 1901, p. 5.
[6] *Editor & Publisher*, 2:3 (Feb. 22, 1902).

tinued to be a subject for ANPA discussion. Although the news-papers had much larger total advertising revenues, the magazines were running an estimated 60 percent of the national advertising space. This competition of magazines in the national advertising market was emphasized at the 1906 annual meeting by President S. S. Rogers of the Chicago *Daily News*. Rogers reported that thirty or more ANPA members were forming a voluntary associa-tion to cooperate more closely with the advertising agencies, in an effort to obtain display advertising then going to the popular magazines. Out of this report grew the Daily Club (called after 1909 the Daily Newspaper Club), a voluntary association of the larger ANPA-member papers whose organization was announced at the 1907 ANPA annual meeting. Members of the club agreed to pay a dollar in dues for each thousand of circulation, up to a maximum of $100, to support a headquarters office. ANPA direc-tors and officers were among the leaders of the plan, but they were unable to convince the general membership that such ac-tion was necessary or that smaller papers would be benefited. Louis Wiley of the New York *Times* told the 1909 convention that the Daily Newspaper Club was spending $25,000 in an ac-tive campaign to promote the newspaper as an advertising medi-um against magazine and billboard advertising. Women's clubs, he said, were being helpful by protesting the appearance of bill-boards along highways.

In 1911 the ANPA membership voted to do a little promotion of newspaper advertising space and detailed a committee to pre-pare a series of fifty-two advertisements, three columns wide, ex-plaining "why newspaper advertising is the best advertising there is on earth." The cost to the association was to be two or three thousand dollars a year. With this encouragement the supporters of the Daily Newspaper Club asked the ANPA to take over its work, and the 1912 convention authorized a committee to inves-tigate the possibilities. Union of the Daily Newspaper Club and two other similar groups, Associated Newspapers and National Newspapers, into an auxiliary bureau of the ANPA was recom-mended and approved at the 1913 ANPA annual meeting.

The Bureau of Advertising thus formed had no financial con-nection with the ANPA, but the committee in charge was an

ANPA committee, augmented by representatives of other interested advertising representatives' groups and non-ANPA papers which were eligible for membership. John F. MacKay of the Toronto *Globe* was the first chairman of the bureau committee, and William A. Thomson, assistant publisher of the New York *Globe*, began a 35-year career as director of the bureau. The bureau set out with a first-year budget of $50,000 to sell the newspaper as an advertising medium. By the end of the year it had 378 members, of whom only 152 were ANPA members. The promotional work the bureau did in its early years with advertising agencies, national advertisers, and newspaper special representatives undoubtedly resulted in advertising gains for dailies. In 1915 national advertising accounted for 55 million dollars in newspaper advertising revenue, only 20 percent of the total advertising income of the papers. In 1919 national advertising in newspapers reached a total of 150 million dollars and jumped to 30 percent of the combined advertising revenue of American newspapers.[7] And for the first time daily newspapers reached equality with magazines in the contest for national advertising.

As the business activities of the daily newspapers became specialized, other national organizations of newspaper executives were formed. The International Circulation Managers' Association met regularly after 1898. The Newspaper Advertising Executives Association was formed in 1900, the Association of Newspaper Classified Advertising Managers in 1919, and the National Newspaper Promotion Association in 1930. Together with the ANPA they worked to promote the business interests of daily newspapers. Regional interests of dailies were served by such growing organizations as the Inland Daily Press Association, the Southern Newspaper Publishers Association, the Northwest Daily Press Association, and the New England Daily Newspaper Association.

Also reaching final form were two major associations of advertisers and advertising agencies. These were the Association of National Advertisers, dating from 1910, and the American Association of Advertising Agencies, so named in 1917. With them and other interested groups the ANPA committee on advertising

[7] ANPA, *The Newspaper as an Advertising Medium*, p. 81.

agents in 1920 worked out a standard contract form to regularize agency practices.[8] The ANPA committee continued to cooperate with the "4-A's" agencies and sought to protect publishers from financially irresponsible or unethical agents. In 1924 the Federal Trade Commission began hearings on a complaint that the American Association of Advertising Agencies, the American Press Association, the Six-Point League of special advertising representatives, the Southern Newspaper Publishers Association, and the ANPA held a "monopoly of advertising" through their regulatory practices, but the suit was dismissed in 1930 without action being taken.[9]

Cooperation of publishers and advertisers in solving the problem of ascertaining circulation figures was stimulated by the passage in 1912 of the Newspaper Publicity Law, which required semiannual statements of ownership and circulation from publishers using the second-class mail service. The legislation spurred publishers and advertisers into forming their own regulatory body to certify circulation claims on which advertising rates were based. The ANPA joined with other publishers' associations, agency groups, and advertising groups in forming the Audit Bureau of Circulations in 1913–14. The ABC now audits more than 90 percent of the total circulation of daily newspapers.

Unethical advertising was curbed indirectly by federal legislation regulating the food and drug industries, and directly by state laws making untruthful, deceptive, or misleading statements a misdemeanor. Nearly all the states adopted such laws after *Printers' Ink* drafted a model statute in 1911, and advertisers and publishers joined in a move to curb the worst abuses of advertising. The ANPA adopted a resolution at its 1912 convention urging regulation of fraudulent and objectionable advertising matter, especially that advertising copy carrying the direct or indirect endorsement of the paper. The section of the Newspaper Publicity Law of 1912 which required the marking of paid reading matter as "advertisement" helped correct another abuse indulged in by some newspapers.

Another problem affecting the business side of newspapers was

[8] *Bulletin 4299*, Oct. 16, 1920.
[9] *Bulletin 5134*, Oct. 24, 1925; *Bulletin 5724*, Jan. 24, 1930.

the development of newspapers which were circuláted free of charge and shopping news publications. In 1908 and 1911 R. E. Stafford of the Oklahoma City *Morning Oklahoman* complained to ANPA conventions about the competition of the newspapers delivered free in his community. He was particularly bitter because the Hearst news services were supplying these competitors with news reports and features. Between 1921 and 1933, according to the ANPA Bureau of Advertising, 187 shopping news publications were started in 154 cities, patterned after the successful Cleveland *Shopping News* of 1921. The general manager of the ANPA was ordered to investigate the situation in 1928,[10] and such remedies were proposed as newspapers' buying control of rival shopping news publications or securing the enforcement of antihandbill ordinances against these "shoppers." The shopping news idea survived, however, and gave many a newspaper a headache during the depression years of the 1930s, when retail merchants used shopping news publications to cut advertising costs.

There are many possible approaches to a consideration of the problem of the use of publicity stories in the news columns of the daily newspaper. The ANPA has approached the subject almost entirely from a business viewpoint, emphasizing the effect of publicity stories on advertising revenues, rather than discussing the editorial principles involved. The association's fight against "free publicity," then, is properly part of a discussion of advertising problems.

The history of the development of publicity and public relations activities may be divided into three major phases. The first phase, ending about 1900, is identified with the figure of the press agent, who created publicity in an opportunistic manner. Some press agents, inspired by the success of P. T. Barnum, operated on the principle of "the public be fooled." As the newspaper became an increasingly important means of communication in the 1880s and 1890s, efforts to use its news columns for private benefit increased.

At the turn of the century, a new and better understanding of the publicity function developed. American businesses and indus-

---

[10] *Report of the Forty-second Annual Meeting* (1928), p. 190.

tries, growing immensely in the decades after the Civil War, had not found it necessary to explain their operations to the public. But the social and economic changes brought about by industrialization and urbanization resulted in widespread demands for reformation and regulation of business practices. Newspapermen, magazine writers, and authors joined in attacks on unethical business activities and insisted that industrialists, businessmen, and financiers were subject to public criticism and regulation in the public welfare. The New York *World's* campaign against insurance companies which did not correctly invest policyholders' premium payments, Ida M. Tarbell's scholarly exposé of the Standard Oil Company monopoly in the pages of *McClure's* magazine, and Upton Sinclair's attack on the Chicago meat-packing industry in *The Jungle* were examples of the widespread efforts which took the name muckraking. The political result of reform activity was the Square Deal legislation of the Theodore Roosevelt administration and the later progressive legislation of the Woodrow Wilson administration.

Businessmen already had found that former newspapermen, free-lance writers, and publicity agencies could obtain space in newspaper columns to publicize products and services. Under the attacks of the muckrakers, business and industry advanced to the second phase of publicity practice — that of informing the public about business activities. The leader in the movement toward informational publicity was Ivy Lee, known best for his association with the Rockefeller family. Business, Lee said, must tell its story promptly and accurately and must inform the public of its motives and policies.

By the time of World War I, the concept of dissemination of informational publicity was well established, although the opportunistic press agent still flourished in many quarters. The application of the principle of informational publicity to the telling of the story of the American war effort, by George Creel and the Committee on Public Information, was a highlight in the development of publicity practices.

The third phase of activity, which brought into being the concept of the public relations counsel, developed in the early 1920s. Edward L. Bernays, Ivy Lee, and other leaders insisted that while the public should be informed of business activities, it was necessary also that business should understand public attitudes and attempt to operate within the defined limits of the public interest. The publicity man not only had a responsibility to his client, but to the general public. Out of this philosophy emerged the modern practice of public relations.

The ANPA campaign against "free publicity" began in earnest in 1908, a year in which earlier press agentry practices were still in vogue, and in which the informational publicity practices of Ivy Lee were gaining favor. Those who organized the ANPA campaign did not distinguish between the motives of these differing publicity efforts. They did know that many of the businesses which had employed publicity writers had deducted the cost from their advertising budgets, and that the newspaper was losing revenue as a consequence. Led by Lincoln B. Palmer, ANPA general manager, and Don C. Seitz, business manager of the New York *World*, they struck out against all forms of what they called "free publicity." They did not listen to the good advice given them by *Editor & Publisher*, which had decided that the dissemination of informational publicity was an established practice, and suggested that the ANPA concentrate on checking the obvious abuses, leaving reputable publicity men alone.[11] Not until the 1930s did the ANPA adequately differentiate between press agentry and properly presented informational publicity.

Seitz made a lengthy report to the 1909 ANPA annual meeting, summarizing conditions at the moment. Some press agents, he said, were making from $6000 to $12,000 a year — quite a handsome income in 1909. Everybody was employing them; even the New York Orphan Asylum was paying a publicity man $75 a month. The advertising agencies — Albert Frank and Company, Lord and Thomas, N. W. Ayer and Son, J. Walter Thompson — had set up publicity departments which took fees for their services, fees diverted from the advertiser's newspaper advertising budget. Automobile manufacturers were sending a page of material each day to the *World*, and the cement, food, insurance, utilities, and other businesses were equally busy. The Metropolitan Life Insurance Company, Seitz said, would not advertise at

[11] *Editor & Publisher*, 8:3 (Aug. 17, 1908).

all, because the company received free all the publicity it wanted.[12]

Other publishers complained about free publicity coming to them on the Associated Press wires in lieu of the news for which they were paying. C. C. Rosewater of the Omaha *Bee* had little interest in an AP dispatch extolling the virtues of a new ship on an ocean steamship line. S. A. Perkins of the Tacoma *Ledger* in Washington received an AP story about a "fish with whiskers," identified by a Stanford University professor at Catalina Island, a southern California resort owned by William Wrigley. Perkins investigated and found that the same publicity bureau represented both the university and the resort.

The ANPA membership thereupon resolved to send a copy of all publicity offered newspapers to the association manager so that he could list the names of publicity-seekers in the bulletin service, and it decided that advertising agencies maintaining publicity bureaus should be warned that they faced loss of ANPA recognition. Harrison M. Parker of the Chicago *Tribune,* who said his paper had banned automobile publicity at a cost of $200,000 in canceled advertising, doubted that many of the members would obey the resolution. One publisher, V. S. McClatchy of the Sacramento, California, *Bee,* spoke for those who were concerned with the ethical principle involved when he tried to make it a matter of honor to stop using free publicity of dubious news value.

"Why Give It Free?" and "Throw Their Offerings on the Floor" became the slogans of the ANPA, as extensive bulletins on free publicity were issued by Palmer and Seitz during 1909 and succeeding years. A 78-page listing of press agents and companies seeking publicity was issued in 1909,[13] and some improvement in the situation was reported by 1910.

Seitz asked the 1911 ANPA convention to take action against advertising agencies which were maintaining publicity bureaus, but he was unsuccessful. The difficulties of curbing free publicity were emphasized by Thomas Rees of the Springfield *Illinois State Register,* who told the convention of reading in Seitz' New York

[12] Metropolitan later became a heavy newspaper advertiser.
[13] *Bulletin 2058,* Sept. 16, 1909.

World about a turtle race aboard a Hamburg-American Line cruise ship, which had humorist George Ade and other notables as judges. The story also related the advantages of taking ocean cruises. Chester Rowell of the Fresno, California, *Republican* said he had received a box of engravings — "a year's supply" — from the Case Automobile Company and surmised that the Sunday automobile section was too well established to be discontinued.[14] In 1913 Seitz offered the ANPA convention what he considered conclusive proof that the Lord and Thomas advertising agency was collecting a sizable commission on publicity printed in newspapers, but punitive action against the agencies still was not forthcoming. An N. W. Ayer and Son executive commented in 1915 that even ANPA members pledged not to accept free publicity were offering to run it if they were given advertising contracts for the companies concerned.[15]

The 1917 ANPA annual meeting resolved that "free publicity in consideration of advertising is illegal, unethical, and seriously interferes with the promotion of newspaper advertising." On many papers, however, the "business office must" continued to flourish. Newsprint shortages after World War I gave the anti-publicity drive impetus, and the New York City and Tulsa, Oklahoma, newspapers curtailed automobile publicity drastically in 1920.[16] The Society for Electrical Development, a trade association representing thirteen hundred firms in the electrical business, reported in 1921, however, that it had obtained the equivalent of 763 pages of newspaper publicity in three months.[17] Various business and trade associations which promoted informational publicity and public relations programs had banded together by 1935 and called themselves "Authentic News and Reference Sources," pointing out that they had a legitimate service to offer the newspapers.[18]

Despite the campaign against free publicity waged constantly by the ANPA, largely through the personal work of General Man-

---

[14] This Sunday feature survived until the newsprint and automobile shortage during World War II.

[15] *Editor & Publisher*, 48:142 (July 17, 1915).

[16] *Bulletin 4218*, Apr. 30, 1920; *Bulletin 4239*, May 29, 1920.

[17] *Bulletin 4503*, Nov. 15, 1921.

[18] *Editor & Publisher*, 68:16 (Dec. 28, 1935).

ager Lincoln B. Palmer, the 1920s saw tremendous publicity developments. The sports and amusement pages of newspapers were the centers of two major drives. More serious were an extensive campaign in behalf of private utilities and the questionable support given by many financial pages to the stock and bond markets during the pre-1929 boom. In 1936, faced with severe advertising losses, publishers in many cities entered into local agreements regulating the most obvious forms of free publicity and the use of the "business office must" on stories submitted by advertisers. Atlanta and Los Angeles were centers of such action.[19] But during the 1930s the slogan of the ANPA, "They don't pay for it if they can get it free," came to be applied especially to radio, a prime advertising menace. The efforts of the publishers to control publicity for this competitor belong in the story of radio-newspaper competition.

[19] *Ibid.*, 69:5 (Apr. 25, 1936).

CHAPTER IX

Association Affairs, 1918–1949

THE American Newspaper Publishers Association had established for itself by 1918 a solid reputation as a trade association which could represent the daily newspapers in their dealings with labor unions, communications competitors, advertisers and advertising agencies, newsprint makers, and the government. Thereafter its story is one of continued action in these fields of economic interest.

Like many of their readers, the daily newspapers lived in a state of relative complacency during the 1920s. After the postwar readjustments the ANPA found its task relatively easy in handling labor relations problems, the competitive advertising situation, governmental actions affecting publishers, and relationships with other businesses. The spirit of the times was reflected in the growth of the tabloid newspaper and the spreading of the influence of "jazz journalism" to the detriment of journalism as a whole. But the sensationalizing of news, or any other editorial problem, was not judged by the ANPA to be of concern to a trade association dedicated to the advancement of daily newspaper business interests.

There were, however, pressing problems confronting the newspapers of the country. As the industrialization and urbanization of the United States continued at an even faster pace after World War I, the patterns of concentration of industrial ownership and standardized mass production became more firmly fixed in American business life. Among daily newspapers these tendencies were also apparent. The number of dailies gradually declined, from a high of 2600 in 1909 to 2441 in 1919 and 2086 in 1929. Their combined circulation, however, rose from 24 million in 1909 to 43 million in 1929.

Then came the great depression. The daily newspapers were doubly hard hit, for the depression years coincided with the growth of a new communications competitor, radio, which cut sharply into advertising revenue. The number of dailies continued to decline, reaching a low of 1744 in 1945 before climbing again to 1781 in 1948. Many forces were at work: inability of communities to support multinewspaper ownership; loss of newspaper individuality as the processes of ,ournalism tended toward standardization; a tendency to combine production of morning and evening papers from the same plant as an answer to mounting costs; and the inevitable elimination of weaker competitors by aggressive papers. The result was that by 1945 only 117 of the 1394 American cities and towns in which dailies were published had separately owned competing daily newspapers.[1] This situation, together with the development of chain ownership, placed the newspaper business in a difficult position and intensified the debate over the social responsibility of communications media. Even though the circulation of the dailies had passed the fifty million mark, publishers and editors found themselves widely criticized as "monopolists," despite their appeals that critics should study the economic facts which had brought about the concentration of newspaper ownership.

The depression had other effects on the public position of the newspapers. The social and economic readjustments which it forced resulted in a demand for political action in behalf of the common welfare. The ANPA, as the trade association of the daily newspapers, asserted itself as never before in the struggle between the contending forces which sought to shape the actions of government. So determined was the resistance with which the association leadership met attempts to widen the degree of government intervention in economic affairs, that one of the most controversial chapters in the association's history was written. And hardly had the intensity of that battle lessened, when the newspapers were plunged into the difficulties of wartime production and postwar readjustment once again.

Through this troubled period the ANPA, like many of the sur-

[1] Raymond B. Nixon, "Concentration and Absenteeism in Daily Newspaper Ownership," *Journalism Quarterly*, 22:97 (June 1945).

viving daily newspapers which constituted its membership, acquired the characteristics which are the mark of bigness: centralized control, a loss of the impact of individuality, and the development of a standardized efficiency. While this change in the ANPA was inevitable as the group grew in size, it reduced the chances for success of those publishers who sought to widen the sphere of the association's official interests to include problems relating to newspaper responsibility.

Membership of daily newspapers in the ANPA, totaling 300 in 1910, rose to a high of 554 by 1922, as publishers were attracted to the association during a postwar period of newsprint shortage. By 1930 membership had leveled off at 503. The depression cut the rolls to 428 in 1933, but ten years later the membership had risen to 586. A great postwar boom then shot the total up to 809 in 1948. What had once been a small organization, with a few score attending its annual meetings, had 1342 publishers and managers of daily newspapers present for the 1949 convention.

The annual meetings of the membership continued to be held each year near the end of April. The sessions were held in the old Waldorf-Astoria in New York City until it was demolished in 1929 and at the new Waldorf-Astoria after 1932. The joint AP-ANPA banquet was discontinued in 1920 in favor of an annual luncheon, which in turn was succeeded in 1922 by an annual dinner sponsored by the ANPA's associate organization, the Bureau of Advertising. These dinners have featured as speakers on the same program such diverse public figures as Charles M. Schwab and Will Rogers, Amelia Earhart and Lewis W. Douglas, William Lyon Phelps and Fiorello La Guardia, Henry Ford and Thomas E. Dewey, and George M. Cohan and Robert A. Taft.

During the 1920s the newspaper publishers conformed to the national trend and held golf tournaments at their conventions. To further this activity, and other social pleasures, the 1925 ANPA convention ordered that a fall convention be held each year "at some Southern watering place." Beginning that year three-day conventions were held each November at White Sulphur Springs, French Lick, Virginia Beach, or Sea Island Beach. The business sessions discussed in more detail the principal activities of the association and operating problems of the publishers which were outlined at the April meetings. In 1931 the fall convention was held in Los Angeles, with a postconvention voyage to Hawaii on the agenda. But as depression shadows lengthened the 1932 annual meeting voted to postpone the fall convention that year, and no more were held. A fall meeting of the association after the close of the presidential campaign of 1936 was suggested by some members,[2] but fortunately for the disappointed supporters of Alfred M. Landon — a majority of the ANPA membership — they did not have to gather for a post-mortem discussion of editorial page effectiveness.

Beginning in 1931 a "small dailies session" has been a feature of the ANPA annual meetings. Held on Tuesday, the opening day of the April convention week, this session has considered the problems of papers published in cities of less than 100,000 population and with less than 50,000 circulation. By 1937 and 1938 an undertone of discontent was felt at ANPA conventions; the *Guild Reporter,* organ of the American Newspaper Guild, said the small daily publishers as a group were not in accord with the aggressive fight made by the ANPA leadership against much of the New Deal social legislation, and they resented metropolitan papers' competing in ever larger geographical areas for circulation.[3] In any event, since the late 1930s the association management has put much emphasis on "small dailies," with noteworthy success. In 1939 the ANPA had only 61 members among the 1302 American daily newspapers with less than 10,000 circulation. By 1948 it had won 149 members among the 1027 dailies left in that circulation bracket, and a separate "smallest dailies session" was organized for them in 1949. Other 1948 figures show that 261 of 375 papers in the 10,000 to 25,000 circulation class were ANPA members, while all but 20 of the 367 dailies with circulations larger than 25,000 were in the fold.

The 28 percent of the membership which might be classed as "metropolitan" — with more than 50,000 circulation — had by the nature of things tended to control the policies of the association, and a conscious attempt has been made since 1938 to increase the interest of the small daily publishers. A larger number of

[2] *Editor & Publisher,* 69:7 (May 2, 1936).
[3] *Guild Reporter,* May 2, 1938, p. 3.

their leaders have been elected to the board of directors, and Linwood I. Noyes, publisher of the Ironwood *Globe,* a Michigan daily of 8500 circulation, became in 1943 the first "small daily" leader to be elected ANPA president. David W. Howe, business manager of the Burlington *Free Press,* a Vermont daily with 24,000 circulation, was elected president in 1947.

The Tuesday small dailies sessions have discussed typical problems of the publishers, in a give-and-take manner reminiscent of the informal atmosphere of earlier ANPA conventions. In 1939 the discussions ranged over topics in the fields of advertising, circulation, merchandising cooperation with advertisers, composing room cost accounting, radio competition, free circulation newspapers, art work, and local pictures. In 1942 the war had changed the topics somewhat, to advertising, circulation, promotion and public relations, reduction in the size of comic strips to save newsprint, government publicity, and service newspapers. The 1947 discussions touched on the topics of merchandising cooperation, national advertising campaigns with dealer tie-ins, copy departments for local advertising, color advertising, newsprint shortages, television and radio developments, and labor relations. The problem of "creating greater interest in editorials" drew some discussion at the 1946 session, but, in general, editorial topics received scant notice. Among the leaders in the small dailies sessions have been Verne E. Joy of the Centralia, Illinois, *Sentinel,* Clare Marshall of the Cedar Rapids, Iowa, *Gazette,* Frank S. Hoy of the Lewiston, Maine, *Sun* and *Journal,* Buell W. Hudson of the Woonsocket, Rhode Island, *Call,* Arthur P. Irving of the Glen Falls, New York, *Post-Star* and *Times,* and Joe M. Bunting of the Bloomington, Illinois, *Pantagraph.*

Association affairs have been controlled largely by the officers and directors, the leading committee chairmen, and the permanent staff. From 1918 to 1949 the following men, all publishers or business managers of daily newspapers, have served as presidents of the ANPA and for a longer time as officers or directors:

	Years as President	Total Years as Officer or Director
Frank P. Glass, Birmingham *News*	1918–20	1906–20
T. R. Williams, Pittsburgh *Press*	1920–22	1918–28
Paul Patterson, Baltimore *Sun*	1922–24	1920–28

	Years as President	Total Years as Officer or Director
Samuel E. Thomason, Chicago *Tribune*.........	1924–26	1922–30
John Stewart Bryan, Richmond *News-Leader*....	1926–28	1912–30
Edward H. Butler, Buffalo *Evening News*.......	1928–30	1920–40
Harry Chandler, Los Angeles *Times*............	1930–32	1913–34
Howard Davis, New York *Herald Tribune*......	1932–35	1921–44
Jerome D. Barnum, Syracuse *Post-Standard*.....	1935–37	1928–42
James G. Stahlman, Nashville *Banner*..........	1937–39	1935–41
John S. McCarrens, Cleveland *Plain Dealer*.....	1939–41	1936–43
Walter M. Dear, *Jersey Journal*................	1941–43	1930–45
Linwood I. Noyes, Ironwood *Globe*............	1943–45	1938–47
William G. Chandler, Scripps-Howard.........	1945–47	1934–51
David W. Howe, Burlington *Free Press*.........	1947–49	1938–51
Edwin S. Friendly, New York *Sun*.............	1949–51	1943–51

Of these sixteen presidents, eight may be classified as primarily interested in business management problems of newspapers — Williams, Thomason, Davis, McCarrens, Dear, W. G. Chandler, Howe, and Friendly. Of the remaining eight, who held the title of publisher while serving as ANPA president, five had extensive working careers on the news and editorial side. They were Glass, Patterson, Butler, Stahlman, and Noyes. Bryan, it might be noted, became president of William and Mary College.

Three veteran directors of the association whose terms of office extended from the earlier period of ANPA history into this later period were Charles H. Taylor, Jr., of the Boston *Globe*, an officer or director from 1896 to 1938; Hilton U. Brown of the Indianapolis *News*, director from 1904 to 1935; and Elbert H. Baker of the Cleveland *Plain Dealer*, officer or director from 1907 to 1928. Other directors serving for considerable periods of time were W. E. MacFarlane of the Chicago *Tribune*, 1930 to 1945; Charles A. Webb of the Asheville *Citizen-Times*, 1927 to 1936; F. G. Bell of the Savannah *Morning News*, 1920 to 1927; S. R. Winch of the Portland *Oregon Journal*, 1929 to 1946; E. M. (Ted) Dealey of the Dallas *News*, 1940 to 1945; and William F. Schmick of the Baltimore *Sun*, 1942 to 1949.

George M. Rogers of the Cleveland *Plain Dealer* served as secretary from 1924 to 1932 and as vice-president from 1932 to 1934. E. H. Harris of the Richmond, Indiana, *Palladium-Item* was secretary from 1932 to 1938, and John S. Parks of the Fort Smith, Arkansas, *Southwest American* and *Times-Record*, a director from 1930 to 1938, was secretary from 1938 to 1940. Norman

Chandler of the Los Angeles *Times*, who became a director when his father retired from the board in 1934, served as secretary from 1940 to 1946. Four men who were later to become presidents, Davis, Dear, W. G. Chandler, and Friendly, held the treasurership from 1921 to 1947.

One Canadian publisher or business manager has been named regularly to the board of directors. John E. Atkinson of the Toronto *Star* served from 1919 to 1923, F. J. Burd of the Vancouver *Daily Province* from 1923 to 1935, and F. I. Ker of the Hamilton *Spectator* after 1935.

Beginning in 1938 with the election of Noyes and Howe to directorships, more publishers of small dailies have been named to the board. J. L. Stackhouse of the Easton, Pennsylvania, *Express* became a director in 1940 and was elected secretary in 1947. JS Gray of the Monroe, Michigan, *News* was named a director in 1945, and J. D. Funk of the Santa Monica, California, *Outlook* followed him onto the board in 1946. William L. Fanning, Westchester County Publishers, Yonkers, New York, was elected treasurer in 1947. Thus on the board of directors in 1949 were five officers or directors from small dailies. The other eight American members were Friendly; W. G. Chandler; George C. Biggers of the Atlanta *Journal*, a director since 1941; Charles F. McCahill of the Cleveland *News*, director since 1944; Elbert M. Antrim of the Chicago *Tribune* and Bert N. Honea of the Fort Worth *Star-Telegram*, directors since 1945; P. L. Jackson of the Portland *Oregon Journal*, on the board since 1947; and Richard W. Slocum of the Philadelphia *Bulletin*, elected in 1949.

A survey of the committee activities of the association since 1918 not only illustrates the nature of the interests of the membership, but also indicates the tendency toward assumption of leadership by the larger papers. The chairmen of the various ANPA committees have had a large part in determining the official stand of the association in matters of policy, and in some cases the committee chairmen have exercised more influence than board members.

The greatest field of committee activity has been that concerning relations with the government and legislative matters. The committee on second-class postage, later called the postal committee, had as chairmen after 1920 three publishers who later became ANPA presidents: Jerome D. Barnum, John Stewart Bryan, and James G. Stahlman. Postal committee chairmen since 1937 have been John S. Parks, Fort Smith, Arkansas, *Southwest American* and *Times-Record*; Silliman Evans, Nashville *Tennessean*; and Josh L. Horne, Rocky Mount, North Carolina, *Telegram*. The committee on paper was led after 1920 by E. P. Adler of the Davenport, Iowa, *Times*, Samuel E. Thomason of the Chicago *Tribune*, and William G. Chandler, general business manager of the Scripps-Howard newspapers. Its duties now have been assumed by the ANPA general manager's office. Other committees in the field of newsprint supply have functioned for shorter periods, considering the problems of conservation of natural resources, newsprint conservation, and newspaper pulpwood supply. The committee on federal laws has had as long-time chairmen Elbert H. Baker of the Cleveland *Plain Dealer* and William F. Wiley of the Cincinnati *Enquirer*. Its chairmen since 1945 have been Raymond B. Bottom, Newport News, Virginia, *Press* and *Times-Herald*, and J. Hale Steinman, Lancaster, Pennsylvania, *Intelligencer Journal*. The committee on freedom of the press, led by Robert R. McCormick of the Chicago *Tribune* since its formation in 1928, was discontinued during World War II but was reorganized in 1948 with George C. Biggers of the Atlanta *Journal* as chairman. A. V. Miller of the New York *Herald Tribune* has been chairman of the social security committee since its formation in 1935. Other committees in this field, now discontinued, have dealt with the problems of the NRA newspaper code, federal taxation, tax depreciation, the securities act, wage and hour legislation, and publicity of court proceedings.

In the advertising sphere the ANPA committee in charge of the Bureau of Advertising has been an important assignment. Chairmen since 1913 have included John F. MacKay, Toronto *Globe*; Fleming Newbold, Washington *Evening Star*; William F. Rogers, Boston *Transcript*; W. E. MacFarlane, Chicago *Tribune*; Edwin S. Friendly, New York *Sun*; Frank E. Tripp, Gannett newspapers; Roy D. Moore, Brush-Moore newspapers; and Richard W. Slocum, Philadelphia *Bulletin*. The committee on advertising agencies, whose technical duties have been taken over by the ANPA central office, has had as chairman since 1944 Harry L. Hawkins of the Philadelphia *Bulletin*. The committee on radio, begun in 1923 and suspended during World War II, had as chairmen Walter A. Strong, Chicago *Daily News*; Elzey Roberts, St. Louis *Star*; E. H. Harris, Richmond, Indiana, *Palladium-Item*; and JS Gray, Monroe, Michigan, *News*. Other short-term committees have been those concerned with shopping news publications, merchandising service, and motion picture productions.

Labor relations of the association have been handled by a department with a paid staff, called the Special Standing Committee. In charge of the department have been H. N. Kellogg, from 1907 to 1926; Harvey J. Kelly, from 1926 to 1936; Eugene MacKinnon, from 1936 to 1942; and George N. Dale, since 1942. A separate labor department, the Open Shop Department, was organized in 1922. H. W. Flagg served as its paid manager until it was dissolved in the early 1940s; committee chairmen were D. D. Moore of the New Orleans *Times-Picayune* and Charles A. Webb of the Asheville *Citizen-Times*. Another long-time committee now discontinued, that on printing trades schools, was dominated by Victor F. Ridder of the New York *Staats-Zeitung* and Ridder newspapers, son of former ANPA President Herman Ridder. The committee on the newspaperboy, begun in 1935, has had as its only chairman Howard M. Stodghill of the Philadelphia *Bulletin*.

The Mechanical Department, organized in 1926 to study newspaper production problems, has had Walter E. Wines as paid manager. Chairmen of the committee in charge have included George M. Rogers, Cleveland *Plain Dealer*; Samuel H. Kauffmann, Washington *Evening Star*; F. H. Keefe, Newburgh, New York, *Beacon-News*; A. H. Burns, New York *Herald Tribune*; Worth C. Coutney, Chicago *Herald-American*; J. L. Stackhouse, Easton, Pennsylvania, *Express*; and Edwin H. Evers, St. Louis *Globe-Democrat*. In 1947 a Mechanical Research Department was begun, with C. M. Flint as research director and William Baumrucker, Jr., of the New York *Daily News* as chairman. The Traffic Department, set up in 1926 to study transportation rates, was managed by W. J. Mathey until 1932 and since then by R. A. Cooke. E. M. Antrim of the Chicago *Tribune* was chairman of

the committee in charge until 1947, when he was succeeded by
Fred J. Byington, Jr., of the Chicago *Tribune*.

The committee on press communications and its predecessors
have periodically represented the ANPA in matters of press rates
and censorship since the 1920s. Its leaders have been Victor F.
Ridder, Ridder newspapers; Elbert H. Baker, Cleveland *Plain
Dealer*; and Julius Ochs Adler, New York *Times*. In 1920 a conference on international communications was sponsored by the
ANPA,[4] and since then the committee has functioned at intervals
to present the views of the association to various international
radio and telegraph conventions.

Another interesting committee has been that on schools of
journalism. After criticism of the teaching of journalism by ANPA
President James G. Stahlman in 1937, a National Council on Professional Education for Journalism was formed, and ANPA participation was approved by the 1939 ANPA annual meeting. The
council, later renamed the American Council on Education for
Journalism, has five educator members from the Association of
Accredited Schools and Departments of Journalism and five
newspaper members representing the ANPA, the American Society of Newspaper Editors, the National Editorial Association, the
Southern Newspaper Publishers Association, and the Inland
Daily Press Association. The council's major activity has been to
establish an accrediting program for schools and departments of
journalism, to which the ANPA has made a substantial financial
contribution. The ANPA also has offered an annual $500 prize and
gold medal to the college journalism student writing the best
monograph on a newspaper subject. ANPA representatives in this
work have been Jerome D. Barnum, Syracuse *Post-Standard*; David W. Howe, Burlington, Vermont, *Free Press*; Charles F. Mc-
Cahill, Cleveland *News*; and Joyce A. Swan, Minneapolis *Star
and Tribune*.

The final current ANPA committee, the library committee,
headed by Linwood I. Noyes of the Ironwood, Michigan, *Globe*,
is engaged in building up a journalism library in the New York
office of the association for research and study activities.

A committee on supplies, headed by John L. Blake of the

[4] *Bulletin 4306*, Oct. 30, 1920.

Scripps-Howard newspapers, was named by the ANPA in 1939, when the war in Europe began. This committee surveyed the war-tightened markets for manufactured products and raw materials used in the production of newspapers, and in December 1940 it advised ANPA members to stock up on supplies which would be restricted by the Office of Production Management established by the government.[5] The committee continued, under Blake's leadership, to report to the membership on the supply situation and to represent the ANPA in discussions with wartime government agencies.

A major change in association leadership took place in 1939 when Lincoln B. Palmer, general manager of the ANPA since 1905 and a leader in daily newspaper affairs, retired from active service.[6] The new general manager selected by the association was Cranston Williams, son of a Georgia newspaper editor, former managing editor of the Americus, Georgia, *Times-Recorder*, and from 1924 to 1939 the secretary-manager of the Southern Newspaper Publishers Association. Williams furthered the emphasis on small daily participation in association affairs and brought an aggressive direction to the ANPA management.

Center of association activities has been the New York office, which moved in 1930 from 270 Madison Avenue to 370 Lexington Avenue, where the ANPA occupies an entire floor. From this central office the various bulletins of the association are issued, answers are given to more than a thousand inquiries from publishers monthly, and advertising credit and collection services are rendered. Through it the affairs of the officers and committees are coordinated and annual conventions of the membership are arranged. The separate departments — Mechanical, Traffic, Newsprint, Credit and Adjustment, and Special Standing Committee — function in cooperation with the general manager. Elisha Hanson, ANPA general counsel, assists in representing the association in legislative and legal affairs.

Under Williams' direction the bulletin series of the association was revised and improved. The bulletins were numbered consecutively, from 1 to more than 7000 up to the year 1941, except

[5] *Bulletin 7385*, Dec. 11, 1940.
[6] Palmer died in 1945 at the age of 79.

for four special series. These were *Bulletins: Labor,* begun in 1908; *Mechanical Bulletin* and *Traffic Bulletin,* both started in 1927; and *Newsprint Bulletin,* begun in 1928. After 1941 all bulletin matter was identified by topics and a new series was begun for each topic each year. Credit ratings for advertising agencies and advertisers are carried in the *A Bulletin* series, while news of new advertising business is reported in the *C Bulletin.* General news of advertising affairs is carried in the *Advertising Bulletin.* General information of interest to all members is reported in the *B Bulletin.* Other new series include the *Convention Bulletin, Federal Laws Bulletin, Circulation Bulletin,* and *Publicity Bulletin.* Bound volumes of the bulletins are prepared for the members' reference libraries each year.

The cost of maintaining the association's activities rose gradually as the ANPA grew in size. A particularly sharp increase came after 1940. Association income — mainly from dues — was $291,-901 that year, while expenses totaled $297,055. In 1947 income amounted to $551,077, while expenses totaled $514,697. The table, "ANPA Expenses, 1940–1947," which is based on the treasurer's statements for those years, breaks down the expenses.

ANPA Expenses, 1940–1947

Item of Expense	1940	1947
General manager's office expense....	$ 85,554.54	$145,825.23
Association general expense.........	74,077.60	75,663.70
Credit Department.................	21,307.77	39,779.24
Traffic Department................	12,327.29	19,673.34
Mechanical Department............	18,083.86	23,981.04
Mechanical Research Department....	. . .	9,055.50
Open Shop Department............	11,281.93	. . .
Special Standing Committee........	59,406.17	171,202.39
Newsprint Department.............	7,526.71	20,088.60
Special committees...............	7,489.84	9,428.83
Total	$297,055.71	$514,697.87

Dues were based on the member's gross minimum advertising rate and the number of typesetting and typecasting machines in his plant. Rates ran from $10 to $35 for each cent of the advertising rate, plus $17 for each machine. The minimum charge was $120 a year.

During the 1930s the activities of the ANPA became more and more centralized in the hands of the paid staff, the officers and directors, and the committees. The annual conventions became more formal, and committee reports and prepared speeches tended to replace debate by the membership. Small daily publishers held their own meeting; the Bureau of Advertising presented an advertising program on another afternoon; and general sessions became limited to a day and a half, with discussion of policies and committee recommendations held to a minimum.

Much was done by the association, nonetheless. The problems of newsprint cost and supply, postal rates and regulations, labor relations, radio as an advertising competitor, mechanical improvements and transportation rates, and governmental actions affecting the publishing business became major issues. Each will be treated individually in the chapters which follow.

CHAPTER X

Newsprint Cost and Supply

PASSAGE of the Underwood Tariff of 1913 marked the end of the long fight of the American Newspaper Publishers Association for duty-free imports of standard newsprint,[1] and thereafter the publishers had little trouble keeping their "white paper" on the free list. American daily newspapers now had unimpeded access to the forest resources of Canada, and American capital rushed in to take advantage of the lower costs of raw materials and production north of the border. As a consequence, the problem of newsprint cost was, in large measure, alleviated for the publishers. But the end result of sacrificing domestic newsprint manufacturing was the creation of a problem of supply during and after World War II. Should the supply shortage prove chronic in the years beyond 1949, the problem of the cost of newsprint would be a headache once again.

Newsprint valued at less than $50 a ton was admitted free of duty by the 1913 tariff provisions. When the price of newsprint threatened to exceed that limit, Congress in 1916 raised the valuation on duty-free paper to $100 a ton. And when the temporary postwar newsprint crisis of 1920 carried newsprint costs above that level, a bill sponsored by Representative Cordell Hull of Tennessee extended the duty-free limit to paper valued at $160 a ton, at the ANPA's request.[2] During the hearings on the high-level Fordney-McCumber Tariff of 1922, S. E. Thomason of the Chicago *Tribune*, chairman of the ANPA committee on federal laws, appeared to defend duty-free newsprint and succeeded in having all standard newsprint, regardless of price, placed on the free list.[3] When the Hawley-Smoot Tariff of 1930 was being

---
[1] See Chapter VI.
[2] *Report of the Thirty-fourth Annual Meeting* (1920), p. 373.
[3] *Report of the Thirty-sixth Annual Meeting* (1922), p. 363.

drafted, the ANPA reported no trouble in retaining newsprint and wood pulp on the free list, despite the otherwise high tariff provisions of the bill.[4] Finally, when publishers during World War II wished to import duty-free newsprint of less than the standard width of sixteen inches, they were accommodated. The bars were down.

The two accompanying tables show the problems of supply and cost which affected publishers of newspapers after 1909. The first, "U.S. Newsprint Supply," illustrates how the newsprint industry became a predominantly Canadian enterprise after the lifting of the tariff barriers. The figures show that American newsprint production reached its peak in 1926, which was also

U.S. NEWSPRINT SUPPLY
(in thousands of tons)

Year	Domestic Production	Imports from Canada	Imports from Europe	U.S. Exports	Total U.S. Supply
1909	1,176	18	1	36	1,159
1914	1,313	310	5	61	1,567
1919	1,375	628	3	111	1,895
1924	1,481	1,217	140	17	2,821
1926	1,684	1,751	100	19	3,516
1929	1,373	2,327	96	19	3,777
1932	1,001	1,647	145	8	2,785
1937	940	3,045	294	17	4,262
1938	816	1,940	243	8	2,991
1945	707	2,666	0	19	3,354
1947	824	3,897	129	7	4,843
1948	858	4,128	267	8	5,245
1949 (est.)	875	4,350	250	9	5,466

SOURCE: Compiled from News Print Service Bureau and Newsprint Association of Canada statistics. Imports from Canada include Newfoundland.

the first year in which domestic production was exceeded by imports from Canada. They also show that there was no recovery in domestic newsprint production after World War II, comparable to that in Canada, because papermaking machines had been shifted to more profitable uses than the manufacturing of newsprint. American imports from Canada slumped sharply during the depression and again during the recession of 1937–38, raising havoc with the newsprint makers' financial position. And while the supply of newsprint available to American publishers by 1949

[4] *Bulletin 5633*, May 9, 1929.

was the largest in history, it still was slightly short of meeting actual needs and far short of filling predicted future needs. Nor were there bright prospects of expanding newsprint production capacity in time to solve the larger problem of world newsprint supply. How this situation came about is one of the threads of this chapter.

The second table, "U.S. Newsprint Prices," lists average prices for newsprint in New York City during these same years and compares those prices with all United States wholesale prices.

U.S. NEWSPRINT PRICES (PER TON)

Year	Approximate Newsprint Price in New York	Index Numbers of Newsprint Prices (1910–14 = 100)	Index Numbers of All Wholesale Prices (1910–14 = 100)
1910	$ 45	103	103
1916	42	96	125
1917	68	157	172
1918	68–80	157–184	192
1919	80	184	202
1920	95–137	218–314	225
1921	137–87	314–200	142
1922	77	176	141
1927	72	164	139
1929	62	142	139
1931	57	130	107
1932	53–45	121–103	95
1933	45–40	103–92	96
1937	42	97	126
1938	50	114	115
1939	50	114	113
1943	50–58	114–132	151
1945	58–61	132–140	155
1946	67–84	154–192	177
1947	90	206	221
1948	90–100	,206–228	242
1949 (June)..	100	228	230

SOURCE: Figures to 1939 compiled by John A. Guthrie in *The Newsprint Paper Industry: An Economic Analysis* (Cambridge: Harvard University Press, 1941), p. 247. The wholesale price index is that of the Bureau of Labor Statistics.

The price of newsprint to publishers was, if anything, slightly to their advantage in the years from 1910 to 1914. Therefore, use of those years as a base to compare the price of newsprint with all United States wholesale prices works to the publishers' advantage. Yet in only thirteen of the thirty-eight years from 1910 to

1948 was the price of newsprint above the general wholesale price level. Those were the years from 1920 to 1932. The sharp price rises during World War I did not get out of line with other wholesale prices until the newsprint "panic" of 1920. And the price jumps after the end of OPA controls in 1946 fell a little short of matching the general wholesale price advance. These indications of price advantage or disadvantage may be kept in mind as the story of ANPA newsprint activities continues.

A report on newsprint supply and cost conditions as America entered World War I is found in the results of an investigation made by the Federal Trade Commission during 1916 and 1917. The inquiry was made under the terms of a Senate resolution calling for an investigation of an increase in the price of newsprint and charges of unfair practices in the sale of print paper. The ANPA in late 1915 had asked its members to supply information concerning price-fixing and selling agreements among the newsprint manufacturers,[5] but it was not pressing for action when the Senate resolution was approved in April 1916. Rather, the complaints were coming from small publishers who found themselves bidding for a tightened supply of newsprint on the open market. Indeed, as the investigation opened, the newsprint manufacturers' representative praised the ANPA and its general manager, Lincoln B. Palmer, for "the fairness and squareness displayed." [6]

The leading newsprint manufacturers in the United States in 1916, the commission reported, were the International Paper Company, with nine mills in New England and New York; the Great Northern Paper Company, with three mills in Maine; the Minnesota and Ontario Paper Company, with mills in Minnesota and Canada; and the Crown Willamette Paper Company, with mills in Oregon, Washington, and British Columbia. Together they controlled 55 percent of the total American output. In Canada the major manufacturers were the Spanish River Pulp and Paper Mills, the Laurentide Company, the Powell River Company, and the Abitibi Power and Paper Company.[7]

---

[5] *Bulletin 3392*, Nov. 27, 1915; *Bulletin 3400*, Dec. 18, 1915.

[6] Ellis, *Print Paper Pendulum*, p. 95.

[7] *Report of the Federal Trade Commission on the News-print Paper Industry*, June 13, 1917, p. 31.

Leading sales agents for newsprint manufacturers, who as agents controlled considerable supplies of paper, were the George B. Mead Company of Dayton, Ohio; the Canadian Export Paper Company, formed in 1916; the H. W. Craig Company; and W. H. Parsons and Company of Maine.[8] Furthermore, the commission found, a Newsprint Manufacturers Association had been formed in April 1915 whose members controlled 86 percent of the 1916 output of newsprint in all North America.

Turning to the price situation, the commission said that while the cost of newsprint production in the mills had increased $5.50 a ton in January 1917, compared to the first six months of 1916, the contract price of newsprint had advanced from $42 to $68 a ton. Some small papers were being forced to pay $150 a ton.[9] In the eyes of the commission this seemed to show that the antitrust laws were being violated. Restriction of competition among the mills, the commission said, had enabled them to maintain a very close balance between supply and demand in the newsprint market. Bidding by disorganized publishers had then produced a sellers' market which was particularly disastrous for small publishers, but not punishing to large contract buyers. The contract price in New York was below the level of all wholesale prices, using the 1910–14 base as a comparison.

The first plan of the Federal Trade Commission was to make an arbitration agreement with the paper manufacturers. In February 1917 eight companies agreed to abide by the results of the Federal Trade Commission investigation and to reduce their contract prices for newsprint to a level determined by the commission. In return their publisher-customers were to agree to release 5 percent of their contracted paper to hard-pressed small publishers. The commission found a fair and reasonable price to be $50 a ton at the mills ($55 a ton in New York) and was preparing to put its agreement with the paper companies into effect, when the Department of Justice brought indictments against the members of the Newsprint Manufacturers Association in April. The newsprint manufacturers thereupon withdrew from the arbitration agreement and fought the antitrust suit, which they lost.[10]

[8] Ibid., p. 42.
[9] Ibid., pp. 132–33.
[10] Ibid., pp. 135–41.

The ANPA, whose larger members had been reluctant to accept the proposal for distribution of 5 percent of their newsprint supplies to small publishers, but whose leaders endorsed the Federal Trade Commission's arbitration plan, protested against the action of the Department of Justice in bringing the indictments.[11]

At the ANPA annual meeting in April 1917 it was announced that the committee on paper had resumed active operations, after it had been practically disbanded in 1913 and its paid executive, John Norris, had retired. Frank P. Glass of the Birmingham *News* had been chairman of the committee during 1916 and had cooperated with the Federal Trade Commission. The committee recommended that newsprint price-fixing be done by the government, since it was evident that the price would be fixed well below the prevailing market price. It also suggested that publishers might be forced to save newsprint by decreasing the number of pages they printed and adopting a ratio of 30 percent news and 70 percent advertising instead of the more usual 50:50 ratio.

A special ANPA meeting, called June 21, 1917, at the Washington *Evening Star* offices, primarily to oppose postal rate increases and a war revenue tax on newspaper profits, also took action in regard to newsprint. Resolutions were adopted urging Congress to pass emergency bills which would provide water power for newsprint production and asking the government to enforce the various newsprint-saving recommendations which had been outlined by the committee on paper. The larger publishers present balked, however, at endorsing the committee's support of the Federal Trade Commission's plan for control of newsprint, and not until a mail ballot had been taken was the committee sustained.[12]

The Federal Trade Commission's report, issued on June 13, had cited the failure of its negotiations with the newsprint manufacturers and publishers and warned that a panic market would develop unless newsprint supplies were controlled in some manner. The commission recommended that Congress pass a war emergency measure containing the following provisions:

1. That all mills producing newsprint and agencies distributing it be operated by their present managements on government account, with their products being controlled and pooled by the

[11] *Bulletin 3647*, Apr. 28, 1917.
[12] *Report of the Thirty-first Annual Meeting* (1917), supplement.

government and distributed with a fair profit to the manufacturers.

2. That the United States seek the cooperation of Canada in joint action along these lines, since 75 percent of Canadian newsprint production was sold in the United States.

3. That if Canada did not cooperate, the government should control the importation of newsprint into the United States.[13]

Unfortunately for the publishers, both large and small, this recommendation that newsprint supplies be allocated equitably at fixed prices was not adopted. A price-fixing system was later instituted by the commission, but it made no provision for control of distribution.

The commission, in its report, commended the ANPA for its cooperation, saying that the association had issued bulletins to its members urging newsprint savings. These suggestions included elimination of waste, curtailment of consumption, disallowance of unsold paper returns by dealers, increases in circulation rates, and advances in advertising rates. The commission also recommended that the 2000 small dailies and 14,000 weeklies depending on the open market for newsprint form buying groups to take advantage of lower contract prices on large amounts of paper. But neither the newsprint manufacturers nor the ANPA showed any concrete interest in thus extending aid to the small publishers until the newsprint panic of 1920 brought belated action.

In November 1917 consumers of newsprint, represented by the Attorney General, agreed to maximum price-fixing with the newsprint manufacturers. The Federal Trade Commission was to set a price effective on April 1, 1918. The commission set the maximum price of carload lots of newsprint at $62 a ton, delivered at the mill. On an appeal by the manufacturers a federal circuit court increased the price to $70, and a supplemental decision authorized a raise to $75 a ton, the court citing increased labor, raw materials, and freight costs to the manufacturers as the basis for its decision.[14] Adding railroad freight charges to New York, this brought the price of newsprint there to $80 a ton by July 1918 — a price still below the general wholesale price level.

---

[13] *Report of the Federal Trade Commission on the News-print Paper Industry, June 13, 1917*, pp. 11–13.
[14] *Report of the Thirty-third Annual Meeting* (1919), p. 12.

The ANPA took an active part in these price-fixing proceedings and opposed the court actions raising the price set by the commission. Special accountants, auditors, and counsel represented the association. The committee on paper collected $48,000 in voluntary contributions from ANPA members during the years from 1916 to 1918, and a compulsory assessment in 1918 raised $99,000 more. The ANPA made extensive efforts to secure a review of the circuit court decisions, but a ruling in November 1919 "brushed aside many months of effort to present evidence."[15]

An unneighborly attitude was expressed at the 1918 ANPA convention, when the War Trade Board was asked to ban all exports of newsprint from the United States and Canada was asked to ship only to Allied countries. The committee on paper claimed much of the newsprint exported was going to unsympathetic Latin-American newspapers. Export shipments to South America and Australia from the United States and Canada had increased considerably, since trade with Scandinavian and other European countries was curtailed by the war. The ANPA was rebuked by *Editor & Publisher* for taking this "selfish attitude," and the magazine asserted that the resolution did not voice the real sentiment of the rank and file membership.[16]

The price of newsprint in New York, set at $80 a ton for 1919, threatened to go completely out of control with the war's end. Dislocation of world trade in newsprint was aggravated by a tremendous demand on the part of American business for advertising space in daily newspapers. When the newsprint manufacturers announced a $95 price in New York, to be effective for the first quarter of 1920, a special paper convention of the ANPA was called for November 12, 1919. The publishers talked about economies in the use of newsprint, ways of increasing production, 50 to 100 percent increases in advertising rates, and rejection of undue amounts of advertising, but nothing concrete was accomplished to benefit the small papers buying in the chaotic open market.

Some papers, among them the New York *Times*, rejected considerable amounts of advertising in order to conserve newsprint,

[15] *Report of the Thirty-fourth Annual Meeting* (1920), p. 228.
[16] *Editor & Publisher*, 51:18 (May 4, 1918).

but the effect of such voluntary action was not great. ANPA President Frank P. Glass summarized the situation effectively when he told the 1920 annual meeting: "The publishers themselves have yielded to the great demand for paper, and have created this skyrocket market by bidding against each other to get the volume of advertising offered, no matter how small the volume of profit."

And a skyrocket market it was. The contract price of newsprint in New York for larger newspapers jumped each quarter of 1920, from $95-105 to $120-137 a ton, putting newsprint prices far out of line with other wholesale prices. Small publishers fared even worse. The ANPA announced in February 1920 that "Scandinavian paper would be available next fall at $150 a ton," [17] and President Glass told the 1920 convention in April that the spot price of newsprint on the open market was $300 a ton.

Elbert H. Baker of the Cleveland *Plain Dealer*, chairman of the committee on paper, reported to the same convention that the committee was urging the government to prorate available newsprint among all customers, was issuing bulletins on the newsprint situation constantly, and was trying to aid small publishers who were caught in the spot price market. The committee was opposing, however, various congressional proposals to control the size of newspapers by excluding from the second-class mail those running above an established maximum of pages. Instead the committee recommended that publishers cut the size of editions voluntarily and cease all extra, early, and late editions. Baker also suggested that publishers increase circulation rates, raise advertising rates at least 50 percent over January 1919 levels, reduce sizes of headlines, eliminate all publicity, and make the ratio of newspaper content 30 percent news to 70 percent advertising.

Determined to take more drastic action, approximately a hundred publishers got together at the 1920 ANPA convention and formed the Publishers' Buying Corporation, with Jason Rogers of the New York *Globe* at its head, to solve the newsprint situation for smaller newspapers.[18] The membership of the group grew to

[17] *Bulletin 4182*, Feb. 7, 1920.
[18] *Editor & Publisher*, 53:6 (June 26, 1920).

250, and it was credited with importing enough Scandinavian newsprint to break the spot market price level.[19] The ANPA also cooperated, giving assistance to 78 small papers in 1920 and obtaining emergency supplies of newsprint for 48.[20]

E. P. Adler of the Davenport, Iowa, *Times*, new chairman of the committee on paper, announced in January 1921 that he could make connections for good contracts. The committee on conservation of paper, headed by W. B. Bryant of the Paterson, New Jersey, *Press-Guardian*,[21] secured pledges from publishers not to use more newsprint during 1920 and 1921 than they had consumed in 1919 and got agreements from the large newspapers that they would stay out of the chaotic spot market. The committee on paper issued charts showing trends in production and consumption of newsprint and in volume of advertising, but Chairman Adler complained, "I have not had very much cooperation from the membership."[22]

The postwar inflation began to subside in 1921 and the wholesale price level declined sharply. The contract price for newsprint in New York fell from $137 a ton to a more normal but still high price of $87 during the year. The spot market price plummeted down to $90 a ton by April 1921.[23] This downward trend continued. In 1922 the contract price in New York was $77 a ton, rising to $82 in 1923, and then declining gradually until it reached a level of $62 a ton in 1929, a price that corresponded almost exactly with the level of all wholesale prices in the United States that year, with the 1910–14 base used for comparison.

Meanwhile the ANPA was engaged in supporting a forest conservation program, so that domestic newsprint manufacturers would have a pulpwood supply. The association established in 1920 a committee on conservation of national forest resources, with Elbert H. Baker of the Cleveland *Plain Dealer* as chairman.[24] The committee encouraged cooperation among publishers, papermakers, and government forest conservation officials

[19] *Ibid.*, 65:25 (Aug. 6, 1932).
[20] *Report of the Thirty-fifth Annual Meeting* (1921), p. 374.
[21] Son of William Cullen Bryant, former secretary-manager of ANPA.
[22] *Report of the Thirty-fifth Annual Meeting* (1921), p. 378.
[23] *Ibid.*, p. 370.
[24] *Bulletin 4299*, Oct. 16, 1920.

and also worked for legislation expanding government control and use of water power resources, which would give cheaper power supplies to some additional American paper mills. The ANPA opposed, however, legislation backed by Gifford Pinchot which sought government ownership of timberlands instead of federal cooperation with private owners.[25] Passage in 1924 of the Clarke-McNary bill extending forest protection and conservation controls was hailed by the ANPA as a victory, and the committee on national forest resources continued to work in behalf of fire prevention measures, forest experiment stations, and state forest policies.

Developments in the newsprint manufacturing industry which occurred during the 1920s indirectly presented the American Newspaper Publishers Association with an embarrassing situation in 1929 and 1930. These developments also brought about a major shift in publishers' attitudes toward the newsprint price problem.

This story begins with the tremendous expansion of the paper industry in Canada after 1920, spurred by the enormous demand for newsprint in the United States and the high prices which developed. The International Paper Company, leading American newsprint manufacturer, entered the Canadian field in 1921. Under the leadership of President A. R. Graustein, International began a great expansion of its mills at Three Rivers and Gatineau, in Quebec province, and the paper company became a subsidiary of the International Paper and Power Company.[26] International became the recognized leader in setting annual price quotations for newsprint, along with the Great Northern Paper Company in Maine and Crown Zellerbach in the western United States, and its contract price announcements were followed by most other companies from 1923 to 1928.[27]

Overexpansion in Canadian newsprint production had unsettled the market by 1928, and when International announced a price of $65 a ton in New York for 1929, only one dollar under the 1928 contract figure, various American publishers balked. In

[25] *Report of the Thirty-sixth Annual Meeting* (1922), p. 360.
[26] Guthrie, *Newsprint Paper Industry*, p. 57.
[27] *Report by the Federal Trade Commission on the Newsprint Paper Industry*, 71st Cong., 2d sess., S. Doc. 214 (1930), pp. 34–36.

October 1928 the Hearst purchasing agency, which bought one eighth of all the newsprint used in North America, drove a bargain with International for $57 a ton in New York, after receiving bids from other newsprint producers.[28] This price, the ANPA declared, would, according to industry custom, become the contract price for all publishers in 1929, and the membership assumed that this would be the case.[29]

But other Canadian newsprint manufacturers, and the premiers of Quebec and Ontario provinces, demanded a stabilization of newsprint prices, warning that the nine-dollar reduction per ton agreed to by International would be disastrous to the paper industry.[30] The statistics show the precarious situation which had developed because of unsound financing. Between 1919 and 1930 investments in Canadian newsprint plants increased 375 percent, while their productive capacity increased 220 percent. Newsprint prices had declined slowly in the middle 1920s, as competition increased between the major manufacturing and sales groups. These included the International Paper Company; the Abitibi Power and Paper Company and its sales agent, the George H. Mead Company; the Canada Power and Paper Company and its partner, the St. Maurice Sales Company; and the Canada Export Company, selling for other mills. In 1927 all these groups except International formed the Canadian Newsprint Company in an effort to control production and allocate sales, but the bidding over the Hearst contract in 1928 broke up this combine. Premiers L. A. Taschereau of Quebec and G. H. Ferguson of Ontario thereupon took the lead and organized in November 1928 the Newsprint Institute of Canada, with all large producers except International again agreeing to restrictive control measures.[31]

Taschereau put pressure on President Graustein of International and on the Hearst interests to renegotiate their contract and stabilize the price of newsprint at a higher level than $57 a ton.[32] Meanwhile the ANPA was sitting tight, although the chairman of its committee on paper, S. E. Thomason of the Chicago *Journal*,

[28] *Ibid.*, p. 41.
[29] *Newsprint Bulletin 21*, Oct. 30, 1928.
[30] *Newsprint Bulletin 22*, Nov. 20, 1928.
[31] Guthrie, *Newsprint Paper Industry*, pp. 57–63.
[32] Ellis, *Print Paper Pendulum*, p. 136.

former ANPA president and then a director, called a meeting of his committee in December and held conferences with Graustein and other newsprint manufacturers.[33] Nothing more was heard by the membership about the newsprint price situation until the end of February 1929, when it was announced that the Hearst interests had agreed to a renegotiated price of $62 a ton in New York. International promptly offered other publishers five-year contracts at that figure. The ANPA committee on paper advised members not to sign five-year contracts without price decrease protection, but did not protest the $62 figure, which was $5 higher than the price anticipated by the committee in October.[34]

When the association's annual meeting convened in April 1929, it was announced that the committee on paper was under heavy fire.[35] E. K. Gaylord, publisher of the *Daily Oklahoman* in Oklahoma City, had written to the ANPA general manager, Lincoln B. Palmer, denouncing the committee on paper. The committee, Gaylord charged, had "lulled the publishers to sleep while allowing the price of newsprint to be raised." And he suggested that the aid given Chairman Thomason by the International Paper Company in the financing of his purchase of the Chicago *Journal* was "a dangerous situation." Gaylord also charged that Elisha Hanson, ANPA counsel in Washington, had opposed a Senate investigation of the newsprint price and monopoly situation and that Hanson had represented the International Paper Company before another congressional committee.

A statement by Thomason explaining his personal position was then read to the assembled ANPA membership. With John Stewart Bryan, publisher of the Richmond, Virginia, *News-Leader* and also a former ANPA president, he had organized the Bryan-Thomason newspapers, holding stock in the Tampa, Florida, *Tribune* and the Greensboro, North Carolina, *Record*. Wishing to return to Chicago, where he had been general manager of the *Tribune*, he purchased with Bryan the financially weakened Chicago *Journal* in 1928. The International Paper Company offered, he said, to market without commissions two million dollars worth of debentures and preferred stock of the *Journal* if Thomason

[33] *Newsprint Bulletin 24*, Dec. 17, 1928.
[34] *Newsprint Bulletin 27*, Feb. 28, 1929; *Newsprint Bulletin 30*, Mar. 9, 1929.
[35] *Report of the Forty-third Annual Meeting* (1929), pp. 177–216.

would sign a ten-year newsprint contract at the prevailing market price and issue International ten thousand shares of common stock. The common stock was to be sold back to the publishers over a five-year period at graduated prices, and Thomason declared that it amounted to only one ninth of the common stock which could be issued by the *Journal*. Thomason said he had told the ANPA board of directors about the situation at the December and March meetings of the group and had offered to resign his committee chairmanship, but his offers had been refused. He also asserted that the committee on paper could do nothing about the Canadian newsprint price situation, because William J. Donovan, first assistant attorney general, had warned the committee not to participate in any price-fixing arrangements.

E. P. Adler of the Davenport, Iowa, *Times*, who had preceded Thomason as chairman of the committee on paper, told the convention that Thomason had merely been acting in the same manner as the ANPA in its newsprint price activities since the decline of the newsprint market price from the postwar panic heights. Adler said he had met with the manufacturers often and had cooperated with them in bringing about an orderly reduction of the price of newsprint, so that there would be no disruption of production facilities. Both Adler and Thomason had taken the view that if publishers took advantage of market conditions to drive the sharpest possible bargains, many paper mills would be forced into bankruptcy, and at some later period they would find the surviving companies charging even higher prices for a lessened supply.

This was a major shift in ANPA policy, as contrasted with the philosophy of the John Norris regime. Former ANPA President Frank P. Glass and others opposed this statement of policy on newsprint activities, but the convention adopted a resolution of confidence in Thomason and his committee. The membership also, after an hour and a half of debate, tabled a resolution offered by Colonel Robert Ewing of the New Orleans *States* which would have put the ANPA on record against ownership of any newspaper by a power or newsprint company as being contrary to sound public policy, to sound journalistic policy, and to principles of press freedom. But J. R. Knowland of the Oakland, California, *Tribune* expressed the sentiments of the majority when he commented: "Any newspaper that may be financed by the International Paper Company in any locality, I believe is handicapped, and most editors would welcome such opposition in almost any city in the United States."

Senator George W. Norris leaped at this chance to investigate power company ownership of newspapers (International Paper being a power company subsidiary), and the Senate ordered the Federal Trade Commission to investigate again the newsprint industry. President Graustein of International explained his plan of securing long-term newsprint contracts by financing various newspapers.[36] He stated that the practice had begun in 1926, when his company had helped to finance the purchase of the Chicago *Daily News* by a group headed by Walter A. Strong, then chairman of the ANPA committee on radio. Besides the Bryan-Thomason newspapers, International had since financed the Boston *Herald* and *Traveler* and to some degree eight other newspapers, including four of the Frank E. Gannett chain. Altogether International had invested $10,849,700 in newspapers between 1926 and 1929. Because of the unfavorable publicity International disposed of nearly all these investments by 1934.[37] Thomason resigned as chairman of the ANPA committee on paper after the 1929 convention closed. He sold the Chicago *Journal* to the *Daily News* and then founded the Chicago *Times*, a lively tabloid which became a strong supporter of the New Deal.

The Federal Trade Commission also noted that some newspapers owned their own newsprint mills, among them the Chicago *Tribune*, New York *Daily News*, New York *Times*, Minneapolis *Tribune*, and St. Paul *Dispatch* and *Pioneer Press*.[38] These papers were not so greatly concerned about the price of newsprint, since its purchase was largely a book transaction. The commission again recommended that publishers of small dailies and weeklies organize buying corporations in order to take advantage of the favorable contract prices, but the publishers and the ANPA took no action.

[36] *Report by the Federal Trade Commission on the Newsprint Paper Industry* (1930), pp. 97ff.
[37] Guthrie, *Newsprint Paper Industry*, p. 104.
[38] *Report by the Federal Trade Commission on the Newsprint Paper Industry* (1930), p. 90.

The price of newsprint in New York for 1929 had finally been set at $62 a ton. In the fall of 1929, with business conditions growing more and more uncertain, the Canada Power and Paper Company and Abitibi announced a price of $67 a ton in New York for 1930, in an attempt to persuade the other members of the Newsprint Institute of Canada and International to make the same five-dollar advance. The ANPA immediately called a special convention of all daily newspaper publishers in New York on December 9.[39]

Three hundred publishers met under the leadership of the new chairman of the ANPA committee on paper, William G. Chandler of the Scripps-Howard newspapers, and denounced the Newsprint Institute of Canada as a monopoly. They asked for federal action to redress the situation and voted not to accept any contracts at the higher rate. International Paper Company then announced that it would maintain its 1929 price of $62 a ton in New York during 1930, and the other companies were forced to yield under the pressure created by the publishers. The publishers had at the same time made it clear that they were willing to pay the 1929 rate during the coming year.

At the ANPA annual meeting in April 1930 Chandler announced that the Newsprint Institute of Canada had suggested that three-and-a-half year contracts be signed, setting a New York price of $62 a ton in 1930, $64 in 1931 and 1932, and $65 in 1933. This, the committee on paper thought, was fair all around, because it stabilized the newsprint production situation to the ultimate advantage of the publishers.

But the deepening depression doomed the stabilization plan to failure. The publishers, who had endorsed the plan to keep the price of newsprint up, saw it fall as the desperate newsprint manufacturers began bidding for customers. This was indeed a queer reversal of the historical position of the two groups. When the Canada Power and Paper Company announced $57 a ton as the price for New York a few days before the 1931 ANPA convention met, starting a break in the newsprint market, Chandler commented that the publishers were less worried about securing a cut in newsprint prices than they were about a disastrous price

[39] *Bulletin 5704*, Dec. 10, 1929.

war which would ruin many mills and allow a few to control the
remaining production and hike prices later.[40]

But there was little anyone could do to save the situation. The
Canadian newsprint manufacturers had been operating at only
84.6 percent of capacity in 1929, when they reached a new peak
of production by making 2,729,000 tons of newsprint. In 1932
Canadian newsprint mills were running at 50 percent of capacity,
producing only 1,914,000 tons.[41] Advertising in American newspapers rapidly declined, until its volume in 1933 was little more
than half the 1929 peak. With their principal customers thus restricting newsprint purchases, the Canadian mills found themselves in a hopeless position. By 1932 seven large Canadian newsprint companies, controlling 58 percent of production, had de-
faulted, leaving International as the only leading manufacturer
still solvent.[42] Price-setting activities were blighted, and the
Newsprint Institute of Canada went into eclipse. The price of
newsprint in New York fell from $53 a ton to $45 during 1932,
and in April 1933 International cut to a rock-bottom price of $40
a ton in New York. This figure, slightly below the over-all United
States wholesale price level, was maintained through 1935 and
was the lowest in the history of the newsprint industry.

American newspaper publishers, now fighting to protect their
own financial position, were no longer able to bolster the sagging
newsprint market through price stabilization agreements. A later
Federal Trade Commission inquiry disclosed that early in 1933
some newsprint manufacturers offered paper to publishers at a
price equivalent to $37 a ton in New York. The commission quot-
ed a letter written at the time by a newsprint manufacturer
which asserted that Chandler's Scripps-Howard organization and
the Hearst papers tried to force the market price down to the $37
figure.[43] ANPA General Manager Cranston Williams, however,
made the following comment about the 1933 market price in his

[40] New York *Times*, Apr. 21, 1931, p. 17; Apr. 24, 1931, p. 16.
[41] Newsprint Association of Canada, *Newsprint Data: 1948* (Montreal: pamphlet, 1948), p. 4.
[42] Guthrie, *Newsprint Paper Industry*, p. 67.
[43] "Newsprint Paper Decree Investigation, A Report Prepared in 1939 by the
Federal Trade Commission," published by the Senate Special Small Business Committee in *Survival of Free Competitive Press*, 79th Cong., 2d sess., Senate Committee Print No. 18 (1947), p. 62.

newsprint report to the 1947 ANPA annual meeting: "Notwithstanding an effort to perpetuate fiction, the $40 price was not a result of publisher chicanery. The facts are that price-determining tonnage was offered at lower prices than $40 a ton and not accepted by publishers who felt the market price should not go lower." The evidence seems clear that the $40 price in New York was set as the natural result of the economic situation and that the publishers and the ANPA were generally willing to accept it as a stabilizing influence.

The next round in the newsprint price situation resulted from the attempt of American manufacturers to utilize the code-making provisions of the National Industrial Recovery Act. The American newsprint makers hoped to stabilize the market and raise prices under an NRA code agreement, and the Canadians hoped to reap some advantage from this New Deal recovery attempt. But the newsprint industry gained little from its participation in the NRA program, because the ANPA opposed any price-fixing agreements. The publishers' opposition stemmed from both their fear of sharp newsprint price increases and their basic opposition to what they considered government interference in economic affairs.

Elisha Hanson, ANPA general counsel and chief association spokesman in legislative matters, opposed the newsprint manufacturers' suggested code, which contained price-fixing provisions, as a "monopolistic effort." [44] The American newsprint makers, who then accepted a code which endeavored to stabilize industry conditions but did not call for price advances, also attempted to set up a joint agreement with Canadian manufacturers. Hanson protested that an "international monopoly" was being proposed, and ANPA opposition prevented any action before the Supreme Court decision invalidating the NRA in 1935. An attempt by Premier Taschereau of Quebec to get the price of newsprint for 1935 raised $2.50 a ton was met by an ANPA threat to boycott Quebec province manufacturers. [45]

The quotation on contracted newsprint in New York rose to $41 a ton in 1936 and to $42.50 in 1937. These prices were set by

[44] *Bulletin 6168*, Sept. 8, 1933.
[45] *Report of the Forty-eighth Annual Meeting* (1934), pp. 254–69; *Report of the Forty-ninth Annual Meeting* (1935), pp. 302–4.

the Great Northern Paper Company, which made early price announcements at levels lower than those desired by other manufacturers. Industry procedure and contract forms called for other newsprint makers to meet the price set by one of the major companies.[46] The International Paper Company, quite justly complaining that newsprint prices had not kept pace with general economic recovery, then jumped the gun in March 1937 and announced a raise to $50 a ton in New York, effective in 1938.[47] When the recession of 1937 became evident in October, the ANPA warned that this rise in the price of newsprint would come close to wrecking a number of newspapers who found their operating costs inflated and their advertising revenue suddenly deflated.

However, after a meeting in New York during November between ANPA General Manager Lincoln B. Palmer, Chairman Chandler of the paper committee, and representatives of the Canadian newsprint companies, it was apparent that the pressure exerted by the premiers of Quebec and Ontario on the manufacturers to maintain wages of Canadian newsprint workers was too great to allow the price increase to be rescinded.[48]

Thus the $50 price in New York was established in 1938, to be maintained until 1943. American daily newspaper publishers were hard-pressed by the business recession, and 160 dailies suspended publication or were consolidated with other papers during the years 1937 to 1939. Canadian newsprint manufacturers, who had operated at 93.9 percent of capacity in 1937 while producing a record total of 3,648,000 tons, had hoped to make real profits at the 1938 price. But production slumped off a million tons in 1938 as newsprint orders from the United States declined, and the manufacturers found themselves operating their mills at 62.4 percent capacity. The percentage of operating capacity used in any one year from 1939 through 1945 ranged between 68 and 78 percent.[49] The price of newsprint had pulled even with the United States wholesale price level after the jump of $7.50 a ton in 1938, but what should have been a profitable market for the

[46] "Newsprint Paper Decree Investigation," pp. 57, 62–63.
[47] *Newsprint Bulletin* 265, Mar. 19, 1937.
[48] *Editor & Publisher*, 70:3 (Dec. 4, 1937).
[49] Newsprint Association of Canada, *Newsprint Data: 1948*, p. 4.

newsprint makers was spoiled first by insufficient demand foɪ
their product and later by wartime production restrictions.

One other prewar occurrence remains to be noted. In April
1938 an ANPA bulletin carried the following headline: "The
Federal Trade Commission Seeks Newsprint Data. Publishers
Not Obligated to Supply Material Sought in Fishing Expeditions
of Government Agencies." [50] The commission's investigation, previously mentioned, was carried out after the Attorney General's
office had received complaints from individual newspaper publishers about the $7.50 jump in the price of newsprint. Its pur-
pose was to ascertain whether or not the terms of the court decree abolishing the Newsprint Manufacturers Association in 1917
had been observed and to search for other possible violations of
the antitrust laws. Reluctance of the ANPA to cooperate with an
investigation of the newsprint industry, as it had been so anxious
to do in the past, may be explained in part by the association's
changed attitude toward newsprint price policies, and in part by
the ANPA leadership's hostile attitude toward activities of the
New Deal administration. In July the American Newspaper
Guild's publication, the *Guild Reporter,* gleefully reproduced the
bulletin quoted above and advanced another reason for ANPA
reluctance to cooperate with the commission. The guild charged
that the ANPA was using the advance in newsprint prices as an
excuse to fight guild-demanded wage increases and the entire
guild unionizing program for editorial employees. [51]

The commission's report criticized the ANPA for its noncoop-
erative attitude. It also pointed out the leadership exercised by
the largest newsprint companies in price-setting activities and
the establishment of a zone price system in 1934. [52] The commission felt that the Canadian provincial governments had laid a

[50] *Bulletin 6618,* Apr. 8, 1938.

[51] *Guild Reporter,* July 18, 1938. The issue of Feb. 21, 1938, carried on page
3 an extensive "exposé" of ANPA newsprint policies. The guild made similar
charges in 1949, when it published a critical study of the newsprint situation:
Clara H. Friedman, *The Newsprint Problem — Ten Questions and Answers* (New
York: American Newspaper Guild, 1949).

[52] The zone system for newsprint pricing established a price for delivered paper
in each of ten areas in the United States. Zone four received the base price, which
was one dollar higher than the price in a score of ports of entry, including New
York. The New York price is used throughout this chapter for the sake of consistency.

heavy hand upon the newsprint manufacturers, but that situation was outside American jurisdiction. No specific evidence of anti-trust law violations was presented.

With the outbreak of World War II in 1939 the American Newspaper Publishers Association bent its energies toward pre-venting a repetition of the "white paper fiasco" of 1920. Cranston Williams, new ANPA general manager, took over direct responsi-bility for newsprint activities of the association. Chandler, How-ard Davis of the New York *Herald Tribune*, and Walter M. Dear of the *Jersey Journal* led in the committee work. The ANPA Me-chanical Department expanded its studies of newsprint waste and, with the newsprint conservation committee, advised various economies in the use of paper.[53] A newspaper pulpwood commit-tee was active in promoting increased cutting of wood for Ameri-can mills. The bulk of the ANPA's activities, however, revolved about the operations of two government wartime agencies, the Office of Price Administration and the War Production Board.

In January 1942 the International Paper Company requested an increase in the price of newsprint, from the $50 figure in New York first set in 1938, to $53 a ton. OPA asked ANPA representa-tives to determine whether or not publishers could absorb the extra cost. The answer was in the negative, and in April the OPA froze the price of newsprint at $50.[54] Nearly a year later, on March 1, 1943, the OPA and the Canadian Wartime Prices and Trade Board announced a $4 increase in the price of newsprint, saying at the same time that Canada thought the price should be still higher to protect the newsprint industry and that studies were continuing. The OPA declared that nine of thirteen Ameri-can newsprint manufacturers had been operating at a loss.[55]

Meanwhile the War Production Board had been studying plans to curtail the use of newsprint and other paper, in order to conserve supplies and allow for decreases in production due to labor scarcity. In October 1942 WPB Chairman Donald M. Nel-son announced the appointment of a Newspaper Industry Ad-visory Committee, with many ANPA leaders among its members,

[53] B *Bulletin 24 – 1944*, Apr. 25, 1944, reports the full list of their recom-mendations.

[54] *Editor & Publisher*, 75:3 (May 2, 1942).

[55] *Ibid.*, 76:7 (Mar. 6, 1943).

to cooperate with the WPB in solving the wartime problems of the American press. William G. Chandler, former chairman of the ANPA committee on paper, was named first director of the printing and publishing division of the WPB. With the advisory committee, he came to the conclusion that various conservation measures, including a reduction in the use of newsprint supplies, were necessary.

Accordingly in January 1943 the WPB issued its famed order L-240, which stated that during the first quarter of 1943 newspapers should use no more newsprint than they did in the corresponding period of 1941 (an average reduction of 10 percent from current use). Magazines were to use 10 percent less paper than they had in 1942. Small papers and magazines were given preferential treatment.[56] The cutbacks in newsprint use were intensified each quarter, as supplies grew more restricted, reaching a basic 23 percent in 1944 and then leveling off until the removal of limitations at the end of 1945. Newsprint reports to the ANPA annual conventions during this period consistently lauded the work of the Newspaper Industry Advisory Committee and the WPB in regulating distribution of newsprint. Congressional critics of the limitation program were advised by *Editor & Publisher* to cease their worrying,[57] but the House established a Newsprint Committee to keep watch on the situation.

The ANPA also accepted without debate a series of OPA-ordered increases in the price of newsprint. A jump to $58 a ton (New York price) was announced in September 1943. The price rose to $61 in April 1945, $67 in January 1946, $74 in August 1946, and $84 in October 1946, just before the death of OPA. The newsprint manufacturers increased the contract price to $90 in April 1947 and to $96 in March 1948. This last figure, the ANPA newsprint report to the 1948 convention said, was a stabilizing price. But in August 1948 newsprint advanced to $100 a ton in New York City, a figure still slightly below the average level of all United States wholesale prices. Meanwhile the spot market price reached $180 a ton before its collapse to near normal figures in early 1949.

The runaway prices of 1920 had been averted, but the demand

[56] *Ibid.*, 76:5 (Jan. 9, 1943), text of the order.
[57] *Ibid.*, 76:36 (Feb. 13, 1943).

from American publishers for additional newsprint to carry large advertising volumes remained unsatisfied. More metropolitan newspapers purchased newsprint mills to obtain control of paper supplies and thus thrust smaller buyers into the open market. Hearings before the Senate's Small Business Committee in 1947 brought a recommendation from the committee for increased voluntary aid to small publishers and others caught by newsprint shortages. In reply, ANPA General Manager Williams explained the operation of the association's "New England Plan." This plan, originating among New England newspapers, made it possible for hard-pressed publishers to meet temporary emergencies by obtaining newsprint on a voluntary loan basis from other publishers. Williams testified that the plan had worked satisfactorily for all daily and weekly newspaper publishers who sought ANPA help when they lacked immediate newsprint supplies.[58] But talk of possible rationing of newsprint supplies remained as an undercurrent. Williams summarized the situation in April 1948 when he said, "The long-range outlook for newsprint indicates a continuing shortage unless production is materially increased by additional machines, the activating of 1,700,000 tons of idle machine capacity overseas, or demand is substantially reduced by a major depression."[59]

The ANPA general manager made this statement despite the fact that American consumption of newsprint exceeded five million tons in 1948, nearly one million tons more than the 1937 prewar high. In April 1949 Williams could report to the ANPA membership that newsprint "supply and demand are nearing a balance," but only because of continued financial inability of most of the world to buy newsprint from Canadian mills. Both the heavy American demand and the extremely short supply in countries outside North America indicated the need for more newsprint production. What were the possibilities?

Canadian production of newsprint shot to an all-time high of 4,983,000 tons in 1948, with the mills operating at 102 percent of capacity. An additional 165,000 tons was scheduled for 1949. But these gains were being made almost solely through improved

[58] *Newsprint Supply and Distribution*, 80th Cong., 1st sess., S. Rept. 150 (1947), p. 13.
[59] *Newsprint Bulletin 28—1948*, Apr. 28, 1948.

production techniques. The Canadian newsprint industry, buffeted by depression and war, had installed only one new papermaking machine since 1930 and had only two new machines under construction in 1948. Although its profits were substantial the industry was wary of being caught in a future newsprint market recession. Large capital investments were being made to improve plants and buy woodlands, but the high cost of installing new papermaking machines (more than double the 1930 cost) was discouraging to publishers who hoped to see additional imports from Canada.[60]

American production of newsprint was 858,000 tons in 1948, and only slightly higher in 1949. This was only half the peak production figure of 1926 and but 150,000 tons above the bottom figure of 1945. Unable to compete with imports from Canada, owners of older American newsprint machines had turned to production of other types of paper products. The one bright spot in the domestic newsprint manufacturing picture was the development of the use of southern pine for newsprint making. Since 1937 the ANPA had watched with interest and encouragement the efforts of the Southern Newspaper Publishers Association to finance construction of newsprint mills in Texas and Alabama. James G. Stahlman, publisher of the Nashville *Banner* and ANPA president from 1937 to 1939, and Cranston Williams, SNPA secretary-manager until 1939, were leaders in the establishment of the Southland Paper Mills at Lufkin, Texas. There the first newsprint successfully manufactured from southern pine was produced in 1940. Southern publishers completed installation of a new papermaking machine at Lufkin in 1948 and provided ten million dollars for the financing of the Coosa River Newsprint Mill in Alabama. These two projects would add 165,000 tons to American production.[61]

Newsprint users also have their eyes on Alaska. Plentiful power supplies and timber stands are available in southeastern Alaska, and surveys were being made for two newsprint companies in 1947. Production could not be expected until 1951 at the earliest,

[60] Newsprint Association of Canada, *Newsprint Data: 1948*, pp. 4–6; *Newsprint Data: 1949*, p. 6. The Canadian production figure includes Newfoundland.

[61] *Newsprint Bulletin 28—1948*, Apr. 28, 1948; *Editor & Publisher*, 81:5 (Nov. 20, 1948).

however.[62] Newfoundland and Scandinavia also offered hope for some additional newsprint production.

Less concern was shown by the ANPA about the problem of the international division of the postwar supply of newsprint. In 1949 Canada, the world's great producer, shipped 84.8 percent of its newsprint to the United States, compared to 72 percent during the years 1935 to 1939. In 1949 the United States was consuming 60.4 percent of the world supply of newsprint, compared to 43.6 percent in the years 1935 to 1939 and 53.8 percent in the years 1925 to 1929. Americans were also taking 80 percent of new production.[63] But other countries, particularly Great Britain, would demand more of the available supply when they recovered their world trade position and obtained dollar credits for newsprint purchases. Those concerned with the problem of international communication of news and opinion felt the need for newsprint abroad was most urgent, as evidenced by the annual reports of the UNESCO Commission on Technical Needs in Press, Film, Radio.

The ANPA has recognized that maintaining reasonable newsprint prices and obtaining adequate supplies will depend upon rapid expansion of existing production facilities. Such an expansion depends in turn, to a great extent, upon the development of cooperative understanding between newspaper publishers, represented by the ANPA, and newsprint manufacturers. The postwar newsprint policy of the ANPA was dedicated to this end. Its successful application remains to be determined.

[62] *Newsprint Supply and Distribution*, p. 16.
[63] Newsprint Association of Canada, *Newsprint Data: 1949*, pp. 8, 18.

CHAPTER XI

The Postal Zone System

THE principle that, as a matter of public policy, newspapers and magazines should be given special service by the United States Post Office Department was well established by 1917.[1] But there was a growing belief that the traditional cent-a-pound rate for second-class mail was too low. Post Office Department claims of annual deficits incurred in the handling of second-class mail ran from 50 to 70 million dollars, with magazines being held responsible for the larger portion of the cost. There seemed to be a plausible argument that both newspapers and magazines should pay a little more of the cost of delivery.

The necessity of raising additional war revenues brought the question of increased postal rates to a head in 1917. The ANPA membership declared itself in favor of the postal zone system, by which a publisher would pay a rate which increased according to the distance of delivery, in preference to an increased flat rate.[2] But the ANPA was not prepared for the proposals Congress had in store.

Word reached Don C. Seitz of the New York *World*, chairman of the ANPA committee on second-class postage, in May 1917 that the Committee on Finance of the Senate was considering adding a second-class postal zone rate provision to the House-approved War Revenue Act. The rates being considered ran from two cents a pound for the first zone (of three hundred miles radius) to six cents a pound for the most distant zone. Seitz immediately exploded into print with a denunciation of these "outrageous proposals" and called Postmaster General Albert S. Bur-

[1] See Chapter VII.
[2] *Report of the Thirty-first Annual Meeting* (1917), p. 23.

leson a "bureaucrat of the narrowest and stupidest sort" for not keeping his finances in order.[3]

Seitz and George A. McAneny of the New York *Times* led the ANPA members who joined with representatives of weekly newspaper and magazine publishers in protests to the Committee on Finance on May 14 and 15, 1917.[4] Asserting that the proposed rates would punish publishers unduly and intimating that there might be some ulterior motive behind them, the publishers used the heavily mailed New York *Times* as an example. The *Times*, then mailing approximately 50,000 copies daily, would be charged more than $250,000 additional postage annually, its manager claimed.[5]

A special ANPA meeting, called for June 21 at the Washington *Evening Star* offices, protested against the proposed postal rate increase and also against any discriminatory war tax on newspapers. The publishers would pay regular war taxes gladly, they said, but not special ones.[6] Nevertheless, the Committee on Finance recommended a 5 percent tax on publishers' profits over $4000, to yield a revenue of $7,500,000. Rejecting a postal zone system, it suggested a rate of 1¼ cents a pound for second-class matter, only a slight increase. The Senate voted down the special tax on publishers' profits, but it adopted an amendment proposed by Senator Kenneth McKellar of Tennessee establishing second-class zone rates of one to six cents a pound.[7]

After a prolonged battle between Senate and House conferees, the War Revenue Act became law on October 3, 1917. During the conferences the publishers had lost much ground, and second-class mail rates under the zone system were distinctly unsatisfactory to newspaper and magazine publishers alike. Publications were to be divided for mailing purposes into editorial and advertising sections. The rate for editorial matter was to be 1¼ cents a pound from July 1, 1918, to July 1, 1919, and 1½ cents a pound after that date, regardless of the zone of delivery. Adver-

[3] New York *Times*, May 10, 1917, p. 3.
[4] *Revenue to Defray War Expenses*, Hearings, 65th Cong., 1st sess., on H. R. 4280 (Washington: Government Printing Office, 1917).
[5] New York *Times*, May 15, 1917, p. 3.
[6] *Report of the Thirty-first Annual Meeting* (1917), supplement.
[7] *Congressional Record*, 65th Cong., 1st sess., Aug. 29, 1917, pp. 6410–16.

tising matter in the publications was to be assessed at the rates shown in the accompanying table.[8]

The ANPA convention of 1918, meeting in April, called these rates "unworkable, unfair, and oppressive" and asked for amendments to the legislation or outright repeal before the rates took effect July 1. Elbert H. Baker of the Cleveland *Plain Dealer*, chairman of the legislative committee, complained, "We didn't work together to fight this — morning, evening, daily, weekly, eastern, and southern papers all presented different views to Congress." The ANPA membership backed a proposed new system of zone rates, ranging from one cent a pound in the first three zones to five cents in the eighth, but despite much agitation by the publishers in Washington, the zone system went into effect July 1, 1918, without modification.

MAILING RATES PER POUND FOR ADVERTISING MATERIAL
(for fiscal years beginning July 1)

Zone	1918–1919	1919–1920	1920–1921	1921 and After
1 and 2	1¼c	1½c	1¾c	2c
3	1½	2	2½	3
4	2	3	4	5
5	2¼	3½	4¾	6
6	2½	4	5½	7
7	3	5	7	9
8	3¼	5½	7¾	10

During 1919 and 1920 the ANPA committee on second-class postage sought constantly to have the second-class rates frozen at the scale set for the period from July 1, 1919, to July 1, 1920. Hearings were obtained by the ANPA on a bill embodying its proposals,[9] but Congress refused to change its decision, and the maximum rates on advertising matter became law in July 1921.

The publishers now took a different tack and encouraged the leaders of the four big printing unions to protest the second-class zone rates. A group of presidents of international unions headed by George L. Berry of the pressmen's union called on President Warren G. Harding in January 1922 to urge a reduction in the second-class postage rates. Such a reduction, they said, would

[8] *Postage Rates 1789–1930*, pp. 21–22.
[9] *Bulletin 4180*, Jan. 31, 1920.

aid in the unemployment situation, acute at that time because of the postwar depression.[10] In March 1922 the American Publishers Conference, with permanent offices in New York, was formed by the ANPA and a group of other publishers' organizations to work for reduction of the zone rates to the 1919–20 level.[11]

No progress was made in Congress during this period, but ANPA President Paul Patterson of the Baltimore *Sun* reported happily to the 1923 annual meeting that five "antagonistic" members of the Committee on the Post Office and Post Roads of the House of Representatives had failed of reelection. The way had been cleared for possible future action.

The struggle over second-class postage rates now became involved with an attempt by Post Office employees to obtain salary increases. S. E. Thomason, then general manager of the Chicago *Tribune*, warned the 1924 ANPA convention that the Postmaster General had declared that newspapers supporting the bill increasing postal employees' salaries could expect to meet some of the cost. A long fight between President Calvin Coolidge and Congress over financing of postal salary increases, during which Coolidge twice vetoed postal bills, finally resulted in a new set of zone rates for second-class matter which varied only slightly, in the more distant zones, from the 1921 rates. During the controversy, members of the ANPA committee on second-class postage conferred with the President and threatened to use other means than the mails to distribute newspapers if some adjustment was not forthcoming.[12] The committee, which had raised $35,000 from ANPA members to finance its activities, was finally satisfied when a Special Joint Subcommittee on Postal Rates, with three senators and three representatives as members, was appointed in February 1925 to canvass the entire second-class mail situation.[13]

The special congressional committee began hearings in July 1925 which extended into the following year. ANPA representatives appeared together with other publishers' spokesmen at many sessions held in various cities across the country.[14] Among the as-

---

[10] Shideler, "Second-Class Matter," p. 95.

[11] *Bulletin 4580*, Mar. 18, 1922.

[12] *Bulletin 4980*, Nov. 22, 1924; *Bulletin 4991*, Dec. 13, 1924.

[13] *Bulletin 5030*, Mar. 2, 1925.

[14] *Postal Rates*, Hearings, 69th Cong., 1st sess. (Washington: Government Printing Office, 1926).

sociation leaders who took part were Jerome D. Barnum of the Syracuse *Post-Standard*, chairman of the ANPA committee on second-class postage; ANPA General Manager Lincoln B. Palmer; Elisha Hanson, ANPA general counsel; Howard Davis of the New York *Herald Tribune*; and Louis Wiley of the New York *Times*.

During the hearings, and throughout this period, the ANPA emphasized that motor trucks and express services were competing with the Post Office Department. The committee on second-class postage declared that 100 pounds of second-class matter could be distributed out of New York City for 50 cents by railroad baggage, 68 cents by truck, $1.00 by express, and $1.80 by mail, in the first and second zones. It also reported that the Indianapolis *News* had established its own "RFD" system, delivering its evening edition on the day of publication at savings of 60 cents on each 100 pounds, and had cut its mail circulation from 19,000 to 9000 copies.[15] The same year, 1927, a study showed that 49 evening papers maintained 249 motor routes totaling 16,000 miles in length, and 37 morning dailies had established 238 routes totaling 19,177 miles. The papers reported circulation increases of 20 to 35 percent along the fast delivery routes.[16] Publishers rapidly adopted these more economic means of distribution with the effect of creating indirect pressure for reduced postal rates.

In 1927, as a result of the special subcommittee's investigation, the Senate voted to return second-class zone rates to the 1919–20 level of 1½ to 5½ cents a pound, and the ANPA postal committee hailed "the first victory for ANPA in this long struggle." [17] The measure failed of final approval by Congress, however. In December 1927 Chairman Barnum of the committee on second-class postage announced that he had been assured by the chairmen of the Senate and House Post Office committees that a bill reducing second-class rates would pass in 1928. The next month Barnum asked ANPA members to send Elisha Hanson, association general counsel, statements as to how much increased use of the mails would result from the reduced rates.[18]

---

[15] *Bulletin 5316*, Jan. 4, 1927.
[16] Lee, *Daily Newspaper in America*, p. 310.
[17] *Bulletin 5317*, Jan. 12, 1927.
[18] *Bulletin 5485*, Dec. 28, 1927; *Bulletin 5491*, Jan. 20, 1928.

The House Committee on the Post Office and Post Roads heard the testimony of ANPA representatives once again on February 10.[19] Hanson, Barnum, and Palmer appeared before the committee, and Hanson testified that member publishers had indicated they would materially increase use of the mails if rates were reduced to the 1919–20 level of 1½ to 5½ cents a pound. The House, however, decided to use the 1920–21 rates of 1¾ to 7¾ cents.

When the ANPA convention met in April the membership was informed that victory was in sight. The Senate had approved an amendment by Senator McKellar putting the 1919–20 rate back into the bill. And when the measure was finally approved in May, with second-class zone rates varying only slightly from the 1919–20 levels, the ANPA committee on second-class postage again urged members to increase their use of the mails.[20] The zone rates continued to apply only to advertising portions of publications; editorial portions were to be charged at 1½ cents a pound in all zones, as before. Free-in-county circulation for weekly papers was maintained, as was the rate of one cent a pound for carrier delivery in the county of publication, and one cent a copy for carrier delivery in the city of publication.[21] The 1928 zone rates compared with previous charges, and with the final ANPA recommendation, as follows:

Zone	1921 Rate	1925 Rate	1928 Rate	Rate Wanted by ANPA
1 and 2	2c	2c	1½c	1½c
3	3	3	2	2
4	5	6	3	3
5	6	6	4	3½
6	7	6	5	4
7	9	9	6	5
8	10	9	7	5½

In 1932 a sudden amendment to a postal revenue bill caught the ANPA committee on second-class postage flat-footed and brought restoration of the 1921 rates of two to ten cents a pound.[22] Designed as a revenue-producing measure, the increase

[19] Regulating Postal Rates, Hearings, 70th Cong., 1st sess., on H. R. 9296 (Washington: Government Printing Office, 1928), pp. 107–28.
[20] Bulletin 5532, June 1, 1928.
[21] Postage Rates 1789–1930, pp. 27, 53–54.
[22] Bulletin 5989, June 2, 1932.

failed of its purpose during the next two years. In 1934 the second-class zone rates of 1928 were again restored and remained unchanged through 1949. Again in 1942 the House seriously considered increases in second-class rates, but after some agitation among the publishers, the proposed increases were abandoned.[23] The ANPA's postal committee continued to guard against attempts to alter the rates.

Throughout this period the ANPA continued to deny Post Office Department assertions that a tremendous "subsidy" was being afforded publishers of newspapers and magazines by the government. In 1935 James G. Stahlman, chairman of the postal group, maintained that the Post Office figure of an 86 million dollar deficit on handling second-class matter was wrong, because costs attributed to the handling of publications were grossly and erroneously assessed.[24] In any event it should be noted that the daily newspapers, which ANPA represented, were charged by the Post Office Department with only about 30 million dollars of the total 86 million dollar deficit.[25] The problems of the magazines have not been touched upon here, but by the 1930s they had come to rely far more on the postal service than the larger newspapers did.

In March 1947 the Post Office Department again made a serious attempt to secure congressional approval of higher second-class postal rates. The Postmaster General proposed that the rate on the editorial portion of publications be raised from 1½ to 2½ cents a pound, and that the zone rates on advertising portions each be jumped one cent a pound. In addition, he suggested surcharges on publications carrying high percentages of advertising.[26]

Josh L. Horne of the Rocky Mount, North Carolina, *Telegram*, chairman of the ANPA postal committee, and Elisha Hanson protested against the Post Office recommendation before the House Post Office and Civil Service Committee on March 19. Horne declared that the second-class mail was not a subsidy but a service. He insisted that Post Office claims of tremendous deficits on

[23] *Editor & Publisher*, 75:3 (July 11, 1942).
[24] *Report of the Forty-ninth Annual Meeting* (1935), p. 296.
[25] Lee, *Daily Newspaper in America*, p. 311.
[26] *Federal Laws Bulletin 14—1947*, Mar. 5, 1947.

handling second-class matter were the result of a faulty accounting system. The various classes of mail had been charged in an arbitrary manner for the costs of various public policy services, such as rural free delivery, free-in-county mail, and star routes to remote sections, Horne said. Thus in 1945, 34 percent of the cost of rural free delivery service had been charged to the second-class mail, accounting for one third of the claimed deficit. Horne also declared the Post Office was giving inadequate service and was assessing "shadow" charges against publishers for sorting, weighing, and transporting services which they themselves performed.[27]

The ANPA also told Congress that in 1946 the Post Office Department had carried 300 million fewer pounds of newspapers than in 1919. The Post Office was still depending primarily upon railroad transportation, and the newspapers were taking to the highways by truck on their own initiative. In 1946 only 12 percent of daily and Sunday newspaper circulation, nearly all on rural routes, was still going through the mails.[28]

The House Post Office Committee approved a bill raising second-class rates, but Congress took no action on it. Instead the House ordered a thorough investigation of the postal service. Through this investigation, the postal committee told the 1948 ANPA convention, it was hoped that a valid accounting system would be established.

However, a fresh attack on second-class mail rates was launched by the Post Office Department in 1949, with the approval of President Truman. Again newspaper and magazine publishers presented their arguments against the sharp increases proposed by the Post Office. No legislation was passed during the year, but committees of both the House and Senate approved bills which would go before Congress early in 1950. These bills would increase the long-standing zone rates of 1½ to 7 cents a pound on the advertising portions of publications to a scale of 2 to 10 cents. Reading portions, charged at 1½ cents a pound since 1919, would jump to 2 cents. The committee recommendations represented substantial reductions of the original Post Office Department proposals.

[27] *Federal Laws Bulletin 16—1947*, Mar. 19, 1947.
[28] *Federal Laws Bulletin 21—1947*, Apr. 9, 1947

The ANPA scored one major point in 1948, when Postmaster General Jesse Donaldson told a Senate committee, "I do not believe that it would be ethical to say that the amount of money we lost on second-class mail would be a subsidy, but it is a loss; it runs to 160 million dollars. . . ." [29]

The ANPA was pleased by the Postmaster General's rejection of the word *subsidy*. Its continuing stand against the department's claim of excessive loss on handling second-class mail is summarized in this statement by the postal committee to the 1948 annual meeting:

The ANPA has taken the position before Congressional committees that newspapers do not object to paying for services comparable to those rendered by private agencies of transportation and distribution, rates which are also comparable to those charged by private agencies. Newspapers do object strenuously, however, to rates which are materially higher for services which are less efficient or, in some cases, for services which are actually not rendered by the postal services.

[29] *Federal Laws Bulletin 31 — 1948*, June 3, 1948.

CHAPTER XII

Troubled Years in Labor Relations

FROM 1900 to 1922 the American Newspaper Publishers Association and the four big mechanical unions representing the printing trades were committed to a negotiatory policy in labor-management relations. International arbitration agreements, given force by local agreements between publishers and unions, had proved mutually advantageous.[1] Daily newspaper publishers and their employees in the closed-shop mechanical unions had conducted their contract bargaining in a manner contrasting sharply with belligerent struggles in many other industries. The gradual deterioration, at the national level, in this labor-management relationship after 1922 forms the theme of this later chapter in association labor relations history.

In 1920 the ANPA had international arbitration agreements with all four major printing trades unions — the International Typographical Union, the International Stereotypers and Electrotypers' Union, the International Photo-Engravers' Union, and the International Printing Pressmen and Assistants' Union. The pressmen had withdrawn from their arbitration agreement in 1912, but rejoined the fold in 1920. A record number of 605 local arbitration agreements were in force, prohibiting strikes, boycotts, and lockouts, and providing for settlement of disputes over wages, hours, and working conditions through processes of negotiation and arbitration.

Despite this record of accomplishment, made possible by constructive leadership in both labor and management groups, there were warnings of trouble to come. The unions had succeeded in writing into the international arbitration agreements a clause which said that provisions of international union law — ex parte

[1] See Chapter V.

statements by the unions — were not subject to arbitration. More and more, publishers insisted that these statements of union practices affected the conduct of the publishers' businesses and should be arbitrable. Particularly under fire were union rulings requiring that all local advertising copy supplied in mat form be reset by machine or by hand, and providing for union control of the training and promotion of personnel in the shops.

Relations between the publishers and the mechanical unions were strained, too, by a series of strikes and labor disturbances including 41 illegal strikes in ANPA member plants during 1919 and early 1920. Such labor-management conflicts were common in the country as it faced the high cost of living and the "Red menace" during the period of postwar reaction. When the typographers and stereotypers announced that they would insist upon a maximum 44-hour week after May 1921, the ANPA queried, "When will the world's work be done?"[2] Publishers of daily newspapers generally avoided strikes over the 44-hour week question, but other publishers and printing firms had 500 strikes on their hands during 1921 and 75 more in 1922 and 1923, while the International Typographical Union spent 14 million dollars for defensive purposes during that period.[3]

All this provided a poor setting for the attempt to renew the five-year international arbitration agreements which expired in May 1922. The 1921 ANPA convention named a committee on arbitrations of twenty-five members and ordered it to insist that all points of difference between publishers and unions — including those covered by union law — be subject to arbitration. Victor F. Lawson of the Chicago *Daily News*, who had argued vainly against the international union law provisions in 1912, was named chairman of the committee. Among its members were two publishers whose names rarely figured in ANPA history — Roy W. Howard and Frank E. Gannett.

Negotiations for the new arbitration agreements foundered over this ANPA stand on the question of union laws. Lawson reported to the 1922 convention that only the pressmen would accept a new five-year agreement on the ANPA's terms. The typog-

[2] *Report of the Thirty-fourth Annual Meeting* (1920), p. 224.
[3] Lee, *Daily Newspaper in America*, p. 149.

raphers' leaders had refused to submit to a union referendum any arbitration agreement not exempting union law provisions, and the stereotypers and photoengravers followed suit. There was no demand from the membership that the ANPA retreat on the issue, and the die was cast. International arbitration agreements with unions other than the pressmen ceased to exist, although local arbitration contracts continued in force, and the international arbitration machinery was left available for use in specific cases by mutual consent.

The Special Standing Committee, headed by H. N. Kellogg, and the committee on arbitrations continued to work for new agreements with the big typographical union and also with the stereotypers and photoengravers. But the only concrete result was a compromise agreement with the International Typographical Union which failed to meet union approval.[4] Strangely enough, the worst labor trouble in this period was caused by an "outlaw" strike of New York City pressmen in 1923, which forced the metropolitan dailies to suspend publication and issue the *Combined New York Morning Newspapers* for a week.[5] However, five-year extensions of the international agreement with the pressmen's union were approved in 1927, 1932, 1937, 1942, and 1947. Harvey J. Kelly, who succeeded Kellogg as Special Standing Committee chairman (a paid position) in 1926, reported to the 1928 ANPA convention that association members had 501 local arbitration agreements still in force, a loss of only 104 from the 1920 peak. Of these, 134 were with pressmen's locals and 367 were with typographers, stereotypers, and photoengravers. Kelly also said that there had been only seven strikes in ANPA member plants during 1927. Thus the arbitration and negotiation principle continued to show strength.

Collapse of all but one of the arbitration agreements on a national scale in 1922, however, opened the way for a minority of the ANPA membership to insist upon a belligerent move — the founding of an Open Shop Division. The United Typothetae of America, representing publishing businesses other than newspapers, had founded an Open Shop Division in 1912,[6] and some

---

[4] *Report of the Forty-first Annual Meeting* (1927), p. 241.
[5] Mott, *American Journalism*, p. 678.
[6] Bonnett, *Employers' Associations*, p. 261.

ANPA members viewed it as a source of strength. They took advantage of the setback to the association's established labor relations policy to obtain passage of the following resolution at the 1922 annual meeting:

. . . the time has arrived when the American Newspaper Publishers Association should set up an Open Shop Division to be maintained and operated without prejudice or opposition to any other department of the organization, such a division to constitute a unit of the organization to which publishers who wish to establish and maintain open shop conditions in their mechanical departments may turn for aid, therefore be it resolved That the Board of Directors be instructed to proceed at once to set up an Open Shop Division of the American Newspaper Publishers Association under such conditions as will enable it to become a substantial aid to members who desire permanently to operate under open shop conditions, it being definitely understood that this department under no circumstances is to be used merely as a strike-breaking organization.

The publishers of papers which had refused to deal with the closed-shop mechanical unions argued that they did not receive much service from the Special Standing Committee. They also pointed out that there was no encouragement of the open-shop theory by the association, although between 10 and 15 percent of the ANPA membership operated open-shop or nonunion establishments.

In June 1922 an open-shop committee was appointed, headed by D. D. Moore of the New Orleans *Times-Picayune* and having as members Harry Chandler of the Los Angeles *Times* and W. A. Elliott of the *Florida Times-Union* of Jacksonville.[7] Herbert W. Flagg was employed as executive secretary in September and the board of directors gave the committee $5000 for expenses.[8]

All members of the ANPA operating open or nonunion shops immediately became members of the new Open Shop Division, the committee in charge reported to the 1923 convention. Of the 534 ANPA members that year, 38 maintained open shops and 18 operated nonunion shops. These publishers pledged themselves to furnish one or more men at the call of the Open Shop Division's executive secretary "to work in any office where there was trouble." The publisher aided was to reimburse the one sending

[7] *Bulletin 4634*, June 8, 1922.
[8] *Report of the Thirty-seventh Annual Meeting* (1923), p. 338.

help and to return the employee when the "trouble" was over. "At least two employers operating open shops have been able to avoid what threatened to be serious trouble through the fact that the Open Shop Division was ready to give prompt assistance," the committee said.

Creation of the Open Shop Division as an official activity of the ANPA of course antagonized the closed-shop mechanical unions. During the early 1920s the ANPA adopted another program which was viewed with distrust by the unions. This was a program of extending aid to printing trades schools training potential employees. To some this action seemed necessary in order to maintain an adequate number of workers in the specialized printing occupations; to others it appeared to be a move to train nonunion men for open-shop publishers and to undermine the apprentice training program of the unions.

The ANPA could point to the fact that in 1913 President James M. Lynch of the International Typographical Union had asked the publishers for aid in schooling apprentices.[9] No action was taken then by the ANPA, but labor shortages in 1919 caused the association to appoint a committee on typesetting machine schools. D. D. Moore of the New Orleans *Times-Picayune* reported for the committee that schools for Linotype and Intertype machine operators should be established and that voluntary payments should be made by ANPA members to support them.[10] By 1922 some seventy members of the Southern Newspaper Publishers Association and fifty ANPA members were supporting a school at Macon, Georgia, which the ITU now frowned upon as a threat to union standards.[11]

A definite policy on printing trades schools was adopted at the 1923 ANPA annual meeting, when it was decided that the association would sponsor a series of regional schools in cooperation with newspapers in the areas. More than $25,000 was collected from the ANPA membership through a special assessment, and a committee on printing trades schools was named, headed by Victor F. Ridder of the New York *Staats-Zeitung*. The committee approved four training centers: the Pacific Northwest School of

[9] *Report of the Twenty-seventh Annual Meeting* (1913), p. 45.
[10] *Bulletin 4251*, Nov. 7, 1919.
[11] *Report of the Thirty-sixth Annual Meeting* (1922), p. 377.

Printing at Spokane, the Empire State School of Printing at Ithaca, the Southeastern School of Printing at Nashville, and the
Southwest School of Printing at Dallas.[12] During 1924 these
schools graduated 178 students, and the ANPA paid them $100
for each graduate, supplementing the tuition fees. The Chicago
Photo-Engravers' School and the New England School of Printing were added to the list in 1927, but the depression eliminated
all but the Ithaca, Nashville, and Dallas schools before 1936.[13]
The expense to the ANPA had reached a high of $22,600 in 1929,
and eventually the association decided that the financial support
of the schools was essentially a regional activity. It ceased its official printing trades school activities in 1943, when war conditions
virtually closed the schools, although the association remained
interested in such projects.

Open-shop activities of the ANPA were expanded in June
1923, when Flagg was made full-time manager of an office in
Philadelphia, and the division became known as the Open Shop
Department. Charles A. Webb of the Asheville *Citizen-Times*
was named chairman of the open-shop committee in 1924, a position he held for the remainder of the committee's lifetime. Webb
pointed out in 1925, when he reported to the annual meeting,
that nonunion and open-shop printing establishments had three
times as many apprentices in proportion to trained men as did
union shops, and declared that the ANPA-supported printing
trades schools were needed to offset union curtailment of apprentices.

Manager Flagg told the 1926 ANPA convention that the Open
Shop Department was giving wage negotiation assistance to its
member employers, similar to that given union-shop employers
by the Special Standing Committee. Concerning his activities in
1925, he said, "In a few instances men have been assembled and
held in readiness . . . on no occasion were they needed." As the
association put it very well in a promotion pamphlet issued in
1926, "The Open Shop Department is enthusiastically endorsed
by members making use of its facilities. While in no sense of the
word a strike-breaking organization, the widespread knowledge
of its operations has frequently had such psychological effect that

[12] *Report of the Thirty-eighth Annual Meeting* (1924), p. 163.
[13] *Report of the Fiftieth Annual Meeting* (1936), p. 378.

many labor union difficulties have resulted in amicable settlement." [14]

Flagg continued to report to the annual meetings on his activities. During 1926 crews were assembled and held for quick call
in several cities, but none was needed. Two Canadian papers used
men sent by the Open Shop Department in 1927, but the strike
ended in two days. Then came the busy year 1928, during which
twenty-six calls for assistance were received by the Open Shop
Department, and the full character of its work was revealed.

During February 1928, Flagg told the 1929 convention, two
New Jersey dailies "changed from union to non-union shops" and
therefore crews were supplied by the Open Shop Department to
work during a strike. In November the ITU called a strike against
four Albany, New York, dailies, and Flagg reported that his department sent substitute typographers within twenty-four hours.
The Open Shop Department sent two hundred men in the first
contingent — a "clean sweep" of the four shops — and increased
the number to three hundred during the next fifteen weeks.
There were fights in the streets and one acid-throwing case,
Flagg said, but the strike came to an end in March 1929, with the
union men reemployed.

Thus the Open Shop Department, which heretofore had been
mainly interested in preventing unionization or other difficulties
in open shops, now definitely was intervening in union shop
areas, in violation of the spirit of the 1922 resolution establishing
the department. The publishers in Albany had declared themselves "open shop" when the ITU members walked out, thus permitting the Open Shop Department to intervene. But they had
promptly declared themselves "closed shop" again at the end of
the strike. Flagg protested that he did not know the intent of the
publishers and had acted in good faith. But the effect was that
many critics viewed the Albany case as a strikebreaking effort
supported by the Open Shop Department.

Manager Flagg received the help of an assistant, R. C. Hallock,
in November 1929,[15] and the expenses of the Open Shop Department increased to $9376 that year. By 1932 they were $14,074,

[14] *Forty Years Record of ANPA.*
[15] *Bulletin 5694*, Nov. 19, 1929.

and Flagg's supply of available nonunion men had been increased by the depression, as were his calls for assistance as union and nonunion men alike fought against pay decreases.

At the 1932 ANPA convention, the Special Standing Committee, headed by Harvey J. Kelly, launched a major attack on wage scales of mechanical employees, using graphs and charts for the first time in the history of ANPA bulletins and annual reports. Taking 1914 as a base year, Kelly reported that the average annual earnings of ITU members had risen as follows: 1914, 100; 1919, 125; 1920, 175; 1923, 200; 1929, 231.9; 1931, 217.8. The cost of living, Kelly said, had averaged 175 during the 1920s in comparison with 1914 and stood at 150 in 1931. Advertising volume, which doubled between 1914 and 1929, had fallen to 150 in 1931. Kelly therefore recommended wage cuts of 20 to 25 percent, or smaller cuts coupled with abolition of "all costly and wasteful labor rules" enforced by the unions. When the ITU announced it would insist on a forty-hour week beginning in January 1933, the Special Standing Committee opposed the move, until the coming of the NRA brought general adoption of the forty-hour week.

How this campaign on the wage and hour question fared is shown by the accompanying tabulation, which gives the average hours worked each week and the average hourly wage received by ITU members in thirty-six leading cities (day wages, six-day week).[16]

Year	Hours Worked	Hourly Wage
1930	46.0	$1.135
1933	45.7	1.094
1934	45.8	1.053
1935	43.6	1.126
1937	39.5	1.188
1940	38.2	1.266
1948	37.2	2.170

While advertising volume decreased drastically during the depression years, circulation of daily newspapers remained comparatively steady, and unemployment among newspaper mechanical employees, except in cases of suspension of publication, was relatively low. And as the figures show, not much of a dent

[16] *Editor & Publisher International Year Book* statistics.

was made in hourly wage payments, in so far as the larger dailies were concerned. Less strongly organized employees of smaller papers and those workers not protected by union contracts suffered more.

Meanwhile the Open Shop Department had advanced to the point where the ANPA said of it, "The savings resulting from its operations are known only to those who have profited by its help."[17] Manager Flagg told the 1933 convention that 1932 had been a "busy and active year" with economy drives and union troubles bringing an increase in open shops greater than in any of the past twenty years. Flagg said: "Crews have been taken to Wichita, Kan.; Paterson, N.J.; Springfield, Ill.; Holyoke, Mass.; Bayonne, N.J.; Minneapolis, Minn.; New Haven, Conn.; Gloversville, N.Y.; New Bedford, Mass.; and San Francisco, Cal."[18] The following year Flagg reported receiving twenty calls for aid and having a large supply of employable printers; in 1935 better economic conditions had cut the supply of men and increased the labor disputes. That year *Editor & Publisher* reported that it "was told unofficially that Mr. Flagg offered the services of his committee to all publishers, members and non-members, for strike-breaking purposes."[19]

The Open Shop Department's activities came to a sudden halt early in 1937 when the Allied Printing Trades Council of Greater New York and the American Newspaper Guild asked the Senate Civil Liberties Committee to investigate.[20] Passage of the Norris-La Guardia Act, forbidding the transportation of strikebreakers across state lines, made it clear that this ANPA activity was contrary to majority opinion. ANPA convention proceedings abruptly ceased to carry reports of the Open Shop Department, although treasurer's reports continued to list expenditures for the department through 1941. Apparently only routine activity continued.[21]

The American Newspaper Guild offered two "exposés" of the

[17] *What the ANPA Means in Dollars and Cents* (pamphlet, 1932).
[18] Also reported in *Editor & Publisher*, 65:66 (Apr. 29, 1933).
[19] *Editor & Publisher*, 67:9 (Apr. 27, 1935).
[20] *Guild Reporter*, Feb. 15, 1937.
[21] When Flagg died in 1948, an ANPA bulletin said he "had been associated with the ANPA since 1922."

Open Shop Department in the August and September 1937 issues of the *Guild Reporter*. The guild claimed that ANPA President James G. Stahlman's Nashville *Banner* was a clearing agency for the "H. W. Flagg Agency (notorious strike-breaking organization)." When Flagg brought a crew to a struck plant, the *Guild Reporter* asserted, he got a sixty-day renewable contract to run the shop, put his key men in as supervisors of a strikebreaking crew, and established an open shop which became a reservoir for later strikebreaking activities. The newspaper paid the expenses of bringing in the new crew and maintaining it "at the best hotels."[22]

Whatever condemnation there may be of the activities of the Open Shop Department, it should be remembered that in the 1930s more than 85 percent of the ANPA membership maintained union shops, and these publishers in the main seemed satisfied with their labor arrangements.

A new labor relations problem was presented to the ANPA in the early 1930s when the American Newspaper Guild came into existence. The story of that organization and its conflicts with the ANPA is more logically told in a later chapter. It should be noted here, however, that by 1935 the guild had advanced its cause sufficiently among editorial and office employees of daily newspapers to attract the attention of the Special Standing Committee. Chairman Harvey J. Kelly commented that the guild was not covered in his report to the annual meeting because it was led by a "round and overstuffed gentleman who delights in preening in public."[23] The guild, Kelly said as a personal prediction, would die within a year under the leadership of this gentleman, who was Heywood Broun.

The following year Kelly warned the association convention that increases in pay for mechanical employees would bring demands from the guild for similar raises for editorial and office workers. Kelly left the ANPA staff later in 1936 to become general counsel on labor for all Hearst newspapers. His successor as Special Standing Committee chairman was Eugene MacKinnon, former editor of the Billings, Montana, *Gazette*. MacKinnon rec-

[22] *Guild Reporter*, Aug. 15, 1937; Sept. 13, 1937.
[23] *Editor & Publisher*, 67:7 (Apr. 27, 1935).

ognized the permanency of the guild and began a policy of studying and reporting the number of contracts between ANPA member publishers and guild units.

Thus the Special Standing Committee and its paid staff in the Chicago office added a new service to the ANPA membership. The greatest accomplishment of the labor relations staff was the building up of cross-indexed files of arbitration decisions and local contracts made since 1901 and the listing of ex parte decisions of the ITU executive council announced since 1913. Use of these files often saved publishers much money, the ANPA states, citing as one notable example an award of $250,000 to Chicago pressmen for excess back time which was reversed when the Special Standing Committee found that back awards could be made only for wages and not for working conditions.[24] The annual expenses of the committee, totaling $25,000 in 1918, rose to $47,000 in 1929, ran between $40,000 and $45,000 during the depression years, and increased to $59,406 by 1940.

During World War II government regulation of labor-management policies brought a period of stability to the newspaper publishing business, as to all other businesses. The wartime wage controls established in 1942 and 1943 brought about the formation of the Newspaper Advisory Council by the National War Labor Board on February 24, 1943. With two employers' representatives, two employees' representatives, and two representatives of the public, it passed upon wage increase requests. John S. McCarrens of the Cleveland *Plain Dealer* and James E. Chappell of the Birmingham *News* were named as publisher representatives. George N. Dale, who in 1942 succeeded MacKinnon as chairman of the ANPA Special Standing Committee, was an alternate employer representative.[25] For the duration of the war the operations of this council in carrying out government wage policies and the existence of labor's no-strike pledge kept daily newspaper labor relations problems at a minimum.

During the war and immediate postwar period the ANPA continued to advocate the principles of negotiation and arbitration which formed its historic labor relations policy. General Manager

[24] *What the ANPA Means in Dollars and Cents.*
[25] *Editor & Publisher,* 76:5 (Feb. 27, 1943).

Cranston Williams told the 1946 ANPA convention that the association would try to restore all the international arbitration agreements, declaring: "Until a better means of determining industrial disputes is available, the ANPA affirms its long-established policy of voluntary arbitration. If conciliation fails in the absence of voluntary arbitration, no other machinery seems available except compulsory arbitration."

The photoengravers in 1947 voted to seek an arbitration agreement covering settlement of existing contracts, but not negotiations of new agreements.[26] The Special Standing Committee reported to the 1948 ANPA convention that it hoped to restore national arbitration machinery for both the photoengravers and stereotypers. Local arbitration agreements were flourishing. They totaled 761 in 1941, reached an all-time high of 1125 in 1943 under wartime labor policies, and stood at 963 in 1947. Of these, 239 were with pressmen who had continued their national agreement, and 373 were with the typographers. The ITU in 1945 barred its locals, however, from using the unofficial international arbitration machinery which had survived the collapse of the 1922 negotiations. This action by the ITU was a setback to the arbitration policy.

Nationwide labor-management disputes over cost-of-living wage increases and maintenance of take-home pay levels in the postwar readjustment period were another indication of new troubles to come. The ANPA in October 1946 therefore engaged the services of Robert N. McMurry and Company to conduct an industrial relations survey for daily newspaper publishers. The survey was to evaluate the functions and activities of the Special Standing Committee, to analyze unsolved problems in newspapers' industrial relations, and to make recommendations for handling those problems effectively. The McMurry report to the ANPA board of directors in July 1947 gives us a picture of ANPA labor relations activity at that moment.[27]

First of all, the report noted an intensification of union activity and effort since the 1930s and the organization of new groups of workers in the nonmechanical departments by the American

[26] *Ibid.*, 80:28 (Aug. 30, 1947).
[27] *B Bulletin 25–1947*, July 9, 1947.

Newspaper Guild. It asserted, as did the ANPA itself, that the international mechanical unions had developed dynamic, aggressive leadership which attempted to dominate local units and determine the character of local settlements. Publishers, whose businesses were of a local character, were opposed to economic bargaining on a national basis. But they often delegated the handling of labor relations problems to unqualified executives who could not deal with the union negotiators or resist the organized union campaigns. The report warned that total newspaper labor costs had risen "well over 100 per cent" since 1941 and, combined with other added costs, threatened the stability of the individual publishing businesses.

The Special Standing Committee, originally organized to facilitate arbitration agreements, now had as its major function the supplying of information about labor problems through its bulletins, loose-leaf wage scale reports, and reports to city publishers' associations. It also provided advice and counsel on labor relations to individual publishers, supplying them with bargaining information and contract forms whenever possible. The report recommended that these services be expanded and tailored to the requirements of specific cases.

The report urged that the Special Standing Committee be renamed and given authority to develop a comprehensive and forceful labor relations program for daily newspapers. The committee must initiate and promote constructive industrial relations policies and programs and sell them to all publishers, the report continued. The activities of city publishers' associations must be coordinated with such a national program. A comprehensive research program in the field of industrial relations, an educational program designed to better individual newspapers' personnel activities, and the establishment of a field service to assist publishers in labor negotiations were other major recommendations. Out of such a program, the report said, could come a new understanding with the union leadership, based upon mutual respect and confidence.

Hardly had the McMurry report been filed with the ANPA board of directors when the gradually deteriorating relationship between the ANPA and the International Typographical Union exploded into a major conflict. The cause was the passage by Congress of the Labor-Management Relations Act of 1947, known as the Taft-Hartley Act, which among other things outlawed the closed shop. The typographers, as a powerful traditional craft union with an organizational history running back for more than a century, were logical candidates among the closed-shop unions to challenge the provisions of the Taft-Hartley law. The ANPA, with sixty years of experience in the daily newspaper labor relations field, was quick to take up the challenge.

During 1947 the ITU was involved in 32 of 39 labor disputes which affected 64 daily newspapers.[28] The ANPA, feeling that relationships between publishers and typographers had reached a crisis point, asked on September 9, 1947, that a conference be held between members of the ANPA Special Standing Committee and the ITU executive council. The offer was made in a letter from George N. Dale, Special Standing Committee chairman, to Woodruff Randolph, president of the ITU.[29] In the letter Dale denied what he termed allegations by ITU leaders that the ANPA was conspiring against the union and reaffirmed ANPA devotion to the principles of collective bargaining and arbitration of disputes. Randolph accepted the offer, and the conference dates were set for September 25 and 26 in Indianapolis. In the meantime Dale strengthened his hand by concluding a new five-year international arbitration agreement with President George L. Berry of the pressmen's union.[30] It might be noted that Berry had been one of the group of union leaders who had actively promoted the original arbitration agreements in the first decade of the century.

When the ANPA and ITU representatives met in Indianapolis, they quickly found their positions irreconcilable. A proposal by the ANPA called for abandonment of the closed shop under the Taft-Hartley Act mandate, curtailment of what it called ITU "featherbedding" practices, and other changes in ITU international union law provisions, as a prelude to the writing of an arbitration agreement. Counterdemands by the ITU were equally

[28] *Bulletins: Labor 5005-A*, Dec. 31, 1947.

[29] *B Bulletin 37–1947*, Sept. 10, 1947.

[30] *B Bulletin 39–1947*, Sept. 24, 1947. Berry died in December 1948, after heading the pressmen for forty-one years.

uncompromising, and the conference adjourned amid exchanges of accusations between the two groups.[31]

The ANPA now decided to take the offensive. General Manager Cranston Williams announced on October 7 on behalf of the board of directors that charges were being filed against the ITU with the National Labor Relations Board. Williams declared that the ANPA had no other recourse than to take this step, which he reiterated was not a "union busting program."[32] On November 21 the Cincinnati office of the NLRB issued a complaint against the ITU charging several violations of the Taft-Hartley Act. On December 3 the ITU filed its answer to the ANPA's charges and the NLRB action, asserting that the Taft-Hartley Act was unconstitutional.[33] Thus the test case challenging the anti-closed-shop provision of the Taft-Hartley law was set upon its devious way through board and court hearings.

The situation worsened with the breakdown of negotiations between Chicago publishers and the ITU on November 24, resulting in a walkout by the typographers. Other mechanical unions remained at work, however, and the Chicago dailies continued to appear by substituting typewritten copy and photoengraved pages for regular makeup processes. By the spring of 1948 more than 2500 typographers were on strike throughout the country, and a half-dozen complaints were on file charging the ITU with defiance of the law. Legal actions and strike benefits were costing the ITU $500,000 a month. The ANPA treasurer, in turn, reported to the 1948 convention that expenses of the Special Standing Committee had increased $70,000 during 1947, to reach an annual total of $171,200. The convention voted a special assessment of 15 percent of the dues regularly payable for the coming year.

Hearings on the National Labor Relations Board complaint against the ITU, in the ANPA-originated case, were conducted intermittently through the spring of 1948 by NLRB Trial Examiner Arthur Leff. Meanwhile Robert Denham, NLRB general counsel, turned to the courts. On March 27 Federal Judge Luther

[31] B Bulletin 42−1947, Sept. 29, 1947.
[32] B Bulletin 43−1947, Oct. 8, 1947.
[33] B Bulletin 52−1947, Dec. 5, 1947.

M. Swygert, sitting in Indianapolis, granted a temporary injunction against the ITU which was to continue in effect until the complaint filed against the ITU had been decided. The injunction directed the ITU not to support or authorize any strikes, slowdowns, or walkouts in furtherance of its closed-shop demands, and to cease efforts to negotiate contracts which perpetuated closed-shop conditions.[34]

After six months of hearings and 5000 pages of testimony, the NLRB trial examiner gave his decision in the ANPA-ITU case. Leff's recommendation to the National Labor Relations Board, announced in August 1948, was based on the same conclusion regarding the closed-shop issue as earlier recommendations in four other hearings involving local complaints against the ITU had been. The union, Leff said, was guilty of violating three provisions of the Taft-Hartley Act by seeking to continue closed-shop conditions. These were the provisions which prohibited a union from trying to cause employers to discriminate against nonunion workers, from coercing or restraining employees in the exercise of their rights, and from coercing employers in their choice of supervisory employees. The latter violation resulted from ITU insistence that foremen be union members, Leff said. The ANPA suffered a setback, however, when Leff recommended dismissal of other charges of ITU legal violations. In particular, the union won a victory when Leff declared he thought the resetting of advertising matter supplied newspapers in mat form did not constitute an illegal "featherbedding" practice.[35]

The ITU, meeting in national convention the same week, retaliated by demanding the removal from office of the NLRB general counsel, Robert Denham, and pledged a fight to the finish against the Taft-Hartley Act.[36] Denham's answer was to ask Judge Swygert to hold the ITU and its officers in contempt of court for violations of the injunction granted in March. This the judge did in October, ordering the union's leaders to "purge themselves of their contempt of court" by ceasing to support all strikes called upon the closed-shop issue and by desisting from

[34] *Bulletins: Labor 5036*, Mar. 29, 1948, text of the decision.
[35] *Editor & Publisher*, 81:5 (Aug. 21, 1948).
[36] *Ibid.*

efforts to secure contracts which perpetuated closed-shop conditions.[37] On November 20 Judge Swygert accepted assurances of the ITU leaders that they were then complying with the court's orders.

This was an ANPA victory on the closed-shop issue. But the situation was still clouded. The general elections of November 2, 1948, resulting in the reelection of President Harry S. Truman and the return of congressional control to the Democratic party, had been a reversal for the supporters of the Taft-Hartley Act. The ITU attorneys informed Judge Swygert that they were reserving the right to insist upon contracts which would provide for immediate reinstatement of closed-shop conditions upon the repeal of the anti-closed-shop provision in the Taft-Hartley Act.[38] In any event the ANPA was more concerned with obtaining a ruling outlawing ITU international union law provisions which affected the conduct of a publisher's business than in upsetting the closed-shop tradition. When the NLRB ruled on the ANPA-ITU case in October 1949, it accepted Leff's recommendations, holding the ITU guilty of violating the closed-shop ban, and followed his lead in declining to rule on disputed union law provisions. The NLRB did agree with the ANPA that union law provisions should be subject to arbitration.[39] Future ANPA-ITU cooperation depended on union acceptance of this viewpoint.[40]

Despite the sound and fury of the ANPA-ITU case, it still seemed true that the prevailing tendency in daily newspaper labor relations policy was negotiatory, with an advocacy of collective bargaining, conciliation, and arbitration. A belligerent attitude toward the mechanical unions has been held by only a small minority. Relationships with unions other than the typographers

[37] *Ibid.*, 81:7 (Oct. 16, 1948).
[38] *Ibid.*, 81:13 (Nov. 20, 1948).
[39] *Ibid.*, 82:10 (Nov. 5, 1949).
[40] Settlement in September 1949 of the 22-month-old strike of typographers against the Chicago daily newspapers brought hope that newspaper relations with the ITU would substantially improve. The ITU and the Chicago publishers agreed on a formula which would satisfy the Taft-Hartley Act ban on the closed shop and yet would assure the union that its members would continue to hold all available jobs through obtaining preference in hiring procedures. Publishers won several modifications of the union's rules requiring resetting of advertising matter. Failure of the Truman administration to obtain repeal of the Taft-Hartley Act in the first session of the Eighty-first Congress brought about the settlement.

continued amicable throughout the postwar period, and ANPA relations with the pressmen were on the closest of terms. This was one of the fruits of the association's policy of dealing only with individual unions and not with allied trades coalitions — a policy facilitated by the craft union organization of the American Federation of Labor. The result of this policy, the ITU discovered, was that newspapers could continue to operate without typographers by the introduction of new printing techniques.

Whether or not the international arbitration contracts, which had proved so mutually advantageous in earlier years, could be restored to full operation remained an unanswered question. Local arbitration contracts with ITU units declined sharply in 1948, but contracts with the other mechanical unions held firm. In the light of the history of publisher-union relationships, a satisfactory newspaper labor relations policy depends upon such traditional cooperative processes being once again fully accepted.

CHAPTER XIII

The Menace of Radio

RADIO was an enjoyable novelty, a competitor with the phonograph, in 1921. Ten years later every newspaper publisher at the annual ANPA dinner smiled wryly when humorist Will Rogers quipped, "I don't know what you have to fear from radio, but if you're worried — why don't you just poison Amos and Andy?" [1] In that decade radio had developed stature enough to menace other communications media in competition for advertising revenue, and it was with that phase of radio that the ANPA was primarily concerned. In the 1940s radio's onward drive impelled the ANPA to revitalize its promotion of the newspaper as an advertising medium. And many newspaper publishers emerged from the fray as owners of standard broadcasting stations, of the new FM radio stations, of facsimile broadcasting facilities, and of television stations.

Newspapers came out of World War I into a great advertising boom that enabled the ANPA president to report to the 1919 convention "boasts on all sides of satisfactory profits," despite rising costs and a newsprint shortage. Advertising volume continued to expand through the 1920s, with newspapers getting their full share in competition with magazines and the outdoor business. But the publishers had their eyes on radio, and each year saw a growing concern expressed at ANPA meetings.

Two firsts in the story of newspapers versus radio came in 1920. That year WWJ and KDKA, the first commercial stations, broadcast presidential election returns, a news novelty. And that year the Detroit *News* became the first newspaper to own a radio station, WWJ. The Kansas City *Star* came on the air with WDAF in 1921; it was the second metropolitan newspaper to decide that

[1] New York *Times*, Apr. 22, 1931, p. 17.

the best way to meet this new competition was to join forces with it.[2]

From its start radio experimented with broadcasting special news events. WWJ announced scores of 1920 World Series baseball games. KDKA, an outstanding leader, aired speeches by several national figures during 1921 and put on the first broadcasts of a prize fight and a baseball game. Occasionally news broadcasts were made, but the potentialities of organized presentation of news over the air were not yet realized. Neither were the advertising potentialities of radio realized; when the Kansas City *Star* offered a combined rate for radio time and newspaper space in 1921, few persons noticed or cared.[3]

Nevertheless by 1922 enough activity had developed so that the Associated Press felt it necessary to warn its member newspapers not to broadcast news or permit others to do so. Since the Associated Press holds rights to local news in member papers, the warning applied to all such news material, as well as that originated by the AP. An ANPA bulletin issued in April 1922 carried complaints of publishers that news was being "lifted" from newspapers for broadcast and that radio reports on baseball games were hurting sales of sports extras. One publisher suggested that notices of radio news broadcasts should not be printed in newspapers. Still another warned that free publicity given to radio was hurting a big newspaper advertiser — the phonograph.[4] But radio was a good and continuing news story, as evidenced by a study made of the columns of the New York *Times*. In September 1922 the *Times* was printing an average of thirty-two column inches daily about radio; by the following June it was averaging forty inches of radio information daily. The number of receiving sets in the United States jumped from some 50,000 in 1921 to over 600,000 in 1922 as a result of the interest thus generated.[5]

By 1924 the ANPA's concern about radio had been quickened. In its preview of the association's annual meeting, *Editor & Pub-*

[2] Mott, *American Journalism*, p. 679.
[3] Mitchell V. Charnley, *News by Radio* (New York: Macmillan, 1948), pp. 4–5.
[4] *Bulletin 4594*, Apr. 8, 1922.
[5] From testimony by Ralph D. Casey, director of the University of Minnesota School of Journalism, before the Federal Communications Commission, reprinted in part by the Newspaper-Radio Committee in *Freedom of the Press* (booklet, 1942), pp. 5–21.

lisher said, "1. Labor. 2. Postage. 3. Radio. In that order stand forth the chief topics of interest before the American Newspaper Publishers Association as it enters its 39th year." [6] A committee on radio had been appointed during the previous year to study "this new phase of newspaper activity," as ANPA President Paul Patterson of the Baltimore *Sun* put it. Walter A. Strong of the Chicago *Daily News* reported for the committee that there was no evidence of news broadcasting affecting newspaper sales, and that while several stations had broadcast paid advertising messages, "attitudes on this question must be based on interests and preferences of the listening public alone." In 1925 the committee told the ANPA convention that the radio log published in newspapers was a "terrific reader puller"; that radio bulletins reporting news events stimulated newspaper sales, but that advertising on the radio was now a worry. Chairman Strong presented a resolution, which the membership approved, stating that "members of the ANPA refuse to publish free publicity concerning programs consisting of direct advertising." Thus the daily newspaper publishers showed their first real concern over the advertising activities of radio—but they could see no harm in radio's broadcasting of the news.

When in later years a major effort was made to curtail radio news broadcasting activities, a complicating factor prevented unified action by the publishers. This factor was the affiliation of many newspapers with radio stations. The committee on radio compiled statistics which indicated that in October 1922 more than 100 newspapers owned stations, most of which were of the 20–50 watt variety. By April 1924, 45 newspapers still maintained radio outlets. [7] A more comprehensive report in 1927 showed that 48 newspapers were owners or part owners of stations, that 18 had studios in stations not owned by them, that 69 sponsored programs from unowned stations, and that 97 at least gave news, scores, market bulletins, and other information over the air. More than half the high-grade stations had some newspaper affiliation. [8]

Two major developments in the history of radio broadcasting now took place, with the result that radio became a much more

[6] *Editor & Publisher*, 57:19 (Apr. 19, 1924).
[7] *Report of the Thirty-eighth Annual Meeting* (1924), p. 185.
[8] *Bulletin 5400*, July 15, 1927.

formidable communications competitor. One was the organization of radio networks; the other, passage of the Federal Radio Act. Formation of the National Broadcasting Company in 1926 and the Columbia Broadcasting System in 1927 meant that radio programs could be vastly improved and that sponsorship of the programs could be sold to national advertisers far more easily. Government administration of the radio frequencies meant an unscrambling of a confused broadcasting situation. It also meant, since the regulatory act called upon radio stations to broadcast "in the public interest, convenience, and necessity," that stations would turn to news programs as one means of satisfying this license requirement. The ANPA helped to obtain this federal legislation, with Walter A. Strong of its radio committee serving as chairman of a Radio Coordinating Committee established in 1926. Radio manufacturers, the National Association of Broadcasters, and other radio groups joined in setting up a Washington headquarters for the committee to promote the passage of the Federal Radio Act. The legislation, establishing the Federal Radio Commission, was approved in February 1927. Government supervision of radio was strengthened in 1934 by passage of the Federal Communications Act, which provided for establishment of the Federal Communications Commission.[9]

The presidential election of 1928 brought the issue of radio competition before the publishers in a clear-cut way once again. The major press associations supplied complete returns to radio on election night and many publishers followed suit locally. Approximately one million dollars was spent by the two major political parties on radio broadcasting during the campaign, to the concern of newspaper publishers who saw potential political party advertising revenue diverted from their papers.[10] Radio took on a new significance. Eight million receiving sets were in American homes; programs were improved; and everything combined to make radio a major threat in the advertising field. ANPA members reported in November 1928 that not only national advertising on network programs, but local advertising as well, was being lost to radio competitors. The Chicago *Tribune*

[9] Charnley, *News by Radio*, pp. 7–8.
[10] Newspaper-Radio Committee, *Freedom of the Press*, p. 18, reporting the Casey statement to the FCC.

reacted by banning the publication of the radio log, except for its own station, WGN.[11]

At the 1930 and 1931 ANPA annual meetings there was extensive discussion of the problem of radio competition for advertising revenue. The reports of Media Records were quoted to the publishers as proof that radio was the villain in the piece. These reports said that in 1930 the 107 leading users of radio time had cut their newspaper advertising 12½ percent from the 1929 volume, while increasing radio expenditures 63 percent and magazine advertising 6 percent.[12] The publishers were well aware that a major business depression was in progress, but they eyed radio as the source of added trouble.

Actually, until 1933 it was the depression, not radio, which was causing the largest shrinkage in newspaper revenue from national advertising. And it was other communications media, not the newspapers, which were losing ground most rapidly to radio. It was not until the late 1930s that newspapers fell victim to the new competitor. The publishers, however, were certain that the advertising budgets allotted to radio each year would have been theirs — and should have been. The accompanying table, "Media Revenue from National Advertising," which gives dollar volumes for national advertising alone and the percentages each medium obtained, illustrates the trend.

National advertising, however, supplies the smaller part of total newspaper advertising revenue (although it should be remembered that national advertising bulks larger for daily newspaper publishers than for weeklies). The second table, "All Newspaper Advertising Revenue," shows that the depression cut just as deeply into revenue from local retail and classified advertising as it did into national volume.

These two tables give a picture of the advertising problem which confronted the ANPA. The World War I period established the newspaper in the national advertising field at a position which was held until the late 1930s. Meanwhile dollar volume increased until 1929, declined 45 percent by 1933, made some recovery which was halted again by the recession of 1937, and then zoomed in the years after World War II.

[11] *Bulletin 5578*, Nov. 20, 1928. It did not continue the policy long, however.
[12] *Report of the Forty-fifth Annual Meeting* (1931), p. 202.

MEDIA* REVENUE FROM NATIONAL ADVERTISING
(dollar volumes in millions)

	All News-papers	All Maga-zines	Radio	Billboards, Car Cards	Total
1929					
Amount	$260	$204	$19	$70	$553
Percent	47.0	37.0	3.4	12.6	100
1933					
Amount	$145	$94	$32	$27	$298
Percent	48.6	31.6	10.8	9.0	100
1935					
Amount	$167	$119	$49	$31	$366
Percent	45.6	32.5	13.4	8.5	100
1939					
Amount	$169	$158	$125	$39	$491
Percent	34.4	32.2	25.4	8.0	100
1948					
Amount	$389	$460	$342	$77	$1268
Percent	30.7	36.3	26.9	6.1	100

SOURCE: Table prepared from figures of the ANPA Bureau of Advertising, *Editor & Publisher*, and A. M. Lee.

* Subdivisions of media, made in later years by the Bureau of Advertising (such as farm journals and spot broadcasting) have not been made here, in order that earlier figures may be compared for the same general categories.

ALL NEWSPAPER ADVERTISING REVENUE
(dollar volume in millions)

Year	Local	National	
1915	$220	$ 55	20.0%
1919	350	150	30.0
1929	600	260	30.2
1933	325	145	30.7
1935	383	167	30.4
1939	441	169	27.7
1947	721	369	33.9

SOURCE: ANPA Bureau of Advertising estimates, in ANPA, *The Newspaper as an Advertising Medium*, p. 81, and in *Editor & Publisher*, 81:5 (June 12, 1948).

The fact that radio was winning new friends and increasing its dollar volume of national advertising in 1931, while all other media were losing heavily, brought definite action by the ANPA annual meeting that year. Elzey Roberts of the St. Louis *Star*, chairman of the committee on radio, said it had been a big mistake for newspapers to treat the growth of radio as a news story, claiming that the publishers had not recognized "the power of the press to popularize radio to the extent that it could carry direct advertising and still not antagonize the listener." This viewpoint was a species of rationalization at this point in radio's history, but it was popular with the publishers. What they needed to do was to accept the position radio had won — admittedly in part due to newspaper coverage of the radio story — and to set out upon a well-organized campaign to prove, by research methods and selling arguments, the effectiveness of the newspaper as an advertising medium. This they did later; but first they tried to undo radio's established position in communications competition. The 1931 ANPA convention resolved that since daily radio program logs related mainly to advertising, such logs, if published, should be handled as paid advertising. The membership also recommended that radio broadcasts of lotteries and gift offers should be regulated by the government as were such offers in newspapers using the second-class mail. And the membership questioned the legal right of radio, operating under government supervision, to compete with other media for advertising at all.

On the question of printing radio logs in newspapers, a 1932 survey showed that 66 ANPA members were publishing logs as paid advertising only; 320 were abbreviating the program listings submitted by the stations, eliminating advertisers' names; and 24 were publishing the program listings in full.[13] New Orleans dailies and other Louisiana papers joined together in late 1932 to forbid any mention of radio programs whatsoever in their columns and claimed that there was little objection from their readers.[14] But the belief expressed in 1925, that radio logs had high readership interest, prevailed with most publishers, who wanted to maintain circulation aids as well as advertising revenue. The

[13] *Bulletin 6009*, Aug. 25, 1932.
[14] *Editor & Publisher*, 65:6 (Dec. 17, 1932).

ANPA did win a victory when Congress forbade broadcasting of any information about lotteries.[15]

Seeking to unify action on the newspaper versus radio question, E. H. Harris of the Richmond, Indiana, *Palladium-Item*, chairman of the ANPA committee on radio, announced in November 1932 the formation of the Publishers' National Radio Committee. Each state was to organize a committee of three members, composed of two publishers who did not own radio stations and one who did. Their ideas were to be transmitted to the ANPA committee on radio.[16]

The furnishing of 1932 presidential election returns to the radio networks by the Associated Press, to forestall sale of election coverage by the United Press, precipitated action on the question of news broadcasting before the new national committee had time to operate. The ANPA board of directors, meeting in December 1932, made a series of recommendations which became the guiding principles of an attempt to remove radio as a competitor in the news communication field. The ANPA recommended that press associations should neither sell nor give away news in advance of publication in the newspapers. Newspaper publishers should take any legal action necessary to protect their property rights in news, before and after publication. Broadcasting of news, the ANPA continued, should be confined to brief bulletins which would encourage newspaper readership, with due credit being given the newspapers for collecting the news. Newspaper-owned stations should also broadcast local news in abbreviated form, for the good of newspapers as a whole. And, the ANPA concluded, radio logs should not be published free of charge. Doubt as to how far newspaper-owned stations would cooperate with this program was expressed by *Editor & Publisher*.[17]

After a spirited fight at the 1933 Associated Press convention, the AP membership voted not to furnish news to the national networks and to limit the broadcasting of news by AP members to occasional thirty-word bulletins not sponsored commercially.[18] The United Press and International News Service bowed to their

[15] *Ibid.*, 66:6 (Mar. 11, 1933).
[16] *Bulletin 6053*, Dec. 8, 1932.
[17] *Editor & Publisher*, 65:5 (Dec. 10, 1932).
[18] *Ibid.*, 66:5 (Apr. 29, 1933).

newspaper clients' desires and announced similar restrictions on use of their news, at the same time stopping sale of news to radio stations. The answer of the radio industry was to undertake the job of gathering the news itself, with the Columbia Broadcasting System leading the way with its Columbia News Service.[19]

The networks found the collection of news difficult and expensive, while the publishers disliked this new competition. By December 1933 the networks, publishers, and press associations decided to seek a solution. Representatives of the ANPA, Associated Press, United Press, International News Service, National Broadcasting Company, Columbia Broadcasting System, and the National Association of Broadcasters met in New York under the chairmanship of ANPA member Edwin S. Friendly of the New York *Sun*. They planned the establishment of the Press-Radio Bureau, which would present two five-minute unsponsored news summaries daily on the networks, the news to be supplied by the press associations. Bulletin coverage of extraordinary news events also would be provided. In return for this concession, the networks would cease news-gathering operations.[20]

But radio news broadcasting could not be so easily curtailed. No sooner had the Press-Radio Bureau begun operating in March 1934 than five new news-gathering agencies jumped into the field, led by Transradio Press Service. Within a year the UP and INS asked to be released from their agreement not to supply full news reports to radio stations, in order to meet the new competition. The 1935 ANPA convention granted them permission to do so, while voting to continue the Press-Radio Bureau arrangement. The UP asserted that failure of newspaper-owned stations to limit their news programs had a part in the breakdown of the cooperative agreement.[21] In any event, the bars were now down and the attempt to curtail news broadcasting had collapsed. UP and INS promoted the sale of news reports to radio stations and were eventually joined by the AP in 1940. The Press-Radio Bureau died quietly. And with the coming of World War II the networks expanded their own news-gathering and spot news coverage enormously, to serve the 45 million now owning radios.

[19] Charnley, *News by Radio*, pp. 15–16.
[20] *Editor & Publisher*, 66:3 (Dec. 16, 1933).
[21] *Ibid.*, 68:3 (May 4, 1935).

The ANPA committee on radio found solace in reporting to
the 1936 annual meeting that "efforts of radio to function in the
field of journalism must fail because a government license de-
stroys the freedom on which any journalistic endeavor rests." But
the ANPA found no solace in the annual reports of advertising
dollar volume. Radio was not only cutting into the national advertising revenues of newspapers, but was steadily increasing its
take in total advertising expenditures. In 1935 advertisers spent
105 million dollars on radio broadcasting. In 1936 the total was
120 million dollars, and in 1937 it reached 145 million dollars.
The recession kept radio at the 145 million mark in 1938, but by
1939 radio advertising revenue reached 170 million dollars. Total
advertising revenue of newspapers increased from 530 million
dollars to 600 million dollars between 1935 and 1937, then
slumped to 520 million dollars in 1938 and 525 millions in 1939.[22]
Newspapers had yielded first place in national advertising dollar
volume to the magazines by 1942 and found radio pressing hard
for second position.

Something had to be done lest newspapers, caught in a period
of increasing costs and declining revenues, become bankrupt in
wholesale fashion. One movement was in the direction of increased restrictions on free publicity for radio. In 1937 only 14
percent of newspapers not owning radio stations required payment for publishing radio logs; a year later the number had increased to 37 percent. Radio gossip columns, publicizing stars of
the air and thus promoting audiences for their radio shows, were
curtailed by many publishers under regional agreements.[23]

But an infinitely more important action was taken by the publishers when they gave increased support and attention to the
ANPA affiliate, the Bureau of Advertising. The bureau had been
organized in 1913 to promote the newspaper as an advertising
medium. It had helped newspapers to gain a healthy proportion
of national advertising revenue, in competition with magazines,
during the 1920s. But it had not been able to match the attrac-
tive sales talk of radio during the 1930s, despite the efforts of its

[22] *Printers' Ink* statistics, used in order to compare newspaper and radio total
advertising revenues. The newspaper revenue figures differ slightly from those of
the Bureau of Advertising.
[23] *Report of the Fifty-third Annual Meeting* (1939), p. 513.

long-time director, William A. Thomson. The bureau had no financial connection with the ANPA and was insufficiently supported by the newspapers and advertising groups which participated in the bureau's program under ANPA leadership.

The year 1938 saw various advertising groups concerned with newspaper space sales join in a "United Front" campaign with the ANPA and the Bureau of Advertising to salvage the position of the newspaper. An intensive drive was launched to obtain new members for the bureau and thus augment its income for promotion and research. As a result Edwin S. Friendly of the New York *Sun,* chairman of the committee in charge of the bureau, was able to report substantial progress in the bureau membership at the 1939 annual meeting. Membership had jumped from 342 in January 1938 to 672 in April 1939. The bureau's annual income had increased from $100,000 to $170,000 and an underwriting committee was raising an additional $230,000. New sales, research, and promotion departments had been established, and the bureau's New York and Chicago offices were augmented by a Pacific Coast division. The most important accomplishment had been the undertaking of a series of publications on the Continuing Study of Newspaper Reading, a careful readership research program paid for by the bureau but directed by the Advertising Research Foundation, under the joint auspices of the Association of National Advertisers and the American Association of Advertising Agencies. The published studies of newspaper readership, which passed the hundred mark in 1947 in the number of newspapers surveyed, provided a wealth of research material, not only for advertising sales staffs and advertisers, but also for editors who could study readership figures for stories and pictures. The bureau also undertook special research studies, particularly in the food products advertising field. The primary target, however, was a selected group of national advertisers to whom the story of the newspaper as an advertising medium was told. The bureau reported a 12-million-dollar upswing in national advertising between 1938 and 1941.

This demonstration of the value of aggressive promotion and research activities in behalf of newspaper advertising sales encouraged a new effort at expansion of Bureau of Advertising activities. Plans for an extensive reorganization of the bureau were laid during the wartime years, under the leadership of Frank E. Tripp of the Gannett newspapers, Roy D. Moore of the Brush-Moore newspapers, and other ANPA leaders in the bureau. The key leader in the drive was Richard W. Slocum of the Philadelphia *Bulletin*, who became chairman of the new governing board of the bureau after the reorganization. Active support was provided by the American Association of Newspaper Representatives and the Newspaper Advertising Executives Association.

At the 1945 annual meeting the Bureau of Advertising of the ANPA, as it became officially known, reported that the reorganization drive had netted the bureau a $750,000 annual income from some 950 newspaper members. The bureau had been divided into three sections: an administrative division, to handle financial affairs and publisher relations; a national division, in charge of national advertising problems; and a retail division, to study selling techniques and promotion efforts in the local field. A research department of seventeen people, spending nearly half the bureau's annual budget, and a promotion department were made part of the national division. The bureau maintained enlarged quarters and a total staff of seventy-five.

By 1949 the bureau's annual income had reached the long-sought one million dollars, under a plan by which each member newspaper contributed 1 percent of its net national advertising revenue. Nearly eleven hundred American and Canadian newspapers were members, representing 87 percent of combined daily circulation. Extensive new research programs were undertaken, and the bureau proudly watched newspaper advertising revenues climb. Newspapers improved their position in the national advertising picture, gaining on the magazines during 1947 and 1948.[24] One factor aided both these media: network radio time had been sold to full capacity after 1944, and radio's national advertising dollar volume gained only through spot sales increases. Total advertising expenditures for radio time, which had amounted to 37

[24] The Bureau of Advertising reported that newspapers received 27 percent of the total national advertising revenue in 1946, and 31 percent in 1947. General magazines had 35 percent in 1946 and 34 percent in 1947. Farm journals, classified in earlier studies as magazines, had 3.1 percent in 1947. Newspaper advertising sales broke all records during 1948.

percent of similar purchases of newspaper space in 1941, had jumped during the war until in 1944 they amounted to 62 percent of total advertising expenditures for newspaper space. During 1946 and 1947 radio's total advertising take was almost exactly half that of the newspapers, as radio broke across the half-billion-dollar mark in 1947, while newspapers crossed the billion-dollar line. Magazines in the postwar years also had total advertising revenues approximately half those of newspapers.[25] In these happy circumstances William A. Thomson resigned as Bureau of Advertising director in 1948, after serving in that post since the bureau's formation in 1913. Alfred S. Stanford, head of the national division, became director, but later in the year he resigned to become advertising director of the New York *Herald Tribune*. Harold S. Barnes, former assistant director, then was named director.[26] John Giesen headed the retail division and William G. Bell the research program.

Newspaper ownership of radio stations still remained a topic for debate. By 1936 newspapers owned, or were affiliated with, 168 stations, amounting to 26 percent of all American broadcasting facilities. Hearst Radio, Incorporated, owned six stations, while the McClatchy newspapers of California controlled five stations, which with its papers gave the McClatchy group a firm hold on its "inland empire."[27] Such chain-ownership situations and an increase in newspaper-affiliated stations to 211 of 728 stations by 1938 gave the Federal Communications Commission "a problem." This was the expression used by JS Gray of the Monroe, Michigan, *News*, chairman of the committee on radio, in discussing the question of newspaper-affiliated stations before the 1938 ANPA annual meeting.

The FCC decided to investigate that problem in March 1941, when it announced that it would seek to determine what statement of policy or rules, if any, should be issued concerning applications for broadcasting licenses made by persons who also published newspapers.[28] When 27 of the first 94 applications for licenses to operate FM stations were found to come from news-

[25] *Printers' Ink* statistics.
[26] *Editor & Publisher*, 81:14 (Oct. 16, 1948).
[27] Lee, *Daily Newspaper in America*, p. 367.
[28] *B Bulletin 16 – 1941*, Apr. 2, 1941.

paper publishers, the FCC decided to study the entire problem of newspaper-radio joint ownership.[29]

Mark Ethridge of the Louisville *Courier-Journal* and station WHAS immediately called for the formation of a Newspaper-Radio Committee. A meeting of 150 publishers owning an interest in radio stations was held simultaneously with the 1941 ANPA annual meeting, but not under ANPA sponsorship. The raising of a $200,000 fund was ordered, and headquarters for the Newspaper-Radio Committee were established in the same building that housed ANPA offices in New York. In the meantime Ethridge was commissioned by President Franklin D. Roosevelt to study the entire press-radio setup, and Harold Hough of the Fort Worth *Star-Telegram* and stations WBAP and KGKO replaced him as chairman of the committee.[30]

When the FCC hearings opened in July 1941, ANPA General Counsel Elisha Hanson and Judge Thomas Thacher, counsel for the Newspaper-Radio Committee, argued unsuccessfully that the commission had no authority to conduct the investigation.[31] Former ANPA President James G. Stahlman of the Nashville *Banner* also showed his disapproval by refusing to appear before the commission, but a court order eventually brought him to the witness stand.[32] The FCC questioned a stream of witnesses about the danger of joint ownership of newspapers and radio stations, especially in cities without other competition. Witnesses for the publishers traced the historical development of radio-newspaper affiliation, the question of press freedom in relation to the use of radio as an added journalistic instrument for conveying news, the competition of outside media in one-publisher newspaper communities, and other related subjects. The legal questions involved were also dealt with.[33]

The commission decided that 249 of 882 radio stations were newspaper-owned,[34] and then adjourned its hearings in February

[29] *Editor & Publisher*, 74:24 (Apr. 26, 1941).
[30] *Ibid.*, 74:24, 74 (Apr. 26, 1941).   [31] *Ibid.*, 74:6 (July 26, 1941).
[32] *Ibid.*, 75:3 (Jan. 31, 1942).
[33] Witnesses for the publishers included Roscoe Pound, former dean of the Harvard Law School, Arthur Garfield Hays of the American Civil Liberties Union, and three journalism school directors, Ralph D. Casey of Minnesota, Frank Luther Mott of Iowa, and Frederick S. Siebert of Illinois.
[34] *Ibid.*, 74:6 (Dec. 6, 1941).

1942 without making any statement of policy. The Newspaper-Radio Committee continued a watch on the FCC for two years, awaiting a decision. In January 1944, however, the commission dropped the matter, commenting only that no further action would be taken and that licenses would be granted on the merits of individual applications, under the guiding rule of as much diversification of ownership as feasible.

The number of newspaper-affiliated radio stations continued to increase. By the end of April 1949, 476 of 1975 standard radio stations had newspaper affiliations, which in most cases meant they were under the outright control of individual publishers or publishing companies. Because the number of stations on the air had more than doubled since 1941, however, the ratio of newspaper-affiliated stations to nonaffiliated ones declined from 28 to 24.1 percent. The publishers took an even keener interest in FM radio stations, holding a special FM clinic at their 1944 annual meeting. By 1949 newspapers had received 39 percent of the FM licenses granted, owning 281 of 724 FM stations. Newspapers also took the lead in establishing television stations after World War II, controlling 28 of the first 60 stations established. The Columbia Broadcasting System in particular concentrated on newspaper-radio ownership and operation of TV outlets.[35]

Discussions of radio in postwar ANPA sessions for small daily publishers showed a marked change of attitude from earlier association policy. Fred Schilplin of the St. Cloud, Minnesota, *Times* told the 1947 session how he had eliminated all expense in circulation renewals by using his radio station to promote the newspaper. His savings, Schilplin said, amounted to between $10,000 and $15,000 a year, and he had a higher rate of circulation increase than when three circulation men had been employed. The small daily publishers felt there was a trend toward getting into radio broadcasting, both standard and FM, in order to protect newspaper properties against new competition and as a precaution in the event facsimile broadcasting became a major factor. As for the once burning question of charging advertising rates for publication of the radio log, less than 5 percent of the pub-

[35] Warren K. Agee, "A Study of Cross-Channel Ownership of Communications Media" (unpublished M.A. thesis, University of Minnesota, 1949), p. 11.

lishers were still continuing this practice or excluding the log from their columns. There was scarcely a newspaper reader who did not own or have ready access to one of the 66 million radio sets in the country, and every reader expected to find program listings in his daily newspaper.

All in all, newspaper publishers held a good position in 1949 in the competition for advertising revenue. They were reminded at ANPA sessions and in other places, however, that during the postwar inflation period, production costs had increased more rapidly for many newspapers than had their incomes from advertising and circulation. A recession similar to that of 1937 might endanger scores of newspaper operations, and of this danger the publishers were well aware. But so long as the great postwar advertising boom continued, everyone could be happy.

CHAPTER XIV

Mechanical Research

IN 1926 the American Newspaper Publishers Association established two new departments to further the business affairs of the members. They were the Mechanical Department and the Traffic Department, both located in the association's New York City office. One studies the most effective and economical methods of producing newspapers; the other constantly watches the various transportation agencies of the country and obtains the lowest possible rates for the raw materials and finished products of the newspaper business. Both are interesting as examples of the work of a trade association.

During the early years of the ANPA's history, much attention was paid to the rapid changes in mechanical processes which accompanied the development of the modern newspaper. Typesetting machines, power presses, stereotyping, mats, photoengraving, electrotyping, and the typewriter all claimed the attention of the association as a group.[1] As the revolution in printing methods subsided and improvements on existing equipment became the principal concern of publishers, mechanical topics took a secondary place on the association's annual agendas. Problems of obtaining more efficient production remained, however. Herman Ridder of the New York *Staats-Zeitung*, ANPA president from 1907 to 1911, was much interested in typesetting machines, in perfecting the Intertype, and in organizing an equipment company.[2] Typecasting machines, the Monotype and Ludlow, joined the Linotype and Intertype; pressmakers strove constantly for higher speeds and improved reproduction; and new advances in other fields of printing came year by year.

After World War I the investment in the plant of a metropoli-

[1] See Chapter III, pp. 42–45.   [2] Mott, *American Journalism*, p. 601.

tan daily newspaper had become so great that it seemed logical
for the ANPA to favor, as it did in 1925, the establishment of a
Mechanical Department "with a view to improving the general
production of newspapers."[3] The department began functioning
in November 1926, with Walter E. Wines as the paid manager.
Wines, who was to serve as manager until 1948, had entered the
newspaper production business in 1899, when publisher William
J. Murphy chose him to rebuild the fire-gutted Minneapolis *Tribune* plant, and to equip it with the most advanced printing machinery. Wines later became mechanical superintendent of the
Chicago *Tribune*, production superintendent of the New York
Times, and a teacher of printing methods, before joining the
ANPA.[4] George M. Rogers of the Cleveland *Plain Dealer* was the
first chairman of the association's advisory committee. His successors included Samuel H. Kauffmann, Washington *Evening Star*;
F. H. Keefe, Newburgh, New York, *Beacon-News*; A. H. Burns,
New York *Herald Tribune*; Worth C. Coutney, Chicago *Herald-American*; J. L. Stackhouse, Easton, Pennsylvania, *Express*; and
Edwin H. Evers, St. Louis *Globe-Democrat*. Vernon R. Spitaleri,
a graduate of the Carnegie Institute of Technology, succeeded
Wines as manager in 1948.[5]

In June 1927 the Mechanical Department held the first of a
continuing series of mechanical conferences for superintendents
and other leading employees from daily newspaper plants. The
conferences, held each year in various cities, have produced
lengthy bulletins reporting discussions of latest composing room
and pressroom developments and have been centers for the exhibit and study of the newest mechanical equipment.

From 1928 to 1933 the ANPA Mechanical Department and the
United States Government Printing Office conducted cooperative
research into paper and ink problems brought about by the use
of high-speed presses. In 1933 the results were published,[6] and
papermakers, ink makers, and publishers were urged to put the
results of the research work into actual practice.

[3] *Report of the Thirty-ninth Annual Meeting* (1925), p. 252.
[4] *Bulletin* 5279, Oct. 20, 1926.
[5] *Editor & Publisher*, 81:55 (Nov. 6, 1948).
[6] B. L. Wehmhoff, D. P. Clark, and D. H. Boyce, *Newsprint and News Ink*
(Washington: Government Printing Office, 1933).

The Mechanical Department has made many other studies of technical printing problems. Among the matters studied are the use of the dry mat, newsprint standardization and waste control, high-speed printing, color printing and rotogravure, stereotyping, cameras and photographic copy, the teletypesetter, pressroom humidity, air conditioning, fluorescent lighting, offset printing, and kindred subjects.

The newsprint waste of 150 cooperating members was reduced from 4½ percent in 1927 to 3¾ percent in 1932, the department asserts, which resulted in annual savings of $500 to $25,000 for individual publishers. Studies of the ink problem saved at least one member $4500 annually.[7] Fluorescent lighting was installed by 165 members after an intensive study of that subject at the 1940 mechanical conference, resulting in improved working conditions for employees.[8] The training of mechanical supervisors which was accomplished by the Mechanical Department undoubtedly justified the annual budget of $15,000 to $20,000 which was provided by the ANPA membership for its use until the close of World War II.

Concern over mounting production costs in the postwar period brought a tremendous expansion in ANPA mechanical research activities in 1947. The interest of members was spurred also by another revolution in printing methods, in which photography was to play the key role. This revolution was initiated by individual publisher experimentation with what became known as the "cold type" process, in which automatically adjusting typewriters replaced typesetting machines and photoengravers replaced makeup men. The object was to find a less costly method of producing newspapers. New funds were provided for ANPA research programs and the board of directors in February 1947 voted to employ a research director. The first short-range project was to be an attack upon the problem of newsprint waste in first impression offset.[9] William Baumrucker, Jr., of the New York *Daily News* became chairman of a five-man subcommittee of the mechanical committee, named the mechanical research committee. In August 1947 the association selected as mechanical re-

[7] *What the ANPA Means in Dollars and Cents.*
[8] *Report of the Fifty-fifth Annual Convention* (1941), p. 108.
[9] *B Bulletin 13 – 1947*, Feb. 26, 1947.

search director C. M. Flint, a former electrical engineer and wartime worker in the Office of Scientific Development and Research.

A statement of the policies of the new Mechanical Research Department was made in September 1947.[10] The association's goal was to conduct research directed toward the improvement of the raw materials, the production elements, and the product of the newspaper business. Research efforts would be concentrated upon the general problems of publishers, while the Mechanical Department would continue to serve members who wished aid in solving individual or immediate problems. The research staff would build up the technical literature of printing, investigate and develop new equipment and processes, and aid in educating printing production men.

The 1948 ANPA convention was satisfied with the start which had been made and voted a 25 percent increase in the annual dues assessment to provide $140,000 annually for the Mechanical Research Department. A laboratory for testing new printing processes and equipment was established in Easton, Pennsylvania, with Roy W. Prince in charge as Flint's assistant.[11] Much of the research program, however, was to be carried on in cooperation with other research institutions, manufacturers, and newspapers. A major step was taken in September 1949, when the Graphic Arts Research Foundation was established in Cambridge, Massachusetts, with the initial objective of developing a photo-composing machine. Other ANPA research included studies of mat packing, linecasting machine productivity, pressroom register control, and allied subjects.

One more innovation was made at the 1948 mechanical conference, which saw for the first time a discussion of industrial relations problems. This educational program for mechanical and production superintendents reflected ANPA recognition of the need for scientific employee relations work and personnel programs which would aid in improving mechanical department productivity.

The work of the Traffic Department has been less dramatic than that of the Mechanical Department, though equally im-

[10] B Bulletin 36 – 1947, Sept. 10, 1947.
[11] Editor & Publisher, 81:24 (Oct. 23, 1948).

portant to the association. As early as 1896 an ANPA committee headed by Milton A. McRae of the Scripps-McRae League of Newspapers was successful in obtaining a reduction in express company charges for carrying newspapers. In 1915 the ANPA had protested increased freight rates for transportation of newsprint and had won a partial victory in hearings before the Interstate Commerce Commission.[12] After having a traffic committee represent it in such matters from 1921 to 1926, the ANPA established a Traffic Department in September 1926, with William J. Mathey, former assistant general freight agent of the Erie Railroad, as paid manager.[13] When Mathey returned to the railroad field in 1932, R. A. Cooke, his assistant, succeeded him as manager. E. M. Antrim of the Chicago *Tribune* served continuously as traffic committee chairman until 1947, when he was replaced by Fred J. Byington, Jr., also of the *Tribune*.

The Traffic Department has analyzed the entire rate structure of each of the common carriers and has negotiated with the railroads and truckers when inequalities affecting newspaper publishers were discovered. It has followed all Interstate Commerce Commission rulings and has argued cases constantly before that body. It also has studied the cheapest and best means of transportation and by 1941 had audited 125,000 freight bills for members, obtaining readjustments on overcharges. Since freight costs on newsprint transportation total some 23 million dollars annually, much attention has been paid to securing the lowest possible rates.[14]

In 1927, for example, the Traffic Department reported to the annual meeting that various ANPA members had been saved from $250 to $2500 annually by the discovery of excessive freight rates on newsprint. The following year the membership was told that a reduction of one dollar a ton on newsprint freight rates from the Pacific Northwest to the Pacific Southwest saved an estimated $40,000 a year for publishers involved. In 1932 reduction of rates west of Chicago, which the ANPA helped to obtain, brought estimated savings to publishers of $250,000 annually.[15]

[12] *Report of the Thirtieth Annual Meeting* (1916), p. 11.
[13] *Bulletin 5258*, Sept. 10, 1926.
[14] *Report of the Fifty-fourth Annual Meeting* (1940), p. 472.
[15] *What the ANPA Means in Dollars and Cents.*

After ten years of service, the Traffic Department reported to the 1937 ANPA convention that at an annual expense to the membership of some $15,000, the department had obtained cost reductions which, when accumulated, meant savings of $2,585,000 annually to ANPA member newspapers.

During the 1940s the Traffic Department turned to another field, when it sponsored a safe-driving contest for newspaper truck drivers, in cooperation with the International Circulation Managers' Association. Like the Mechanical Department, the Traffic Department has been a typical business service of a trade association, guarding the publishers against unnecessary costs and securing advantages for them whenever possible.

CHAPTER XV

Freedom of the Press, the New Deal, and the Guild

FREEDOM of the press is a liberty vital to the life of a democratic people and to the advancement of their common welfare. The American Newspaper Publishers Association has always stood ready to defend the right to publish news and opinions freely, under the protection provided by the Constitution and expanded through usage and legal decisions. Since the late 1920s the ANPA has systematically offered encouragement to newspapers which have found themselves harassed by a Huey Long or by an overly zealous legislature or judge, and which therefore have appealed to the courts to uphold the historic right to freedom of expression without prior restraint and without punitive action by government.

Praise has been properly accorded to this association activity of opposing all actions that attempt to restrain or censor publication illegally, or that impose special burdens upon newspapers as a means of restricting their influence or muzzling their voices. But during the 1930s a controversy developed which centered around the ANPA's expansion of its definition of what freedom of the press, as provided by the Constitution, properly entails. In those years of economic and social readjustment, the association's spokesmen exhibited pronounced anxiety for the maintenance of press freedom, and they found a greatly increased number of situations which they felt involved basic concepts of freedom of the press. Out of this trend in thinking developed a determined contention that a large portion of the New Deal legislative program abridged the rights of the free press and an equally strong opposition to the unionization of editorial employees by the American Newspaper Guild on the grounds that press freedom was thereby endangered. Since ANPA spokesmen argued that both government and guild were encroaching upon constitutional freedoms, the account of this period of ANPA history can best be told in a single recital.

ANPA legislative and anti-guild activities during the 1930s aroused interest and no doubt aided in stimulating public discussion of the rights and obligations of the press. In a period of economic stress and social insecurity, it is not to be wondered at that the press, business, and other institutional activities came under scrutiny. In this debate the newspaper publishers had a valid, basic argument to present. They asserted that should the prevailing tendency toward closer government regulation of business continue unabated, a press that was regarded solely as a business enterprise might find its freedom of economic action so restricted that it would wither. If society wished to continue to have a free press, the publishers felt, it must safeguard newspapers against restrictive actions which would endanger their economic security and would curtail their enterprise as forceful organs presenting news and opinions.

The ANPA did advance this argument against specific federal legislative proposals which association spokesmen thought would impair the financial integrity — and therefore the freedom — of the press. Too often, however, the argument was lost because the association's leadership talked more loudly about the issue of the constitutional guarantee of press freedom than about the problem of maintaining a healthy newspaper economy. If during this controversial New Deal era some legislation did seriously threaten the economic stability of the newspapers, the ANPA failed to make the facts clear because of its preoccupation with the "press freedom crusade." The ANPA's arguments thus appeared to the general observer to be only surface deep. The impression was left that newspaper publishers were not attempting to make reasonable adjustments to new conditions and to carry out their business operations within the framework of post-1929 economic and social beliefs and changes.

This impression was heightened because ANPA spokesmen did not concentrate their opposition upon those legislative proposals which, if adopted, would seemingly seriously jeopardize press freedom. Rather, they attempted to oppose a great variety of New Deal measures of varying potential effects upon newspapers' well-being, with the result that in some instances the validity of their opposition to measures of wide public interest seemed questionable. Some voices within the press itself expressed the fear that such indiscriminate opposition to legislation and constant appeals for protection of press freedom would dissipate public support — upon which that freedom eventually depends — and would render the press unable to fight effectively against the governmental actions that could be shown clearly to endanger the welfare of newspapers, and therefore the public welfare.

Official acts of the ANPA were by no means the major points stimulating public discussion of newspapers, however. The controversy which was steadily developing centered mainly around the widespread editorial opposition, particularly outside the Democratic South, to the successive candidacies of Franklin D. Roosevelt for the presidency, and about some conspicuous examples of misuse of the news columns during the coverage of political issues. No thoughtful person could deny that newspapers have a right to express their honest editorial opinions. But those who supported Roosevelt were not always inclined to remember this, particularly when concentration of newspaper ownership in many cities had left only a single editorial voice. And when readers observed the partisan extremes of important sections of the press their sympathy for a "press freedom crusade" went up in smoke.

Why did not the ANPA become more sensitive to the rising criticism of press behavior, stimulated by the obvious partisanship of many newspapers? Why did it not accept the justness of some of the public criticism of the press and stress a more responsible handling of the news and a less partisan treatment of political questions? The ANPA's answer may be summed up as follows: The ANPA is a voluntary organization. At any time a newspaper may resign from the ANPA, for any or no reason. The ANPA has never attempted to force a newspaper, whether it is a member or not, to follow any policy. The newspapers evolve their own policies. The ANPA has not tried nor could it try to dictate to a newspaper publisher how his newspaper is to be run.[1] Self-regulation of newspapers is not a problem for a trade association to consider, the majority of ANPA members agreed, and there the matter stood.

This was the complex situation, then, with which the ANPA was forced to deal. What it did do, what it did not do, and what its critics said, can now be related to the problem as a whole.

The ANPA membership's first official directive asking for constant watchfulness on matters affecting press freedom was voted at the 1922 annual meeting, where it was resolved that "the Committee on Federal Laws be authorized and directed to exercise its utmost effort to maintain the freedom of the press whenever and wherever it may be threatened." The specific issue which had inspired the resolution was not particularly impressive: Congress had been considering a bill which would have made publication of news about betting on sports events a federal offense for newspapers using the second-class mail. Protests by several ANPA members had sufficed to kill the proposed measure.[2] But during the debate over the ANPA resolution, the point was made that a "free press" issue involves struggles on major, and not superficial, attacks on freedom of expression. In the years immediately following World War I, freedom of expression had been threatened by the growth of public opposition to those espousing radical causes, and by the tendency of government officials and courts to continue to act as they had under extraordinary wartime conditions. These were types of questions, it was argued, that demanded ANPA intervention.

The name of Elisha Hanson first came into ANPA records as a result of this desire by the membership to provide a formal means of assuring the protection of press freedom. He was retained by the committee on federal laws as the Washington representative of the association in 1923.[3] Then thirty-five years old, Hanson had attended Bradley Institute in Peoria, Illinois, from 1906 to 1907, had been a reporter for the Peoria *Journal* from 1907 to 1910, and had enrolled at Cornell University from 1910 to 1911. He then went to Washington, where he was a clerk in

---

[1] This is a statement of position made to the author by an influential ANPA spokesman.
[2] *Bulletin 4547*, Jan. 18, 1922.
[3] *Report of the Thirty-seventh Annual Meeting* (1923), p. 350.

the document room of the House of Representatives from 1911 to 1913, a Washington correspondent for the Chicago *Tribune* from 1913 to 1917, and secretary to Senator Medill McCormick from 1917 to 1922. Hanson completed his law studies at George Washington University in 1924 and was admitted to the District of Columbia bar. He practiced law thereafter as a member of the firm of Hanson, Lovett and Dale and eventually became general counsel of the ANPA.[4] During the 1930s Hanson became a leading spokesman for the publishers, representing some individually as well as the ANPA collectively in legislative and legal matters. He also came to eclipse Robert R. McCormick of the Chicago *Tribune* as the leading exponent of freedom of the press.

McCormick became chairman of a committee on freedom of the press established by the ANPA in 1928,[5] a position he retained into the 1940s. The first case for the new committee was already under way. What was known as the Minnesota "gag law" of 1925, permitting the suppression of malicious and scandalous publications, had been applied by a court to the *Saturday Press* of Minneapolis. Calling the law a threat to all newspapers, no matter how unworthy the *Saturday Press* might be, McCormick retained counsel to carry its case to the Supreme Court.[6] The high tribunal, in a 5–4 decision handed down in 1931, held the Minnesota law unconstitutional because it permitted prior restraint upon publication.[7] This was a landmark case, for it marked the first application of the freedom of the press guarantee of the First Amendment against the states through the due process clause of the Fourteenth Amendment.

Huey Long, the Louisiana political boss, provided McCormick with his next major case in 1934. The Long machine had obtained passage of a special 2 percent tax on the gross advertising income of Louisiana papers with a circulation of 20,000 or more. Twelve of the thirteen papers affected were opposed to the Long

[4] *Who's Who in America.*

[5] *Report of the Forty-second Annual Meeting* (1928), p. 146.

[6] *Bulletin 5578,* Nov. 12, 1928. McCormick generally has been given personal credit for providing the legal counsel, but in an address made in 1933 he said the case was appealed "with the financial assistance and moral support" of the ANPA. *The Case for the Freedom of the Press* (Chicago: The Tribune Company, 1933), p. 18.

[7] *Near* v. *Minnesota ex rel. Olson,* 283 U.S. 697 (1931).

regime. This punitive tax was found unconstitutional by the Supreme Court two years later,[8] after the ANPA had cooperated with the publishers from Louisiana in the presentation of their case.

The ANPA freedom of the press committee later intervened in various contempt of court cases affecting newspapers; it condemned the seizure of telegrams — particularly those of William Randolph Hearst — by the Black committee investigating lobbying practices; and it protested the "political murder" of Editor Walter Liggett in Minnesota. Soon the ANPA, with McCormick and Hanson as the principal spokesmen, became a constant participant in cases involving the constitutional rights of newspapers.[9]

The phrase *freedom of the press* was being interpreted in many other ways than it had been in the examples already cited. The association leadership increasingly advanced the argument that business activities of newspapers either were exempted under the First Amendment from government regulation, or should be protected against any adverse effects of federal general business laws. A bill which would have placed advertising claims as well as product labels within the scope of federal food and drug regulation was called "legal censorship of advertising" by the committee on federal laws in 1930.[10] This contention that advertising has constitutional protection was persistently advanced by the ANPA, although the Supreme Court twice flatly denied the claim.[11]

More ANPA legislative activity was in evidence during the early 1930s. When Congress barred certain types of puzzle contests from the mails in 1932, Hanson was influential in having such puzzles appearing in newspapers exempted from the ban.[12] The following year the committee on federal laws reported to

[8] *Grosjean* v. *American Press Co., Inc.*, 297 U.S. 233 (1936).
[9] For an exhaustive treatment of this subject see J. Edward Gerald, *The Press and the Constitution, 1931–1947* (Minneapolis: University of Minnesota Press, 1948). For differing views on the consistency of McCormick's freedom of the press philosophies see his own book, *The Freedom of the Press* (New York: D. Appleton-Century, 1936), and the dissents of John Tebbel in *An American Dynasty* (New York: Doubleday, 1947).
[10] *Report of the Forty-fourth Annual Meeting* (1930), p. 204.
[11] Gerald, *The Press and the Constitution*, p. 75.
[12] *Report of the Forty-sixth Annual Meeting* (1932), p. 189.

the ANPA convention that it had obtained the exemption of
newspapers from the application of a Senate-approved law for a
thirty-hour work week on the grounds that marginal publishing
operations would be put out of business, and that larger papers
could not adjust themselves to a six-hour day. The committee
protested the regulation of financial advertising copy in newspapers as proposed by sponsors of the Federal Securities Act in order to protect investors. And it asserted various food and drug
regulation bills under congressional consideration "involved censorship."

The advent of Franklin D. Roosevelt and the launching of the
New Deal resulted in many federal proposals which seemed to
the ANPA leadership to have a direct bearing on newspaper
publishing. The first round between the newspaper publishers,
the Congress, and the President came with the passage in June
1933 of the National Industrial Recovery Act, which called for
establishment of NRA codes of fair competition for all industries.
Two sections of the law in particular affected the publishers.
One was the famous section 7-a, which guaranteed the right of
collective bargaining and freedom of labor union organization.
Under the shelter of its provisions the American Newspaper
Guild came into being. The other was the licensing section,
which gave the President power to license individual companies
in an industry not cooperating under the NRA program and to
revoke such licenses for continued noncompliance if he deemed
it necessary and proper. Operation of a business without a license under such conditions would be unlawful.

Deciding that there was work to be done to protect newspapers from the NIRA legislation, the ANPA took the lead in the
writing of a voluntary code for daily newspapers. President Howard Davis, of the New York *Herald Tribune*, became chairman of
a committee on the newspaper code, which set out to write into
a code the safeguards and requests which the committee thought
publishers wanted. The association's general counsel, Hanson,
played a leading part in the code negotiations and influenced the
course which the ANPA followed.

The publishers feared the licensing provisions of the NIRA
legislation and, at the urging of McCormick, correctly insisted

that their code deny the application of the licensing power to newspapers. But their other reservations, disclosed when the temporary code was submitted to the NRA administrator, General Hugh S. Johnson, in August, raised objections not only from the outspoken former cavalry officer, but from some newspapers which felt that the ANPA was asking a privileged position for daily newspapers that was not in keeping with the recovery effort.[13]

After eyeing the NIRA's guarantee of the right to collective bargaining, Hanson and the committee had written into their code an open-shop provision assuring any employer or employee the right to bargain individually. The code also proposed that newsboys be exempted from NIRA provisions limiting child labor. Reporters and other editorial workers who were doing "professional work" were not to be subject to the maximum hour provisions of the law. Capping the requests of the publishers was their insistence upon this famous clause: "Nothing in the adoption and acceptance of this code shall be construed as waiving, abrogating, or modifying any rights secured under the Constitution of the United States or of any state, or limiting the freedom of the press."

Those surrounding Roosevelt regarded the inclusion of such a statement in the proposed code as an insulting gesture, and a vigorous debate ensued over the intentions of the New Deal toward the newspapers, in which some publishers and editors rejected the freedom of the press clause as both unnecessary and unwise. General Johnson accepted the code, after obtaining modification of the child labor and open-shop clauses, commenting, "I don't want to fight the press of America but I can't afford to lay down for them."[14] President Roosevelt, approving the final draft of the daily newspaper code in February 1934, contributed his part to the developing controversy by issuing an executive order which declared that the modified freedom of the press clause appended to the code was "pure surplusage." The order continued: "The freedom guaranteed by the Constitution is freedom of expression and that will be scrupulously respected — but

---

[13] *Editor & Publisher*, 66:3 (Aug. 12, 1933).
[14] *Ibid.*, 66:38 (Aug. 19, 1933).

it is not freedom to work children, or to do business in a fire trap or violate the laws against obscenity, libel and lewdness." [15]

This was strong medicine, which many publishers refused to swallow. It was their turn, as it had been the President's earlier, to feel unjustly and falsely accused. The result was that Hanson and other ANPA leaders who proposed to fight the New Deal legislative program down the line, objecting whenever they felt press security was endangered or the constitutional rights of newspapers were being violated, were strengthened in their control of ANPA policy.

The final version of the daily newspaper code provided for a forty-hour week only for employees of newspapers published in cities of more than 50,000 population. A minimum wage scale was set up, ranging from $15 a week for employees of papers published in cities of more than 500,000 population down to $11 a week in cities of less than 25,000 population. "Learners" would receive at least 70 percent of the scale. Mechanical employees were guaranteed a minimum wage of forty cents an hour. The minimum age for newsboys remained at twelve (subject to regulations in the various states), with the added provision that publishers were not to employ children under sixteen except for daylight work which would not impair their health or interfere with their schooling. Employees were guaranteed collective bargaining rights, and the "professional worker" clause was clarified so that ordinary news-editorial employees came under the maximum hour clause. An NRA Code Authority of ten publisher members was established, five members to be chosen by the ANPA and five by various regional publishers' associations. Four representatives of employers and four representatives of the mechanical unions were to compose the Newspaper Industrial Board. [16]

President Roosevelt, when he signed the code, asked that all newspapers with more than 75,000 circulation, published in cities of more than 750,000 population, adopt a five-day, forty-hour week, in order to increase employment of newspapermen. Most of the metropolitan dailies adopted the five-day week as re-

[15] *Ibid.*, 67:3 (Feb. 24, 1934).
[16] *Ibid.*, 67:36 (Feb. 24, 1934) gives the text of the code.

quested. The President also asked that the child labor provision
of the code be made more stringent, since many other industry
codes had raised the minimum age for employment to fourteen.
But the ANPA committee on the newspaperboy, named to consider child labor regulations and to foster progressive newspa-
perboy-training programs, came to the conclusion that "action
on the use of boys 12 to 16 for selling and delivering newspapers
must be voluntary with the publishers to preserve the opportunities and educational work done by the newspapers for the
boys." [17]
Wage and hour provisions of the daily newspaper code were
received with little enthusiasm by newspaper workers, who complained that the $11 to $15 weekly salary minimums were far too
low. Reporters and desk men on dailies in various sections of the
country had already begun to form bargaining units in the summer of 1933 when the trend of the code negotiations became apparent. The American Federation of Labor had chartered some
newswriters' locals in earlier years, but no national organization
was in existence.[18] This belated organization of editorial employees was climaxed by the founding in December 1933 of the
American Newspaper Guild, which reporter-columnist Heywood
Broun was to lead as president until his death in 1939. The newspapermen and women were seeking, they said, "to preserve the
vocational interests of the members and to improve the conditions under which they work by collective bargaining, and to
raise the standards of journalism. . . ." [19] A union publication, a
tabloid-size newspaper named the *Guild Reporter*, began to appear fortnightly almost immediately.
The first contract to be signed by a publisher and a guild unit
included a guild objective that was to meet determined opposition from the ANPA. J. David Stern, liberal-minded publisher of
the Philadelphia *Record*, signed a contract in April 1934 which
provided for a guild-shop agreement. The contract stipulated

[17] *Report of the Fiftieth Annual Meeting* (1936), p. 370.
[18] For details of these AFL unions, see National Labor Relations Board, *Collective Bargaining in the Newspaper Industry* (Washington: Government Printing Office, 1939), pp. 104–13. The ANPA was not concerned with unions of editorial employees before 1933, treating them as local matters.
[19] *Collective Bargaining in the Newspaper Industry*, p. 117.

that all editorial employees must join the guild within thirty days of initial employment.[20] Another form of the guild-shop agreement which was later used required that only 80 percent of the employees covered by the contract must become union members. In either case the publisher was free to hire whomever he chose, without regard to prior guild membership, thus differentiating the guild shop from typical closed shops. And in many cities the guild-shop agreement was not included in local contracts.

Other publishers were watching the guild movement warily. They were antagonized when the guild, which now had eight thousand members, decided at the June 1934 convention to take the form of a trade union organization. Arguments had been advanced that newspapermen should limit themselves to a professional club type of organization, but the guild leaders felt they needed the strength of the union movement to obtain wage and working condition advancements. Publishers resented the action of the guild in preparing and publicizing a list of what it regarded to be harmful practices by newspapers: carrying publicity disguised as news; requiring reporters to write stories which newspapermen knew to be false or misleading; acceptance of money by newspapermen for obtaining publicity stories; sometimes requesting newspapermen to use their influence with public officials in matters other than the gathering of the news.[21] The publishers' objection to this listing was that all newspapers were being accused of these faults in a general indictment regardless of the degrees of individual newspaper integrity.

Hanson now proceeded to give the publishers legal advice on the guild situation. In July 1934 the ANPA suggested to its members that although the NIRA gave their employees the right to bargain collectively, it did not *require* that the employer sign a contract. Various tips on how to avoid the making of guild-shop agreements were included in the bulletin.[22] The *Guild Reporter* obtained a copy of this confidential message and printed it in April 1935, commenting angrily: "The publishers were, in effect,

[20] *Editor & Publisher,* 67:5 (Apr. 14, 1934).
[21] Lee, *Daily Newspaper in America,* p. 685.
[22] *Bulletin 6305,* July 27, 1934.

to confer but to arrive at no agreement."[23] As a result of these actions, relations between the guild and employers worsened. The guild's first major strike was called against the Newark, New Jersey, *Ledger* in November 1934 after publisher L. T. Russell discharged eight guildsmen. The guild retaliated with mass picketing, public boycott, and a secondary boycott of advertisers. Russell called upon the ANPA for aid, but the only answer was an assurance from the Special Standing Committee that the association was doing all within its power to support publishers against the guild. The eighteen-week strike finally broke the newspaper, forcing Russell to sell, and thus was only a moral victory for the newspapermen involved. But it was a powerful demonstration by the guild.[24]

A crisis was reached in government-publisher relations when the National Labor Relations Board tried to break a stalemate which had been created in guild-publisher negotiations. The NLRB, operating under NIRA authority, ordered William Randolph Hearst's San Francisco *Call-Bulletin* to reinstate Dean S. Jennings, who claimed he had been discharged for guild activity. Weary of inaction by the Newspaper Industrial Board, which was deadlocked with four employer and four employee representatives, the NLRB had issued the order in the Jennings case without going to the Newspaper Industrial Board for approval.[25] ANPA President Howard Davis immediately called a national meeting of newspaper publishers for January 28, 1935, to protest this violation of code procedure and threatened to withdraw the papers from their NRA code. President Roosevelt overruled the NLRB, and the publishers canceled their protest meeting, but another bitter exchange had resulted.[26] The publishers were generally opposed to continuing the daily newspaper code after its scheduled expiration on June 15, 1935, but the Supreme Court decision finding the National Industrial Recovery Act unconstitutional, handed down in May, made any further action unnecessary. The collective bargaining rights of employees were pre-

[23] *Guild Reporter*, Apr. 1, 1935, p. 1.
[24] *Collective Bargaining in the Newspaper Industry*, pp. 64, 120.
[25] *Ibid.*, p. 151.
[26] *Editor & Publisher*, 69:1 (Jan. 26, 1935).

served and strengthened, however, by the passage of the Wagner Labor Relations Act that year.

It was at the association's 1935 convention that Chairman Harvey J. Kelly of the ANPA Special Standing Committee called the guild president, Heywood Broun, a "round and overstuffed gentleman who delights in preening in public" and predicted that the guild would waste away under his leadership.[27] But the newsmen's union failed to oblige and was to cause publishers infinitely more trouble in 1936 and 1937.

Meanwhile the ANPA committee on federal laws and Elisha Hanson were discovering more and more New Deal legislation which, they thought, struck at the foundations of the press. In 1934 the committee warned the ANPA convention about a new thirty-hour work week bill which did not exempt newspapers; about the Wagner labor bill; about new proposals for child labor legislation which did not exempt newsboys; and about the proposed social security bill. Lincoln B. Palmer, general manager of the association, told the same convention that Rexford Tugwell's theories on curbing false or misleading advertising had found their way into forty-five NRA codes, the Securities Exchange Act, pure food and drug legislation, and other New Deal proposals which Palmer thought were aimed at injuring the press through restriction of advertising.

Opposition to federal legislation, either because it affected the business interests of newspapers or because it was deemed unconstitutional as applied to them, reached a peak at the 1935 ANPA annual meeting. A committee on the Securities Exchange Act reported that it had sought revisions in the advertising safeguards of the act — written to prevent a repetition of the financial fiasco of the 1920s — because of a drying up of financial advertising in newspapers. The report of the committee on federal laws, made by chairman William F. Wiley of the Cincinnati *Enquirer*, was particularly complete. Wiley referred to the Wagner Act, which the ANPA was unsuccessfully fighting, as "one of the most obnoxious bills." He said Hanson and Chairman Kelly of the Special Standing Committee had opposed the Wagner Act and the thirty-hour work week bill at congressional hearings. A

[27] *Ibid.*, 69:7 (Apr. 27, 1935).

brief had been filed by the ANPA against the Copeland pure
food, drugs, and cosmetics bill because amendments advocated
by the ANPA and designed to modify the proposed advertising
safeguards of the bill had not been included. Wiley was watching pending copyright legislation and proposed tariffs on newsprint and wood pulp. He warned the publishers against Agricultural Adjustment Act amendments which would "control advertising of farm products." A bill regulating truck transportation
exempted from its provisions carriers of agricultural products,
livestock, fish, and newspapers. Finally, Wiley suggested that
since newspapers maintained a high degree of employment during depression as well as prosperity, they should receive the
same compensatory consideration in the assessing of payroll taxes
on employers under the Social Security Act as would employers
who paid unemployment insurance claims.

Heywood Broun complained in his syndicated column, after
attending this ANPA convention, ". . . they did not talk of journalism but of the industry. If a man from Mars had happened in,
I think he might have spent an hour and still remained puzzled
as to whether he had happened in upon a convention of bankers,
cotton-mill owners, or the makers of bathroom supplies. . . ."[28]

Should Broun, as president of the guild, be disqualified as an
impartial observer, then the sentiments of a member of the
ANPA committee on freedom of the press can be recorded. Arthur Hays Sulzberger, publisher of the New York *Times*, suggested at the 1936 annual meeting that perhaps the association
was going too far in its campaign. He said that while safeguard-
ing of press freedom was necessary he was not convinced "the
present administration has or had designs upon the freedom of
the press." And he declared that the freedom of the press guarantee in the Constitution "is the statement of an essential liberty
of a free people and not a grant of immunity extended to a particular trade or profession . . . the responsibilities that the fran-
chise entails are greater than the privileges it bestows." If the
press was in trouble, he suggested, perhaps it had some contributing faults: slanted "interpretations" and inaccuracies in the

[28] As quoted by George Seldes in *Lords of the Press* (New York: Messner,
1938), p. 7.

reporting of news; putting the personal interests of publishers ahead of public service; failure to present both sides of arguments, especially during election campaigns; and overeditorializing in news columns.[29]

This was wise and needed counsel, both for the ANPA and for some newspapers. But it was not heeded by those who needed it most during the 1936 presidential election campaign and the post-election struggle over the Supreme Court "packing bill." Among the newspapermen who wrote explanations of the overwhelming victory of President Roosevelt over Alfred M. Landon, despite the opposition of editorial writers for a great majority of the daily press, was Virginius Dabney, noted editor of the Richmond, Virginia, *Times Dispatch*. Said he of the ANPA:

My candid opinion is that its record in recent years has gone far to arouse the public against the newspapers. One does not have to go all the way with the *Christian Century* in its celebrated post-election blast against the American press — in which it charged that press with arrogance, tyranny, greed, and scorn of fair play — to feel that the dailies of this nation are under strong suspicion, and that their influence, in consequence, is on the wane. This, I believe, is as much due to the American Newspaper Publishers Association as to the activities of individual papers.

The publishers' association has indulged in an unabashed campaign of self-laudation; it has over-emphasized the "freedom of the press" to a ludicrous extent, thereby incurring the suspicion that it is using this shibboleth as a red herring; and its members have banded together to defeat legislation, such as the Child Labor Amendment, and have thereby created the impression in many minds, whether justly or not, that they put their own private profit above the general good.[30]

General Counsel Hanson, undertaking to answer these strictures, dealt with the three points in Dabney's second paragraph.[31] "The first charge is so silly there is no use to discuss it," Hanson began. He answered the second point by reviewing the laudable activities of the committee on freedom of the press in the Minnesota gag law and Louisiana tax cases, but ignored the association's attempts to connect press freedom with newspaper

[29] The full text of his remarks is recorded in *Editor & Publisher*, 69:4 (Apr. 25, 1936).
[30] *Public Opinion Quarterly*, Apr. 1937, p. 124.
[31] *Ibid.*, Jan. 1938, p. 124.

business operations, which had inspired Dabney's charge. Coming to the final point, he made this assertion:

Insofar as legislation is concerned, the Association, during the 15 years that I have been connected with it, has steadfastly adhered to a policy of refusing to seek any legislation which would give to the newspaper publishing business of this country any business or commercial advantage. The Association has not hesitated to oppose measures designed to affect the newspaper publishing business injuriously or to restrict the people's right to have a press free from governmental restraint.

There is no reason to presume that this statement did not represent Hanson's honest estimate of the ANPA legislative activities which he then so strongly influenced. The record of such activities written into the history of the association would indicate that Hanson either had a strained conception of the rights and responsibilities of the press or an unusual fear of government encroachment on the press.

Certainly Hanson had a deep fear of the New Deal, and particularly of what he regarded as its ability to hoodwink the Washington news corps. In an article written for the *Annals* of the American Academy of Political and Social Science and published in May 1935, he made these observations about "Official Propaganda and the New Deal":

Any Government propaganda bureau to be wholly successful must have full control over the agencies for the dissemination of information. In Europe, dictators have complete control over both the press and the radio. In the United States, while the administration in office has full control over radio, if it cares to exercise it, no administration can exercise any form of control over the press if the press resists, as it did in 1933 and 1934. However, there are methods of indirection which at times are even more effective than direct action. These were the methods tried in Washington.

By setting up publicity divisions in departments and agencies which had not had them theretofore; by expanding offices of information already in existence; by hiring more newspaper men to write news for the Government than were employed by the newspapers and press associations to write for them; by bottling up sources of news so that any subordinate who gave out any information except through channels was subject to immediate dismissal; by retaining advertising agencies skilled in handling promotional copy to advise it in the selling of its programs — by these and various other methods, the New Deal sought to get its program before the people. For nearly a year there was no opposition — no counter-propaganda. . . .

While news was being bottled up in the departments, it was being opened up after a fashion at the White House. An entirely new system of dealing with newspaper men was installed there. The President met the correspondents and freely discussed matters with them. Mrs. Roosevelt looked after the ladies of the press. An *entente cordiale* was established between the correspondents and the White House which embraced the families of the correspondents as well. . . .

Washington columns present an interesting field for study of propaganda and counter-propaganda. How many of them are being sent out daily is any man's guess. The rate of mortality is high. But a comparison of what is being published today with that published two years ago by the same columnists reveals this interesting fact: Whereas in 1933 practically all the columns read like pro-Administration propaganda, today the reverse is substantially true.[32]

It is not surprising then that Hanson rejected the comments of the Sulzbergers and the Dabneys and seemed to be in consonance with the freedom of the press committee chairman, whose Chicago *Tribune* exhibited deepest distrust of the motives of the federal government.

While this debate was in progress, Hanson and the ANPA continued to tilt with the American Newspaper Guild. It was a time of decision for the guild. Between February 1936 and June 1938 the newsmen conducted twenty strikes, having a major labor dispute in progress at all times.[33] Two of the biggest battles were against Hearst's Seattle *Post-Intelligencer* and Chicago *Herald & Examiner*. But the most significant struggle, because it ended in a vital Supreme Court decision, involved only one Associated Press staffman, Morris Watson.

Watson, who had been discharged by the AP in 1935, asserted he had been discharged for guild activities. He appealed to the National Labor Relations Board for an order compelling his reinstatement under the provisions of the Wagner Act. When the NLRB ruled against the AP in 1936, the press association carried the case to the Supreme Court, contending that the Wagner Act was unconstitutional and that in any event it did not apply to newspapers or press associations. Hanson entered the ANPA in

[32] Harwood L. Childs, ed., "Pressure Groups and Propaganda," *Annals*, May 1935, pp. 176–86.

[33] *Collective Bargaining in the Newspaper Industry*, p. 121.

the case as *amicus curiae* and asserted that unionization of editorial employees under government compulsion destroyed freedom of the press.[34] The Supreme Court heard the arguments on the case in October.

Hanson, however, did not await the court's decision before telling the membership and other publishers to "flatly refuse to have anything to do with the National Labor Relations Board, other than to notify it that it is without power under the Constitution to interfere with their business."[35] The *Guild Reporter* cried: "Hanson an Anarchist!"[36]

A flat statement that a publisher who agreed to a guild shop thereby destroyed or restricted freedom of the press was issued by the ANPA board of directors in December 1936. Carrying out Hanson's thesis, the board said that the guild shop was in effect a closed shop, and it argued that the inclusion of all editorial employees in the guild would lead to biased news writing and consequently to violation of freedom of the press. The board advised publishers not to sign contracts which established guild shops, recognized the check-off system for collecting dues, established salaries on a time basis, or provided for arbitration of dismissal cases. These recommendations opposed nearly all the guild program.[37]

An outraged protest from J. David Stern, publisher of the Philadelphia *Record* and the earliest signer with the guild, greeted this ANPA statement of policy. Stern resented the implication that he had tossed aside his freedom of the press guarantees by agreeing to a guild shop. Resigning from the ANPA, he said: "Ever since the NRA code, the American Newspaper Publishers Association has been using the pretext of protecting the freedom of the press to gain special privilege in purely business obligations. That is why I say *you* are endangering the freedom of the press, one of the most important essentials of our democracy."[38]

The 1936 general election demonstrated that the principle of

[34] *Collective Bargaining in the Newspaper Industry*, p. 63.
[35] *Editor & Publisher*, 69:7 (Oct. 10, 1936).
[36] *Guild Reporter*, Oct. 15, 1936, p. 1.
[37] *Editor & Publisher*, 69:12 (Dec. 12, 1936).
[38] *Ibid.*, 69:57 (Dec. 19, 1936).

236 NEWSPAPER PUBLISHERS ASSOCIATION

collective bargaining was on the statute books to stay. Newspaper publishers, recognizing this situation and desiring to abide by the majority decision, shied away from the ANPA's guild policy in growing numbers, without awaiting the Watson case ruling. The New York *Daily News*, the country's largest newspaper, signed a contract for a guild shop, and Hearst ended the long Seattle *Post-Intelligencer* strike, putting President Roosevelt's son-in-law and daughter, John and Anna Boettiger, in charge of the paper.[39] There was widespread granting of higher wages and shorter hours by metropolitan publishers who wished to beat the guild to the punch.

Then the Supreme Court added its voice to those rejecting the ANPA's concept of freedom of the press. On April 12, 1937, the court read a series of decisions upholding the constitutionality of the Wagner Act. Among the cases decided was that of Morris Watson. A majority composed of Justices Hughes, Brandeis, Stone, Cardozo, and Roberts found in favor of the NLRB and ordered the Associated Press to reinstate Watson in his job.[40] The five justices ruled that Watson had been illegally discharged for union activity, and it was upon this point that the case turned. They also had this to say about freedom of the press:

The publisher of a newspaper has no special immunity from the application of general laws. He has no special privilege to invade the rights and liberties of others. He must answer for libel. He may be punished for contempt of court. He is subject to the anti-trust laws. Like others, he must pay equitable and nondiscriminatory taxes on his business.

Hanson could find some comfort in the fact that a minority of four justices agreed with him that freedom of the press was being endangered if the AP could not discharge Watson for his union activity. But it is significant that these four justices were then under bitter attack as being out of step with the country's dominant economic and social philosophies. They were Justices McReynolds, Butler, Van Devanter, and Sutherland.

The upholding of the Wagner Act was a great guild victory. It assured the American Newspaper Guild a permanent place in

[39] *Ibid.*, 69:3–5 (Dec. 5, 1936).
[40] *Associated Press* v. *NLRB*, 301 U.S. 103 (1937).

newspaper life. There was to be one more major explosion, however, before publisher-guild relations settled down to a routine
labor-management activity. Flushed with success, the guild held
its 1937 convention in St. Louis from June 7 to 11. There the
delegates voted to leave the American Federation of Labor and
to join the Congress of Industrial Organization. At the same time
the guild broadened its membership base to include commercial
office and other nonmechanical employees. Guild leaders also
decided to insist on guild-shop provisions in all future contracts.
Finally, the convention adopted several resolutions defining the
guild's stand on national and international issues.[41]

To the publishers, this was the last straw. They did not like
the CIO affiliation, or the guild-shop mandate, or the proposed
unionization of their business office employees, or the guild taking stands on public issues that might conceivably affect impartial reporting and news handling. The ANPA called a mass meeting of all newspaper publishers, to be held in Chicago on June
29. Joining the ANPA in sponsoring the convention were the
American Society of Newspaper Editors, the Inland Daily Press
Association, the Southern Newspaper Publishers Association, the
New England Daily Newspaper Association, the Pacific Northwest Publishers Association, and the state associations of New
York, Ohio, Pennsylvania, Texas, and California. The 555 newspaper executives who attended declared they would present a
solid front against the guild-shop demand, which they said was
"threatening the impartiality of reporting." A national committee
was organized, with ANPA President James G. Stahlman as
chairman and ANPA General Manager Lincoln B. Palmer as secretary.[42]

If the publishers were angered by the aggressive stand taken
by the guild leadership, so were some of their employees. The
American Federation of Labor sponsored various local newspaper unions after the guild joined the CIO, and on some dailies
independent professional groups were organized. The conservative element within the guild itself forced a toning down of guild
stands on public issues after 1939, and the *Guild Reporter* gradu-

[41] *Guild Reporter,* June 20, 1937, p. 1.
[42] *Editor & Publisher,* 70:3 (July 3, 1937).

ally ceased using the letters *ANPA* as an epithet. Guild organizational activity, particularly the drive to win guild shops, was slowed for a time by the publishers' "solid front" agreement made at the Chicago convention. ANPA Special Standing Committee statistics show this trend in guild contracts held with individual newspapers, nearly all published in larger cities:

Type of Contract	1938	1939	1940	1941	1946	1947	1948
Open-shop	46	70	67	65	69	61	76
Guild-shop or modified guild-shop.	10	13	28	35	100	132	111
Total	56	83	95	100	169	193	187

Figures for 1946 and later include maintenance of membership contracts in the guild-shop and modified guild-shop contract totals. The guild drive to organize newspaper commercial offices netted it 27 contracts by 1939, 57 by 1941, and 92 by 1948.

Quite normal labor-management relationships existed between the guild and metropolitan publishers during World War II and the postwar years. One victory was scored for the guild when the War Labor Board ruled that its maintenance of membership formula legally applied to newspapers. The maintenance of membership plan, formulated to stabilize union membership under disrupted wartime working conditions and thus prevent strikes, required an employee to remain in his union for the period of a contract agreement unless he resigned within an "escape" period at the start of the contract. The Harrisburg *Patriot* carried a case to the WLB, protesting application of the maintenance of membership clause to newspaper employees, but received an adverse ruling in 1944. Freedom of the press was not infringed upon, the WLB said, pointing out that the employer could discharge any newsman who did not fulfill his journalistic obligations correctly.[43] The publishers still contended, however, that the danger of biased news handling was increased by the existence of a powerful guild organization.

After the end of the war guild units succeeded in obtaining higher wages and better contracts with a minimum of difficulty. There was one sharp setback which embarrassed the guild, however. The union's first supporter and long-time friend, J. David

[43] *Bulletins: Labor 4632*, Mar. 10, 1944.

Stern, liquidated his Philadelphia *Record* rather than submit to what he called unfair wage demands by the guild. After this shock the union proceeded with more caution in its campaign to win $100-a-week minimum salaries for newsmen on larger papers with five years' experience, and by 1949 half of the 23,000 membership was covered by such contracts. The ANPA, preoccupied with its troubles with the International Typographical Union in the immediate postwar years, did pause to note with satisfaction the decline in guild contracts recorded in 1948. It also attempted, without success, to revive its claim that nearly all newsmen should be regarded as professional workers, exempted from wage and hour regulations.[44]

Meanwhile the ANPA continued to keep a close watch on the government in Washington. The committee on the Social Security Act, headed by A. V. Miller of the New York *Herald Tribune*, reported annually on developments in unemployment insurance and old age pension legislation, viewing with disfavor various attempts to expand social security benefits which would mean added cost to employers. This committee also told the 1939 ANPA annual meeting that "there is no warrant or justification" for passage of legislation establishing a national health insurance program with an initial annual cost of 80 million dollars.

"Dangers and problems of the Washington ambush" was the topic of the committee on federal laws at the 1936 annual meeting. The committee thus described life in the capital after being beaten back during 1935 on the Wagner Act and the social security issue. It gave its approval to the considerably softened Copeland pure food, drugs, and cosmetics bill. But it found that the Nye antiwar profits bill as passed by the House would give the President power to license the press. And it joined with Hanson in protesting legislation giving the Federal Trade Commission authority to ban unfair or deceptive acts or practices in commerce. Hanson had filed a statement with the Senate Interstate Commerce Committee opposing the granting of this increased authority to the FTC.[45] The association, however, was unsuccessful in its efforts to prevent passage of the Wheeler-Lea

[44] *Editor & Publisher*, 80:15 (Jan. 17, 1948).
[45] *Bulletin 6555*, Mar. 4, 1936.

legislation giving the FTC power to regulate unfair or misleading advertising of products in interstate commerce. The committee on federal laws was able to obtain the release of newspapers from responsibility for any false advertising the FTC might find.[46]

ANPA legislative representatives also were unsuccessful in opposing passage of the Fair Labor Standards Act, popularly known as the Wage and Hour Law. This act looked forward to the establishment of a forty-hour week and forty cents an hour minimum pay. Congress exempted weekly newspapers with a circulation of three thousand or less from the provisions of the bill, but some other publishers felt that they, too, should be free from the application of this legislation. Their argument was that their ability to operate was affected, along with that of the small weeklies, and therefore the press freedom guarantee of the First Amendment took precedence over the law. Evidence was presented that small dailies were being burdened with difficult financial problems by the Wage and Hour Law provisions, but the publishers were unable to obtain relief either from Congress or from the courts. The committee on federal laws insisted in its 1941 ANPA convention report that the Wage and Hour Law "was not intended to apply to the newspaper publishing business," and the ANPA supported publishers who went to court rather than let federal investigators inspect their financial records.

Apparently this ANPA activity was not popular with the membership. Hanson, warning the 1944 annual meeting about the effects of the Wage and Hour Law upon the newspaper business, made this comment:

The question is, do you want such a life and death power asserted over you? I can't conceive of your wanting it. Yet I have been utterly amazed that in the four years these issues have been before the courts, with isolated exceptions, practically all the editorial comment that I have seen has been editorial comment giving this Association plain unshirted hell for even challenging the power of Congress to destroy the press.

Here was evidence that the opinions of the rank-and-file mem-

[46] *Bulletin 6786*, Feb. 1, 1938; *Bulletin 6794*, Feb. 28, 1938.

bership were having their effect upon ANPA policy. After 1939
new association management direction, a broadening of membership on the board of directors and committees, and increased
participation of small dailies in association affairs tended to re-
orient the extreme policy, adopted by the ANPA leadership of
the 1930s, which had brought about criticisms of the "press freedom crusade." Association committee reports and bulletins now
became more informative in their nature and only occasionally
asserted positive opinions concerning government acts and legislation, in contrast to the salty comments of the mid-1930s.
When the Supreme Court ruled against two newspapers which
had fought the Wage and Hour Law, the committee on federal
laws told the 1946 annual meeting quietly, "publishers, for the
first time since the law was enacted, know just where they
stand." They had to produce their books for inspection and meet
the requirements of the law, the committee said.

Two other factors were involved in this softening of ANPA
policy. One was the cessation of "reform" legislation as New
Deal control of Congress weakened after 1938. The other was
the coming of war, which shifted the government's energy from
the domestic scene to wartime and international problems. Newspaper relations with the government during World War II went
quite smoothly. When a state of national emergency was pro-
claimed by President Roosevelt, the ANPA board of directors
called representatives of all other leading newspaper associations to a meeting in New York on February 4, 1941. The following statement, which was approved by the 1941 ANPA annual
meeting, was issued:

1. The newspapers recognize their primary obligation to further
national defense in every possible manner;
2. The newspapers also recognize their essential duty to furnish
complete and accurate information compatible with military neces-
sities;
3. The newspapers in the performance of these obligations be-
speak the cordial consideration and cooperation of federal and state
authorities concerned with national defense.[47]

With few exceptions both newspapers and government au-

[47] *Report of the Fifty-fifth Annual Convention* (1941), p. 51.

thorities carried out the injunctions of this statement. After Office of Censorship duties were put under the direction of a veteran newspaperman, Byron Price, the voluntary censorship of military and war production information was carried out by the newspapers with a minimum of friction. Naming of another veteran newspaper and radio man, Elmer Davis, to head the Office of War Information eased concern over the activities of the government's information agencies. The newspapers of America, with the ANPA aiding in organizational work, helped sponsor a national scrap metal and rubber drive, a wastepaper collection campaign, and a massive advertising campaign in behalf of government war bond sales. And they covered the war effort on all fronts in a manner unequaled in history.

Postwar problems of the ANPA can be summarized by surveying the list of association committees and departments as of 1949. Labor relations with the mechanical unions and the guild were handled by the Special Standing Committee's Chicago office. The committee on advertising agencies, the Credit and Adjustment Department, and the ANPA's affiliate, the Bureau of Advertising, were concerned with advertising problems. The Mechanical and the Mechanical Research departments, and their respective advisory committees, were promoting better methods of newspaper production. Operating in specialized fields were the committee on press communications, the schools of journalism committee, and the library committee.

Governmental and legislative affairs still occupied the attention of the largest number of committees and departments. Included were three old stand-bys: the Newsprint Department, the postal committee, and the Traffic Department, with its advisory committee. The social security committee, still headed by A. V. Miller of the New York *Herald Tribune,* apparently had achieved permanent status. One of the most active groups was the committee on the newspaperboy, led continuously by Howard W. Stodghill of the Philadelphia *Bulletin.* This committee worked with the International Circulation Managers' Association to publicize the values of newspaperboy delivery systems. It contended that the newspaperboy problem could best be met by the papers themselves taking responsibility for the welfare of their carriers, operating under child labor provisions of state laws and local ordinances. The remaining committees in this field were the committee on federal laws and the committee on freedom of the press, which continued their work in behalf of newspaper business interests and press freedom, in cooperation with ANPA General Counsel Hanson.

One victory was scored by the committee on federal laws when Congress overrode a veto by President Harry S. Truman in 1948 and enacted into law a bill excluding vendors of newspapers and magazines from the benefits of the Social Security Act. The Supreme Court had ruled in 1944 that adult news vendors working in fixed locations were employees of the newspapers, rather than independent contractors as the papers claimed, and approved a Los Angeles vendors' collective bargaining unit.[48] Hanson protested the decision at the 1944 ANPA annual meeting, and the association undertook with other interested groups to support legislation establishing the vendors as independent contractors for social security purposes. Their point was finally won, after President Truman had twice vetoed bills on the grounds that they violated the spirit of the Social Security Act by removing a group of workers from the protection of that law.[49]

The ANPA also endorsed passage of the Taft-Hartley Act over the President's veto in 1947, since it drastically revised provisions of the Wagner Act to which the ANPA had long been opposed.

In the area of freedom of the press Hanson participated for the ANPA in nearly every case involving constitutional rights of the press. Two of these were major contempt of court cases, involving the Los Angeles *Times* and the Miami *Herald*.[50] Out of these legal battles came the Supreme Court's "clear and present danger" definition, to be applied to contempt of court charges. This definition gave newspapers much more latitude in commenting upon court activities, by stating that a judge could take no action unless press comment created so great and immediate a danger that his court could not continue to function. The committee on freedom of the press, inactive during the war, was re-

[48] *NLRB* v. *Hearst Publications, Inc.*, 322 U.S. 111 (1944).
[49] *Federal Laws Bulletin 22 – 1948*, Apr. 28, 1948.
[50] *Bridges* v. *California*, 314 U.S. 252 (1941); *Pennekamp* v. *Florida*, 328 U.S. 331 (1946).

vived in 1948, the chairmanship passing from the Chicago *Tribune's* McCormick to George C. Biggers of the Atlanta *Journal*.[51]

The biggest problem which confronted the daily newspapers of America at the close of 1949, however, was not yet being faced by the ANPA. This problem, defined at the start of this chapter, involved growing public criticism of newspapers, which, it was maintained, did not serve the public interest fully. Much of the criticism actually centered around the questionable activities of a relatively few newspapers, but the effect of the controversy was felt by all newspapers and newspapermen. Intensifying the problem was the fact that in all but 117 American cities and towns, one publisher controlled the local daily newspaper or newspapers, bringing forth cries of "monopoly," no matter how conscientiously the individual publisher might seek to maintain a proper balance. And stimulating the controversy in late 1948 and 1949 was the startling reelection of President Truman, who had enjoyed the active editorial support of only 15 percent of American dailies, with 10 percent of the country's total circulation.[52] Many newspaper publishers and editors had worked hard to present honest editorial opinion during the campaign and to have their newspapers conscientiously report the issues in the news columns. They were dismayed by the wide publication of a photograph of the victorious President, holding high over his head a newspaper whose banner line read: DEWEY DEFEATS TRUMAN. This masterpiece of Chicago *Tribune* "enterprise" was the most striking bit of evidence that newspapers needed to engage in a constructive program of self-criticism. But newspapermen agreed during the election aftermath that there was much other evidence of the need for newspapers to study the problem of their relationships with the public.

Editor & Publisher, trade journal for the daily newspapers, took one step in March 1949 when it sponsored a meeting of a panel on the press, composed of ten newspapermen and educators, including publishers Barry Bingham of the Louisville *Courier-Journal* and Philip Graham of the Washington *Post*. The panel, while wary of endorsing any precipitate actions, approved

---

[51] *B Bulletin 23 – 1948*, May 12, 1948.
[52] *Editor & Publisher*, 81:11 (Oct. 30, 1948).

tentative proposals for a "joint appraisal of the self-improvement possibilities of American newspapers through studies of specific problems."[53] The American Society of Newspaper Editors, which defined the rights and obligations of the press in its "Canons of Journalism" adopted in 1923, named a committee in September 1949 to "examine the desirability of sponsoring an appraisal of self-improvement possibilities of American newspapers" as an outgrowth of the *Editor & Publisher* panel meeting.[54] The National Conference of Editorial Writers, at its third annual meeting in October 1949, adopted a basic code of principles for the conduct of editorial pages "to stimulate the conscience and the quality of the American editorial page."[55]

In addition to these group decisions pointing toward mutual study of newspaper behavior, there were many appeals for increased recognition of newspapers' social responsibilities made by individual journalists, notably Arthur Hays Sulzberger of the New York *Times*, Barry Bingham and James S. Pope of the Louisville *Courier-Journal*, Erwin D. Canham of the *Christian Science Monitor*, and Herbert Brucker of the Hartford *Courant*. The publications of the Commission on Freedom of the Press and those of journalism educators and communications research specialists made further contributions.[56] Their goal was best expressed as factual, unemotional analysis of press behavior in relation to public questions and scientific analysis of the content of the press, to be accomplished without the intervention of government. Such a program of analysis would hearten responsible newspapermen and would stimulate those who need to reform both their outlook and their journalistic practices.

As a trade association for daily newspapers, the American Newspaper Publishers Association had by 1949 more than borne

---

[53] *Ibid.*, 82:5 (Mar. 26, 1949).

[54] *Ibid.*, 82:8 (Oct. 1, 1949).

[55] *Ibid.*, 82:8 (Oct. 29, 1949).

[56] Noteworthy among these publications are Herbert Brucker's *Freedom of Information* (New York: Macmillan, 1949) and *Communications in Modern Society*, edited by Wilbur Schramm (Urbana: University of Illinois Press, 1948). Essays of major importance to this subject in the latter volume are those by Paul Lazersfeld, "Role of Criticism in Management of Mass Communications," Ralph D. Casey, "Professional Freedom and Responsibility in the Press," and Robert J. Blakely, "The Responsibilities of an Editor."

out the expectations of its founders. In the various fields of ANPA activity which this study has examined, the achievements of the association in advancing the business welfare of newspapers have been substantial. Perhaps the most imaginative and praiseworthy of all the association's actions was the establishment of a policy of voluntary arbitration in cooperation with the printing trade unions. The creation of this pioneering labor relations policy in 1900 was a bold step. A decision by a majority of ANPA members to lend the influence of their association to a carefully planned program of study of newspaper behavior would perhaps be judged another bold step. It is a step which, if taken, could lead to the greatest single public service of the American Newspaper Publishers Association.

Appendix

Officers and Directors of the American Newspaper Publishers Association, 1887-1949

Asterisk indicates current officer or director, 1949

* Antrim, Elbert M. Chicago *Tribune*. Director, 1945–51.
Atkinson, John E. Toronto *Star*. Director, 1919–23.
Austin, C. E. Buffalo *Express*. Director, 1901–2.
Baker, Elbert H. Cleveland *Plain Dealer*. Secretary, 1907–12; president, 1912–14; director, 1915–28.
Baker, Lewis. St. Paul *Globe*. Director, 1890–92.
Barnum, Jerome D. Syracuse *Post-Standard*. Director, 1928–34; vice-president, 1934–35; president, 1935–37; director, 1937–42.
Bell, F. G. Savannah *Morning News*. Director, 1920–27.
* Biggers, George C. Atlanta *Journal*. Director, 1941–45, 1946–50.
Brearley, William H. Detroit *Evening News*. Permanent secretary, 1887 convention; secretary, 1887–88.
Bridgman, Herbert L. Brooklyn *Standard-Union*. Vice-president, 1911–14; president, 1914–16; director, 1916–18.
Brown, Hilton U. Indianapolis *News*. Director, 1904–35.
Bryan, John Stewart. Richmond, Virginia, *News-Leader*. Secretary, 1912–24; vice-president, 1924–26; president, 1926–28; director, 1928–30.
Bryant, William B. Paterson, New Jersey, *Press-Guardian*. Director, 1928–29.
Bryant, William Cullen. Brooklyn *Times*. Treasurer, 1887–89; director, 1889–92; secretary and New York office manager, 1892–1905. (Father of William B. Bryant.)
Burd, F. J. Vancouver *Daily Province*. Director, 1923–35.
Bush, F. W. Athens, Georgia, *Messenger*. Director, 1928–29.
Butler, Edward H. Buffalo *Evening News*. Director, 1920–26; vice-president, 1926–28; president, 1928–30; director, 1930–40.
Butler, James Ambrose. Buffalo *Evening News*. Director, 1887–89, 1891–95; vice-president, 1895–99. (Uncle of Edward H. Butler.)
Cabaniss, Henry H. Atlanta *Journal*, Augusta *Chronicle*. Director, 1902–6.
Call, Edward P. Boston *Herald*, New York *Evening Post*, New York *Mail and Express*, New York *Commercial*, and *Journal of Commerce*. Permanent treasurer, 1887 convention; director, 1887–88; treasurer, 1899–1908, 1914–20.
Campe, R. H. Pittsburgh *Chronicle-Telegraph*. Secretary, 1890–91.
Chandler, Harry. Los Angeles *Times*. Director, 1913–28; vice-president, 1928–30; president, 1930–32; director, 1932–34.
Chandler, Norman. Los Angeles *Times*. Director, 1934–40; secretary, 1940–46. (Son of Harry Chandler.)

* Chandler, William G. Scripps-Howard newspapers. Director, 1934–39; treasurer, 1939–43; vice-president, 1943–45; president, 1945–47; director, 1947–51.
Clapp, William W. Boston *Journal.* Vice-president, 1887–88.
Davis, Howard. New York *Tribune,* New York *Herald Tribune.* Treasurer, 1921–30; vice-president, 1930–32; president, 1932–35; director, 1935–44.
Dealey, E. M. (Ted). Dallas *News.* Director, 1940–45.
Dear, Walter M. Jersey City *Jersey Journal.* Treasurer, 1930–39; vice-president, 1939–41; president, 1941–43; director, 1943–45.
Driscoll, Frederick. St. Paul *Pioneer Press.* Director, 1893–1900.
* Fanning, William L. Westchester County Publishers. Treasurer, 1947–51.
Farrell, J. H. Albany, New York, *Press & Knickerbocker.* Director, 1888–90.
* Friendly, Edwin S. New York *Sun.* Treasurer, 1943–47; vice-president, 1947–49; president, 1949–51.
* Funk, J. D. Santa Monica, California, *Outlook.* Director, 1946–50.
Ganz, C. E. Albany, New York, *Journal.* Temporary secretary, 1887 convention.
Glass, Frank P. Montgomery *Advertiser,* Birmingham *News.* Director, 1906–16; vice-president, 1916–18; president, 1918–20.
* Gray, JS. Monroe, Michigan, *News.* Director, 1945–51.
Gunnison, Herbert F. Brooklyn *Eagle.* Permanent vice-president, 1887 convention; treasurer, 1894–99; secretary, 1905–7.
Haldeman, Bruce. Louisville *Courier-Journal.* Vice-president, 1909–11; president, 1911–12.
Haldeman, John H. Louisville *Courier-Journal.* Permanent vice-president, 1887 convention. (Uncle of Bruce Haldeman.)
Hamlin, Condé. St. Paul *Pioneer Press,* New York *Tribune.* Director, 1907–13.
Harris, E. H. Richmond, Indiana, *Palladium-Item.* Director, 1929–32; secretary, 1932–38.
* Honea, Bert N. Fort Worth *Star-Telegram.* Director, 1945–50.
Hornick, Charles W. St. Paul *Dispatch,* San Francisco *Chronicle,* San Francisco *Call.* Director, 1902–13.
* Howe, David W. Burlington, Vermont, *Free Press.* Director, 1938–45; vice-president, 1945–47; president, 1947–49; director, 1949–51.
* Jackson, P. L. Portland *Oregon Journal.* Director, 1947–50.
Jones, Charles H. Jacksonville *Florida Times-Union.* Temporary president, 1887 convention; director, 1887–88; vice-president, 1888–89.
Kauffmann, Samuel H. Washington *Evening Star.* Director, 1887–90; vice-president, 1890–91; director, 1893–99; president, 1899–1902.
* Ker, Frederick I. Hamilton, Ontario, *Spectator.* Director, 1935–51.
Knapp, Charles W. St. Louis *Republic.* Director, 1890–95; president, 1895–99; director, 1900–12, 1914–15.
Laffan, William M. New York *Sun.* Treasurer, 1889–93.
Larke, G. H. New York *World.* Treasurer, 1919–21.
McAneny, George A. New York *Times.* Vice-president, 1918–20.
* McCahill, Charles F. Cleveland *News.* Director, 1944–49; vice-president, 1949–51.
McCarrens, John S. Cleveland *Plain Dealer.* Director, 1936–37; vice-president, 1937–39; president, 1939–41; director, 1941–43.
McCormick, A. A. Chicago *Times-Herald,* Chicago *Record-Herald.* Director, 1899–1902; vice-president, 1902–4.
McCormick, Medill. Chicago *Tribune.* Vice-president, 1907–9.
MacFarlane, W. E. Chicago *Tribune.* Director, 1930–45.
MacKay, John F. Toronto *Globe.* Director, 1913–20.
McLean, William L. Philadelphia *Bulletin.* Director, 1899–1905; vice-president, 1905–7.

McManus, William. Philadelphia *Record*. Permanent vice-president, 1887 convention.

McRae, Milton A. Cincinnati *Post*, Cleveland *Press*. Director, 1891–99; vice-president, 1899–1901.

Manship, Charles P. Baton Rouge *State Times* and *Advocate*. Director, 1945–46.

Meigs, M. C. Chicago *Herald-Examiner*. Director, 1928–30.

Misch, F. K. San Francisco *Call*. Secretary, 1889–90.

Moore, D. D. New Orleans *Times-Picayune*. Director, 1916–20.

Morgan, L. L. New Haven *Register*, Boston *Post*. Secretary, 1888–89; director, 1889–91; secretary and New York office manager, 1891–92.

Nevin, Joseph T. Pittsburgh *Leader*. Director, 1900–6.

Noyes, Linwood I. Ironwood, Michigan, *Daily Globe*. Director, 1938–41; vice-president, 1941–43; president, 1943–45; director, 1945–47.

Palmer, C. M. New York *Journal*, St. Joseph *News*. Director, 1899–1903.

Parks, John S. Fort Smith, Arkansas, *Southwest American* and *Times-Record*. Director, 1930–38; secretary, 1938–40.

Patterson, Paul. Baltimore *Sun*. Vice-president, 1920–22; president, 1922–24; director, 1924–28.

Pattison, William J. New York *Evening Post*. Treasurer, 1908–14.

Pease, Arthur S. Woonsocket, Rhode Island, *Reporter*. Director, 1892–93.

Richards, W. J. Indianapolis *News*. Permanent vice-president, 1887 convention; director, 1887–90.

Ridder, Herman. New York *Staats-Zeitung*. President, 1907–11.

Rogers, George M. Cleveland *Plain Dealer*. Secretary, 1924–32; vice-president, 1932–34.

Rogers, Hopewell L. Chicago *Daily News*. Director, 1912–14; vice-president, 1914–16; president, 1916–18; director, 1918–22.

Rogers, Jason. New York *Globe*, New York *Commercial Advertiser*. Director, 1913–19.

Rogers, S. S. Chicago *Daily News*. Vice-president, 1904–5; president, 1905–7.

Schmick, William F. Baltimore *Sun*. Director, 1942–49.

Scott, James W. Chicago *Herald*. Director, 1888–89; president, 1889–95.

Seif, W. H. Pittsburgh *Times*. Director, 1895–99, 1906–7.

Seymour, J. S. New York *Evening Post*. Treasurer, 1893–94.

Singerly, William M. Philadelphia *Record*. President, 1887–89.

* Slocum, Richard W. Philadelphia *Bulletin*. Director, 1949–51.

* Stackhouse, J. L. Easton, Pennsylvania, *Express*. Director, 1940–47; secretary, 1947–51.

Stahlman, James G. Nashville *Banner*. Vice-president, 1935–37; president, 1937–39; director, 1939–41.

Stone, Melville E. Chicago *Daily News*. Permanent vice-president, 1887 convention.

Taylor, Charles H. Boston *Globe*. Vice-president, 1889–90.

Taylor, Charles H., Jr. Boston *Globe*. Director, 1896–99, 1900–1; vice-president, 1901–2; president, 1902–5; director, 1905–38.

Thomason, Samuel E. Chicago *Tribune*, Chicago *Journal*, Chicago *Times*. Vice-president, 1922–24; president, 1924–26; director, 1926–30.

Townsend, John B. Philadelphia *Press*. Director, 1908–13.

Webb, Charles A. Asheville *Citizen-Times*. Director, 1927–36.

Weston, S. P. Seattle *Post-Intelligencer*. Director, 1903–8.

Whiting, Fred E. Boston *Herald*. Director, 1895–96, 1899–1904.

Williams, T. R. Pittsburgh *Press*. Director, 1918–20; vice-president, 1920; president, 1920–22; director, 1922–28.

Winch, S. R. Portland *Oregon Journal*. Director, 1929–46; secretary, 1946.

Winslow, David. Boston *Journal.* Permanent president, 1887 convention.
Woods, E. H. Boston *Herald.* Director, 1890–91; vice-president, 1891–95.

Managers of the Association

James S. Metcalfe, 1887–89.
G. M. Brennan, 1889–91.
L. L. Morgan, 1891–92.
William C. Bryant, 1892–1905.

Lincoln B. Palmer, 1905–39. (First general manager.)
Cranston Williams, 1939–

Bibliography

Publications of the American Newspaper Publishers Association

Bulletin. Issues numbered consecutively from 1887 to 1940; separate annual series begin in 1941 for *A Bulletin, B Bulletin, C Bulletin, Advertising Bulletin, Circulation Bulletin, Federal Laws Bulletin, Publicity Bulletin;* bound volumes available since 1894.

Bulletins: Labor. 1908–49.

Mechanical Bulletin. 1927–49.

Newsprint Bulletin. 1928–49; issues numbered consecutively from 1928 to 1940; annual series after 1940.

Traffic Bulletin. 1927–40; after 1940 combined with *B Bulletin.*

"Proceedings of the Convention of Newspaper Proprietors held at the City of Rochester, New York, on Wednesday and Thursday, February 16, 17, 1887." The typewritten manuscript of stenographic record is in the New York office of the ANPA.

Minutes of the Third, Fourth, Fifth, and Seventh Annual Meetings of the American Newspaper Publishers Association. 1889–91, 1893. Printed. Minutes for the 1888 and 1892 meetings are not available.

Reports of Proceedings of the Eighth to Thirteenth Annual Conventions of the American Newspaper Publishers Association. 1894–99.

Reports of the Fourteenth to Fifty-fourth Annual Meetings of the American Newspaper Publishers Asssociation. 1900–40. Included in the *Bulletin* series since 1920.

Reports of the Fifty-fifth to Sixty-third Annual Conventions of the American Newspaper Publishers Association. 1941–49.

American Newspaper Publishers Association, Its Works and Purposes. Pamphlet, 1915.

Forty Years Record of ANPA. Pamphlet, 1926.

What the ANPA Means in Dollars and Cents. Pamphlet, 1932.

The Newspaper as an Advertising Medium. New York: Bureau of Advertising, 1940.

The Continuing Study of Newspaper Reading. New York: Advertising Research Foundation, 1939–49.

Magazines and Newspapers

Editor & Publisher
Fourth Estate
Guild Reporter
Journalist
Journalism Quarterly

New York *Herald*
New York *Times*
Printers' Ink
Public Opinion Quarterly
Publishers' Guide

251

Government Documents

Congressional Record.

North, Simeon N. D. *History and Present Condition of the Newspaper and Periodical Press of the United States,* 47th Cong., 2d sess., H. Doc. 42. Washington: Government Printing Office, 1884.

U. S. Congress. House. *Tariff Hearings before the Committee on Ways and Means,* 54th Cong., 2d sess., H. Doc. 338 (1897). 2 vols.

U. S. Congress. House. *Tariff Acts Passed by the Congress of the United States from 1789 to 1897,* 55th Cong., 2d sess., H. Doc. 562 (1898).

U. S. Congress. House. Select Committee under H. Res. 344, *Pulp and Paper Investigation,* 60th Cong., 2d sess., H. Rept. 2206 (1909).

U. S. Congress. House. *Pulp and Paper Investigation Hearings,* 60th Cong., 2d sess., H. Doc. 1502 (1909). 5 vols.

U. S. Congress. House. *Tariff Hearings before the Committee on Ways and Means of the House of Representatives,* 60th Cong., 2d sess., H. Doc. 1505 (1909). 7 vols.

U. S. Congress. House. *H. R. 1438,* 61st Cong., 1st sess., H. Doc. 92 (1909).

U. S. Congress. House. Committee on Ways and Means. *Reciprocity with Canada,* Hearings, 61st Cong., 3d sess., on H. R. 32216 (1911).

U. S. Congress. House. Committee on Ways and Means. *Reciprocity with Canada,* 61st Cong., 3d sess., H. Rept. 2150 (1911).

U. S. Congress. House. *Report of the Special Commission on Second-Class Postal Rates,* 62d Cong., 2d sess., H. Doc. 559 (1912).

U. S. Congress. House. *Tariff Schedules: Hearings before the Committee on Ways and Means,* 62d Cong., 3d sess., H. Doc. 1447 (1913). 6 vols.

U. S. Congress. House. Committee on the Post Office and Post Roads. *Regulating Postal Rates,* Hearings, 70th Cong., 1st sess., on H. R. 9296 (1928).

U. S. Congress. Postal Rates Special Joint Subcommittee. *Postal Rates,* Hearings, 69th Cong., 1st sess. Washington: Government Printing Office, 1926. 2 vols.

U. S. Congress. Senate. *Reciprocity with Canada: Hearings before the Committee on Finance of the United States Senate on H. R. 32216 An Act to Promote Reciprocal Trade Relations with the Dominion of Canada and for Other Purposes,* 61st Cong., 3d sess., S. Doc. 834 (1911).

U. S. Congress. Senate. *Report by the Tariff Board Relative to Pulp and Newsprint Industry,* 62d Cong., 1st sess., S. Doc. 31 (1911).

U. S. Congress. Senate. *Reciprocity with Canada: Hearings before the Committee on Finance of the United States Senate on H. R. 4412 An Act to Promote Reciprocal Trade Relations with the Dominion of Canada and for Other Purposes,* 62d Cong., 1st sess., S. Doc. 56 (1911). 2 vols.

U. S. Congress. Senate. Committee on Finance. *Revenue to Defray War Expenses,* Hearings, 65th Cong., 1st sess., on H. R. 4280 (1917).

U. S. Congress. Senate. *Report by the Federal Trade Commission on the Newsprint Paper Industry,* 71st Cong., 2d sess., S. Doc. 214 (1930).

U. S. Congress. Senate. Special Committee to Study Problems of American Small Business. *Survival of Free Competitive Press,* 79th Cong., 2d sess., Senate Committee Print No. 18 (1947).

U. S. Congress. Senate. Special Committee to Study Problems of American Small Business. *Newsprint Supply and Distribution,* 80th Cong., 1st sess., S. Rept. 150 (1947).

U. S. Federal Trade Commission. *Report of the Federal Trade Commission on the News-print Paper Industry, June 13, 1917.* Washington: Government Printing Office, 1917.

U. S. National Labor Relations Board. *Collective Bargaining in the Newspaper Industry.* Washington: Government Printing Office, 1939.

U. S. Post Office Department. *Postage Rates 1789–1930, Abstract of Laws Passed Between 1789 and 1930 Fixing Rates of Postage and According Free Mail Privileges.* Washington: Government Printing Office, 1930.

U. S. Statutes at Large.

U. S. Supreme Court Reports.

U. S. Tariff Commission. *Reciprocity with Canada: A Study of the Arrangement of 1911.* Washington: Government Printing Office, 1920.

Other Works

Agee, Warren K. "A Study of Cross-Channel Ownership of Communications Media." Unpublished M.A. thesis, University of Minnesota, Minneapolis, 1949.

Ayer, N. W. and Son, Inc. *Directory of Newspapers and Periodicals.*

Bleyer, Willard G. *Main Currents in the History of American Journalism.* Boston: Houghton Mifflin, 1927.

Bonnett, Clarence E. *Employers' Associations in the United States.* New York: Macmillan, 1922.

Broadcasting Yearbook.

Brucker, Herbert. *Freedom of Information.* New York: Macmillan, 1949.

Charnley, Mitchell V. *News by Radio.* New York: Macmillan, 1948.

Childs, Harwood L., ed. "Pressure Groups and Propaganda," *Annals* of the American Academy of Political and Social Science, May 1935.

Dictionary of American Biography.

Editor & Publisher International Yearbook.

Ellis, L. Ethan. *Print Paper Pendulum: Group Pressures and the Price of Newsprint.* New Brunswick: Rutgers University Press, 1948.

Ellis, L. Ethan. *Reciprocity 1911: A Study in Canadian-American Relations.* New Haven: Yale University Press, 1939.

Friedman, Clara H. *The Newsprint Problem — Ten Questions and Answers.* New York: American Newspaper Guild, 1949.

Gerald, J. Edward. *The Press and the Constitution, 1931–1947.* Minneapolis: University of Minnesota Press, 1948.

Guthrie, John A. *The Newsprint Paper Industry: An Economic Analysis.* Cambridge: Harvard University Press, 1941.

Herbert, B. B. *The First Decennium of the National Editorial Association of the United States.* Chicago, 1896.

Lee, Alfred McClung. *The Daily Newspaper in America.* New York: Macmillan, 1937.

Loft, Jacob. *The Printing Trades.* New York: Farrar and Rinehart, 1944.

Lynch, James M. *Epochal History of the International Typographical Union.* Indianapolis, 1925.

McCormick, Robert R. *The Case for the Freedom of the Press.* Chicago: The Tribune Company, 1933.

McCormick, Robert R. *The Freedom of the Press.* New York: D. Appleton-Century, 1936.

McRae, Milton A. *Forty Years in Newspaperdom: The Autobiography of a Newspaper Man.* New York: Brentano's, 1924.

Mott, Frank Luther. *American Journalism.* New York: Macmillan, 1941.

Newspaper-Radio Committee. *Freedom of the Press.* New York, 1942.

Newsprint Association of Canada. *Newsprint Data: 1948.* Montreal, 1948.

Newsprint Association of Canada. *Newsprint Data: 1949.* Montreal, 1949.

Paxson, Frederic L. *Recent History of the United States.* Boston: Houghton Mifflin, 1929.

Presbrey, Frank. *The History and Development of Advertising.* New York: Doubleday Doran, 1929.

Rowell, George P., and Co. *American Newspaper Directory.*
Schlesinger, Arthur M. *The Rise of the City.* New York: Macmillan, 1932.
Schramm, Wilbur, ed. *Communications in Modern Society.* Urbana: University of Illinois Press, 1948.
Seldes, George. *Lords of the Press.* New York: Messner, 1938.
Shideler, James H. "Second-Class Matter: The American Press and the Subsidy, 1879–1933." Unpublished M.A. thesis, University of California, Berkeley, 1938.
Sullivan, Mark. *Our Times.* New York: Scribner's, 1926. 6 vols.
Tarbell, Ida M. *The Nationalizing of Business.* New York: Macmillan, 1936.
Taussig, Frank W. *The Tariff History of the United States.* 8th ed. New York: Putnam's, 1931.
Tebbel, John. *An American Dynasty.* New York: Doubleday, 1947.
Weeks, Lyman H. *A History of Paper-Manufacturing in the United States, 1690–1916.* New York: Lockwood, 1916.
Who's Who in America.
Who's Who in Journalism. 1928.

Index

Abitibi Power and Paper Company, 147, 155, 159
Adler, E. P., 138, 153, 157
Adler, Julius Ochs, 140
Advertising, 5–6, 22–23, 25–26, 29, 34–42, 54–55, 115–17, 119–30, 138–39, 196–211: national development, 5–6, 22, 38, 41, 119–20, 121, 123, 199–201, 205–8; retail store advertising, 5–6, 38, 119, 121, 125, 201, 207; ANPA relations with advertising agencies, 22–23, 25–26, 36–38, 120–21, 123–24, 127–29, 139, 206; newspaper advertising revenue, 29, 54–55, 119–20, 123, 196, 199–201, 205–8; patent medicine advertising, 38–41, 119, 124; magazine competition, 41, 120–23, 200–1, 205, 207–8; outdoor and car-card advertising, 41–42, 120, 122, 201; promotion of newspaper advertising through *Newspaper Record*, 42; identification of paid reading matter, 115–17, 124; circulation statements and auditing, 115–18, 124; Daily Newspaper Club, 122; Bureau of Advertising, 122–23, 133, 138, 143, 205–8; monopoly of advertising charges, 124; truth in advertising, 124, 223–24, 230, 239–40; shopping news competition, 125; effects of publicity on advertising, 125–30; association committees, 138–39; radio competition, 199–201, 205; Continuing Study of Newspaper Reading, 206; "United Front" campaign, 206-8
Advertising Research Foundation, 206
Agnus, Felix, 89
Akron *Beacon-Journal*, 68
Albany, N.Y.: *Press*, 17; *Evening Journal*, 17, 23; *Argus*, 47; *Times-Union*, 49
Aldrich, Nelson W., 97–99, 103

American Association of Advertising Agencies, 121, 123–24, 206
American Association of Newspaper Representatives, 207
American Council on Education for Journalism, 140
American Newspaper Guild: criticisms of ANPA policies, 134, 163, 186–87; labor relations with publishers, 187–88, 190, 218, 227–30, 234–39
AMERICAN NEWSPAPER PUBLISHERS ASSOCIATION
Association development: reasons for, 3–14; formation, 15–27; New York office, 19, 23, 27, 30–31, 56–57, 141; privacy of affairs, 20–21, 33–34; incorporation, 26, 55; officers and directors, 26, 30, 31–33, 57–58, 135–37, 247–50; annual meetings, 30–31, 55, 59–60, 133; association managers, 30–31, 56, 141, 250; bulletin services, 30–31, 34–36, 44, 56, 141–42, 241, 251; membership growth, 31, 55, 133–34; annual budgets, 56–57, 142; committee chairmen, 58–59, 137–41; legal counsel, 61, 88, 116–17, 141, 221–22; fall conventions, 133–34; small dailies sessions, 134–35; library, 140; mechanical conferences, 213; current committees, 242–43; publications, 251
Attitude toward news and editorial policies of newspapers, 30, 125–30, 131–32, 135, 149, 151–52, 218–21, 244–46
Legislative activities: patent medicines, 39; before *1900*, 49–53; censorship, 61; newsprint, 72–73, 82–83, 86–87, 90, 93–94, 97–99, 105–8, 144, 149–51, 153–54, 156, 161, 163; postal rates, 112–13, 115–18, 169–77;

262 NEWSPAPER PUBLISHERS ASSOCIATION

Prescott, George F., 17, 20, 23, 25

Press communications, 140

Press-Radio Bureau, 204

Price, Byron, 242

Prince, Roy W., 215

Printers' Ink, 42, 124

Printing trades schools, see Labor relations

Printing trades unions, see Labor relations

Publicity: development of publicity practices, 125–27; ANPA campaign against "free publicity," 127–30

Publishers' Buying Corporation, 152

Publishers' National Radio Committee, 203

Pulitzer, Joseph, 7, 13, 16, 28, 43–44, 88

Radio, 139, 196–211: association committee chairmen, 139; early development of radio, 196–98; newspaper-radio affiliation, 198, 208–10; federal supervision of radio, 199; chain broadcasting, 199; effect on newspaper advertising revenues, 199–201, 205; curtailment of radio logs, 202–3, 205, 210; Publishers' National Radio Committee, 203; curtailment of radio news, 203–4; Press-Radio Bureau, 204; rejuvenation of Bureau of Advertising by newspapers, 205–8; press-radio investigation, 208–10; Newspaper-Radio Committee, 209–10; newspaper FM and television affiliations, 210

Raleigh News, 89

Randolph, Woodruff, 191

Reciprocity with Canada, 103–7

Red Wing, Minn., Daily Republican, 18

Reed, Thomas B., 60, 79

Rees, Thomas, 128

Regional newspaper trade associations, 123, 226, 237

Richards, W. J., 17, 21, 23, 26, 33, 39

Richardson, Friend W., 93

Richmond, Ind., Palladium-Item, 136, 139, 203

Richmond, Va.: News-Leader, 58, 136, 156; Times Dispatch, 232

Ridder, Herman: interest in mechanical processes, 43, 212; elected president from convention floor, 57; labor relations activities, 63–64, 66, 68, 71–72, 75; newsprint activities, 88–94, 98, 102, 108; father of V. F. Ridder, 139

Ridder, Victor F., 139–40, 182

Ridder newspapers, 139–40

Roberts, Elzey, 139, 202

Rochester, N.Y.: Post Express, 17; Union and Advertiser, 17

Rocky Mount, N.C., Telegram, 138, 175

Rogers, George M., 136, 139, 213

Rogers, Hopewell L., 58

Rogers, Jason, 58, 152

Rogers, Sherman S., 57, 122

Rogers, William F., 138

Roosevelt, Franklin D., 209, 220, 224–27, 229, 232, 234, 236, 241

Roosevelt, Theodore, 39–40, 54, 89–90, 103, 126

Rosewater, C. C., 128

Rowell, Chester, 129

Rowell, George P., 22, 25, 59

Russell, L. T., 229

Sacramento, Calif., Bee, 128

St. Cloud, Minn., Times, 210

St. Louis: Post-Dispatch, 16; Republic, 16, 32, 57, 64, 74–75, 86, 113; Star, 64, 66, 139, 202; Globe-Democrat, 139, 213

St. Paul: Pioneer Press, 32, 49, 59, 63, 65, 86, 88, 158; Dispatch, 58, 158; Globe, 247

San Francisco: Call, 32, 58; Call-Bulletin, 229; Chronicle, 248

Santa Monica, Calif., Outlook, 137

Savannah Morning News, 136

Schilplin, Fred, 210

Schmick, William F., 136

Schools of journalism, 140, 209n, 245

Scott, James W., 13, 31–33, 46–47, 57

Scott, Marsden G., 57

Scripps, E. W., 6, 14, 16–17, 29, 40, 59

Scripps, James E., 14, 19

Scripps-Howard newspapers, 136, 138, 141, 159

Scripps-McRae League of Newspapers, 17, 32, 39–40, 86, 112, 216

Seattle Post-Intelligencer, 58, 70, 234, 236

Second-class mail, see Postal rates

Securities Exchange Act, 224, 230

Seif, W. H., 64

Seitz, Don C.: prominence in association, 58–59; labor relations activities, 64, 75; newsprint activities, 88, 90, 93, 98, 105; and postal rates, 113, 115–